Shifting Perspectives on the European Public Prosecutor's Office

Willem Geelhoed · Leendert H. Erkelens
Arjen W.H. Meij
Editors

Shifting Perspectives on the European Public Prosecutor's Office

ASSER PRESS

Springer

Editors
Willem Geelhoed
Department of Criminal Law
University of Groningen
Groningen
The Netherlands

Leendert H. Erkelens
T.M.C. Asser Instituut
The Hague
The Netherlands

Arjen W.H. Meij
T.M.C. Asser Instituut
The Hague
The Netherlands

and

University of Luxembourg
Luxembourg

Authors contributing to this volume were invited to submit their chapters by February 2017 at the latest.

Generally speaking, references in the chapters to provisions of the EPPO proposal under negotiation at the time of the preparation of these chapters therefore relate to the version available on http://extras.springer.com. It should be noted that the final text as adopted by the Council upon consent of the European Parliament may differ slightly on certain points. This final text can be found here: http://data.europa.eu/eli/reg/2017/1939/oj

Additional material to this book can be downloaded from http://extras.springer.com.

ISBN 978-94-6265-215-6 ISBN 978-94-6265-216-3 (eBook)
https://doi.org/10.1007/978-94-6265-216-3

Library of Congress Control Number: 2017952912

Published by T.M.C. ASSER PRESS, The Hague, The Netherlands http://www.asserpress.nl
Produced and distributed for T.M.C. ASSER PRESS by Springer-Verlag Berlin Heidelberg

Printed on acid-free paper

This T.M.C. ASSER PRESS imprint is published by Springer Nature
The registered company is Springer-Verlag GmbH Germany
The registered company address is: Heidelberger Platz 3, 14197 Berlin, Germany

Foreword

Parturient montes, ...[1]

The foreword to this second T.M.C. Asser Instituut volume on what should have been the first, non-intergovernmental, European body responsible for criminal investigations into large-scale fraud with regard to the Union's financial interests, must unfortunately begin, this time, with a sad remark.

After years of studies, green papers, reports and lectures and seminars held all over Europe, and after more than 3 years of intensive legislative work done in the context of a procedure involving the European Parliament, the Council and the European Commission (the so-called "special legislative procedure"), the "mountains" (i.e. the sovereign Member States), gathered far from public eyes in a room of the Council in Brussels (7 February 2017), have finally acknowledged the lack of required unanimity to adopt the regulation on the European Public Prosecutor's Office (EPPO). A quite predictable outcome, as several Member States, and not only one, expressed their concerns about such a proposal, and not all for the same reasons.

The European taxpayers and the autonomous legal order of one of the most important, united, economic inter-states realities in the world will therefore be deprived, for quite some time, of a European key instrument in the judicial configuration of the Union.

Even so, the EPPO is not yet officially dead.

During an informal meeting of the JHA Council in Malta, a few days before the above-mentioned European "surrender", seventeen Member States were said to be ready to carry on the project and to submit the proposal to the European Council, in view of establishing an enhanced cooperation allowing no less than nine Member States to have their own EPPO, so reported Věra Jourová, the Commissioner in charge of this file (see Agence Europe, 8.2.2017, N°11°720). It was 10 March 2017 when the European Council, due to the impossibility of reaching a consensus on the

[1] *Parturient montes, nascetur ridiculus mus.* (Horatius, *Ars Poetica, v.* 139). (*The mountains are in labor,* [and] *an absurd mouse will be born*: Merriam Webster Dictionary).

creation of a European Public Prosecutor, gave rise to the birth of *an absurd mouse*, as Horatius, the poet, would have said. A tiny and therefore weak EPPO, operating within a limited number of EU Member States, and which will therefore be even less able to investigate fraud in the sophisticated and border-free single market, where very efficient criminal organizations will probably play with this "fancy" EPPO, like the cat plays with a little mouse!

However, from the legislative point of view, the major downside to the foreseen enhanced cooperation procedure would be how to justify the EU democratic legitimacy of such an "intergovernmental" body. Indeed, according to Article 86(1) second indent, TFEU, if at least nine Member States wish to establish an enhanced cooperation on the basis of the draft regulation concerned, *they shall notify the European Parliament, the Council and the Commission accordingly* [and] *the authorization to proceed with enhanced cooperation ... shall be deemed to be granted ....*

This means that the EPPO legal text could be entirely put in the hands of a few Member States and adopted without any further substantial involvement of the Commission, the European Parliament or even of the Council. Such a result is probably not fully in line with the EU legality standards on criminal matters. Therefore, to avoid such a risk, it could be advisable, on one side, to adopt the regulation establishing the above-mentioned enhanced cooperation on the basis of the Commission's initial legislative proposal, the only one which has already gone through the National Parliaments subsidiarity test. On the other side, due to the significant changes introduced by the Member States sitting on the Council, the Commission should submit, for the purposes of this particular enhanced cooperation, a public revised text of its proposal, to be then submitted to the European Parliament for consent before the final adoption by the Council.

According to the Treaty (see Article 20 TEU), enhanced cooperation means *to further the objectives of the Union, protect its interests and reinforce its integration process*. Establishing a Council's "homemade" Public Prosecutor between, now, seventeen Member States could be, I guess, politically meaningful, but it does not correspond, in this case, to the very objectives of an enhanced cooperation. From such a perspective, it could even be preferable to put aside, for a while, this proposal and really reinforce Eurojust and OLAF, in order to better pave the way for a future, genuine EPPO.

An alternative option to this state of play could be to connect the role of the EU General Court with the EPPO's activity.

Due to its recent December 2015 reform, the General Court of the European Union will be composed, by the end of 2019, of 56 judges, two for each Member State.

Could this new General Court be charged, within the legal structure of the Court of Justice (see Articles 86(3) and 263(4) TFEU), to review also the legality of EPPO's procedural acts and/or to examine preliminary questions that national courts could raise before the Union's judge (see Article 36(2) of the draft EPPO regulation)?

The time has probably come to look ahead towards an efficient European Prosecutor, operating in the entire area of freedom, security and justice, and not only in some Member States. All in all, a European Prosecutor who must be, as Viviane Reding and Robert Badinter have recently declared to Le Monde (27.10.2016), *European not only in name but also in acts.*

Be that as it may, this book, which collects the various contributions submitted by great EPPO experts, is exactly what is needed to properly understand all the nitty-gritty of the pending EPPO's proposal. Indeed, the draft text examined by these connoisseurs corresponds largely to the text finally "rejected" by the Council under the Maltese Presidency on February 2017, which could become the future text of the EPPO-enhanced cooperation.

My suggestion, if I may, would be to read each of these critical analyses bearing in mind the reasons why EPPO has been so far an unsuccessful European story. The reader will catch and appreciate all the legal and practical implications raised by these authors, and therefore be persuaded that what is nowadays needed by the Union and its citizens is an efficient European Public Prosecutor. A body which will not take away from the Member States a piece of their sovereignty, but which, on the contrary, will efficiently help these countries and the Union to fight against the currently increasing European scourge, i.e. fraud and corruption.

Luxembourg
April 2017

Ezio Perillo
Judge at the General Court of the European Union[2]

[2] The opinions expressed here are strictly personal and under the sole responsibility of the author.

Contents

Chapter 1
Introduction

Willem Geelhoed, Leendert H. Erkelens and Arjen W.H. Meij

Contents

In July 2013, the European Commission presented a legislative proposal for a regulation establishing a European Public Prosecutor's Office (EPPO).[1] The T.M.C. Asser Instituut organised, shortly thereafter, the first conference in which this proposal was discussed.[2] The main point of departure for that conference was the idea that the establishment of the EPPO would be a step in the direction of bestowing the European Union with the exercise of criminal law competences. The conference focused on constitutional, institutional, legal and operational questions arising from that idea. These issues also comprised the main part of a book delivering the results of the 2013 EPPO conference.[3]

At that moment, the legislative initiative appeared to be a major breakthrough in the rather lengthy process of strengthening the protection of EU finances against fraud.[4] Undeniably, the Commission's proposal provoked many serious comments. However, the scholarly world reacted quite favourably to the proposal. It was considered to be a reasonable attempt at creating a European Public Prosecutor's

[1] Commission 2013.
[2] TMC Asser Instituut 2013.
[3] Erkelens et al. 2015.
[4] A brief history of the EPPO is provided in Erkelens 2015.

W. Geelhoed (✉)
Department of Criminal Law, Oude Kijk in 't Jatstraat 26,
9712 EK Groningen
The Netherlands
e-mail: w.geelhoed@rug.nl

L.H. Erkelens · A.W.H. Meij
R.J. Schimmelpennincklaan 20–22, 2517 JN The Hague, The Netherlands
e-mail: leendertherkelens@casema.nl

A.W.H. Meij
e-mail: awhmeij@xs4all.nl

W. Geelhoed et al. (eds.), *Shifting Perspectives on the European Public Prosecutor's Office*, https://doi.org/10.1007/978-94-6265-216-3_1

Office, though the proposal was deemed to be in need of improvement. This was thought to be particularly necessary in order to establish the Office in such a way that it would be able to function effectively. It was suggested that the effectiveness of the Office could be improved through increasing the level of harmonisation of the rules that the Office would need to apply, whether these rules related to procedure or substantive criminal law or to the determining of its competences *ratione materiae*.[5] In that respect, the so called *Corpus Juris* study served as a point of reference providing for a homogeneous, transnational set of rules on substantive criminal law concerning offences against the financial interests of the Union and procedural rules concerning the functioning and the competences of an EPPO.[6] The Commission's proposal underlined the concept of European territoriality: for the purposes of investigation, prosecution and trial, the European Union should constitute a single, judicial area. Though the Commission proposal embraced this principle, it still relied on national criminal procedure, on nationally determined competences of the Office[7] and on the mutual recognition of judicial decisions between the Member States. The Office was intended to be hierarchically organised, in a two-layer system with a European prosecutor (and his/her staff) at the top, and European delegated prosecutors in each of the Member States.

Subsequent deliberations in the Council appeared to deviate in many respects from the Commission's proposal. This resulted in a thoroughly revised text. In a nutshell, the Council preferred shared competences over exclusiveness, abolished the principle of a single legal area, and opted for a five-layer institutional setup, combining Delegated Prosecutors in the Member States with a central Office consisting of a College, a European Public Prosecutor, Permanent Chambers, and single European Prosecutors. Besides this, the functioning of the Office and the powers to be conferred upon it would be almost entirely determined by the national laws on criminal procedure and substantive criminal law.[8] In hindsight, it can be concluded that this intergovernmental approach was heavily influenced by a Franco-German common position which, among other elements, advocated a collegial model.[9] Alternatively, that position expressed a generally accepted view among EU Member States that intergovernmental cooperation should remain a dominating principle of governance in the Area of Freedom, Security and Justice (AFSJ).

The Council's multiple adaptations of the original proposal inspired the organisers to set up a second gathering of scholars, legislators and policy-makers in order

---

[5] *Supra* note 3. Among many, many other comments on the proposal, see Caianiello 2013.

[6] *Corpus Juris* 2000.

[7] PIF Directive 2017. EPPO competences are to be determined through implementation by the Member States of this directive.

[8] Ibidem.

[9] French/German Common Position 2013 (of the 20th March) stating in the accompanying letter: 'Nous pensons que la structure collégiale est à même de garantir l'efficacité opérationnelle et l'indépendance de ce Parquet européen, tout en assurant un ancrage fort en une vraie légitimité dans les États Membres.'

to scrutinise the draft text of the regulation. It was decided not to wait for the adoption of the final legislative instrument, as it became clear that—after almost three years of negotiations—the Dutch Presidency of the Council was able to reach a partial agreement on the main body of the text at the end of its term.[10] This partial agreement on EPPO, together with the draft PIF directive, constituted the basis for discussions at the second EPPO conference held in The Hague on 7 and 8 July 2016.[11] The main targets of this conference were threefold: to take stock of the current state of the Council negotiations, to provide a scholarly examination of the draft EPPO Regulation as it stood and to present an inside assessment of that draft by informed members of two institutions and a highly involved agency—Eurojust.[12]

The EPPO Conference of 7 and 8 July 2016 started with introductory remarks and a first panel session, in which the state of play was sketched, and in which representatives from presidencies and institutions reflected on major issues in the negotiations. This set the scene for the second part of the conference, starting with a second panel, in which three normative perspectives were unfolded, intended to scrutinise the EPPO proposal: the idea of better regulation, the benchmark of human rights, and the foundations of criminal law and criminal procedure. The third panel, dealing with issues of substantive criminal law, discussed the links between the EPPO proposal with the proposed PIF directive and the *Taricco* case, as well as the subject of ancillary offences and *ne bis in idem* issues. The fourth panel shifted the discussion to the procedural realm, focusing on forum choice and judicial review, and on the question of applicable law and the admissibility of evidence. The fifth panel discussed the institutional elements of the proposed regulation: the decision-making procedures within the EPPO, its cooperation with OLAF and its cooperation with Eurojust. The conference's third part consisted of a final panel reflecting on the *raison d'être* of the future EPPO, both from the point of view of several institutions as well as from an academic perspective.

This volume of proceedings aims at disseminating the results of the conference in order to inform the ongoing debate on the EPPO. Preceded by a highly topical foreword by General Court Judge and conference panel chair **Ezio Perillo**, this volume is composed of three parts, corresponding to the three parts of the conference.

Part I, entitled 'General Perspectives on the EPPO: From the Outside and the Inside' provides introductory remarks and institutional views on the state of the project. In Chap. 2, **John Vervaele** places the basic idea of the EPPO project against the background of the fight against fraud affecting the EU's financial interests. He questions the legitimacy of the establishment of EPPO both from a

[10] EPPO partial general approach 2016. This draft text was published on 3 June 2016.

[11] T.M.C. Asser Instituut and Leiden University 2016. The organisers thank OLAF for a project grant helping to make this conference possible.

[12] EPPO Conference report 2016. This report provides a comprehensive summary of the Conference discussion.

point of view of effectively fighting fraud, and from a political perspective. According to his idea, the EPPO should only be established if it is clear that it can effectively fight the as yet not very well understood problem of EU fraud, and if its establishment is in the interest of citizens and suspects. In Chap. 3, **Marnix Alink** and **Nicholas Franssen** describe the progress that was made in the negotiations during the Dutch Presidency of the Council in the first half of 2016. They refer to three topics: the relationships between EPPO and its strategic partners OLAF and Eurojust, the protection of personal data, processed by the EPPO, and the provisions on simplified prosecution procedures. Council discussions on these topics were complicated, but nevertheless acceptable solutions were found, sometimes undeniably having the character of a compromise. In Chap. 4, **Wouter van Ballegooij** presents a view on the negotiations from the perspective of the European Parliament. He summarises the involvement of the Parliament, which was quite active given the nature of the legislative procedure. In substance, the European Parliament stressed that the EPPO should be set up in such a way that it is able to operate effectively and efficiently, and that its operations conform to fundamental rights. Equality of arms is—when it comes to the latter aspect—one of the most important rights to pay attention to when deliberations progress.

Part II, titled 'Scholarly Perspectives on the EPPO: Constitutional, Regulatory and Institutional Issues', contains pieces of academic reflection, relating to major aspects of the prospective EPPO. The first two contributions strive to suggest particular benchmarks that can be used to evaluate the legislative draft. In Chap. 5, **Ester Herlin-Karnell** takes the Better Regulation Agenda as a point of departure for her analysis of the EPPO framework. Additionally, she discusses the proposed EPPO framework from a subsidiarity perspective. According to her analysis, it might be the best solution to grant the EU more competences in order for the EPPO to be a workable institution. In Chap. 6, **Valsamis Mitsilegas** and **Fabio Giuffrida** evaluate the draft EPPO Regulation against human rights standards. To that end, they identify four relevant viewpoints: the Charter of Fundamental Rights, the procedural safeguards within the draft Regulation, the possibilities for judicial review of the acts of the Office, and the specific needs of cross-border investigations. They perceive a strong tension between upgrading the fight against fraud and not downgrading the protection of human rights in supranational proceedings.

The remainder of Part II is dedicated to substantive, procedural, and institutional issues. Chapters 7 and 8 deal with substantive criminal law. In Chap. 7, **Rosaria Sicurella** essentially focuses on the quite unsatisfactory results of the negotiations on the PIF Directive, devoting special attention in this context to the ECJ judgment in the *Taricco* Case. This judgment turned out to be of crucial importance for the negotiations. At the same time, as this contribution demonstrates, it may have a rather complicating impact on the role of the national legality principle, thus giving rise to a fresh preliminary reference of the Corte costituzionale. In Chap. 8, **Eric Sitbon** analyses the different categories of offences which may be included in the material competence of the EPPO: offences defined by the PIF directive, participating in a criminal organisation with a specific focus, and offences inextricably linked to offences falling within the previous categories. He then evaluates the relevant provisions in the light of the *ne bis in idem* principle. Chapters 9 and 10 discuss matters of procedural criminal law. In Chap. 9, **András Csúri** compares the investigations of the prospective EPPO with the mutual cooperation based on the European Investigation Order. He is of the opinion that the draft Regulation envisages an increasingly hybrid scheme of cross-border investigations that echoes the European Investigation Order (EIO) Directive without borrowing the necessary elements from it. The EPPO would work better were it to use the EIO in its cross-border investigations. In Chap. 10, **Michiel Luchtman** deals with the issue of forum choice, which he regards as a both important and problematic topic. While it affects all the actors involved in criminal proceedings, there are few remedies available. Luchtman analyses the proposed legal framework on forum choice and judicial review, which was heavily debated in negotiations, and proposes some amendments based on the system in place in Switzerland. The last chapter focuses on institutional issues. In that chapter, Chap. 11, **Anne Weyembergh** and **Chloé Brière** analyse the relationship between the future EPPO and Eurojust. They examine the envisaged institutional relationship between both bodies, their management and administrative links, and their operational cooperation. Since they experience difficulties in seeing Eurojust as EPPO's privileged partner, as it should be, they recommend clarifying the relationship between both actors in their respective regulations.

Part III, titled 'Summa Summarum: Assessing EPPO's *Raison d'Être* in the Light of the Debates', revisits the issue of *raison d'être* that was raised in Part I. The text of the two chapters closely reflects the discussions at the conference, where the panel topic was introduced by John Vervaele. In his opening words, he commented on the legislative process, including the possibility—in the meantime activated by 16 Member States[13]—of enhanced cooperation and the fundamental questions this entails. Vervaele also raised the intriguing question whether the draft as it stood—and in the meantime is referred to enhanced cooperation—corresponds to the added value that an EPPO based on Article 86 TFEU is supposed to produce as compared to a reformed Eurojust finding its basis in Article 85. In other words, does the present text fit within Article 86? Furthermore, the chair of the final panel pinpointed the question whether in the set-up of the present text the independent authority of the office and its chief in organised hierarchy can be guaranteed in a way corresponding to the Council of Europe's 2000 Recommendation on the role of public prosecution and criminal justice systems.[14] In Chap. 12, **Hubert Legal** stresses that the multiple changes made during Council negotiations improved the structure of the EPPO and, in doing so, its prospects as an operational Office. Furthermore, its legitimacy is strengthened because it rests on the solid foundation of the Member States' democratic decisions. In Chap. 13, **Alex Brenninkmeijer** paints a different picture: he foresees that the EPPO will turn out to be a failure in terms of an effective fight against fraud. Already now, the Member States seem to be unwilling to take the

[13] Press Release 184/17 (2017).

[14] Council of Europe 2000.

principle of loyal cooperation seriously and opt for a very nationalistic approach. The EPPO, when it is established according to the draft regulation, will not change much and consequently offer little value for money for EU citizens. This contribution can be seen as related to a recent report by the Court of Auditors.[15]

A final comment on the concept '*raison d'être*', the central issue of Part III, is in place here, given the fundamental legal and political questions that surround the EPPO project. The concept '*raison d'être*' originates from the Union's legislative process. It refers back to the most fundamental objective(s) for the realisation of which a legislative measure should be taken and proposed by the Commission accordingly. In the course of the legislative process, it may occur that the Commission reaches the conclusion that the original proposal has been robbed of the appropriate instruments to achieve these fundamental objectives. When that happens, the draft legislative instrument transforms into an object that is susceptible to being 'discontinued', that is: withdrawn by the Commission.[16]

At the time of writing this introduction, the negotiations on the EPPO have moved into a stage where enhanced cooperation has started, as the Council could not reach unanimity. It can be questioned in what way the Commission's rights to withdraw this proposal still apply during the procedure for enhanced cooperation. The answer to that question could be made dependent on the relationship between the prior legislative procedure, ending inconclusively in the Council, and the subsequent procedure for enhanced cooperation. One way of looking at this is that the start of enhanced cooperation marks the beginning of an entirely new legislative procedure, which is governed by Article 20 TEU and Title III on Enhanced Cooperation of Part Six TFEU. In this view, Article 86(1) TFEU only slightly adapts that framework by providing that the authorisation to proceed with enhanced cooperation shall be deemed to be granted. Otherwise, the regular provisions on enhanced cooperation apply, which provide for detailed rules on the procedure to be followed. In this view, it would not be very logical to suppose that the Commission's right to withdraw a proposal would equally apply in a procedure for enhanced cooperation started on the basis of Article 86. After all, that procedure is started on the basis of an initiative of the Member States participating in the cooperation and not on the basis of a legislative proposal submitted by the Commission, which is the regular method for starting enhanced cooperation as provided for in Article 329, para 1 TFEU.

Another way of looking at the relationship between the two procedures is, evidently, to regard them as a coherent whole. In that view, Article 86(1) provides the linking pin between the two, stating that enhanced cooperation can be requested '… on the basis of the draft regulation concerned, … '. In this view, therefore, there is only one continuous procedure, consisting of a regular stage and a stage of

---

[15] European Court of Auditors 2015.

[16] The competence of the Commission to may discontinue pending legislation is laid down in Article 293(2) TFEU. See further *Council v Commission*, Case C-409/13. Among others, scrutinised by Ritleng 2016.

enhanced cooperation and the Commission's withdrawing rights will remain intact during the enhanced cooperation procedure. Such an approach is corroborated by the fact that it is not self-evident, as particularly shown in the case of the EPPO, that the original combination of fundamental objectives and appropriate instruments to achieve these, which inspired the initial proposal, still inspires the object of the enhanced cooperation. In such a perspective even the Commission may not necessarily be in a position to support and pursue enhanced cooperation.

Perhaps the EPPO will be established using enhanced cooperation. But even if that attempt fails, the legal basis for its establishment will remain, and so will the need for its introduction. Therefore, it is to be expected that the contents of this volume will remain useful in order to inform future debates on the nature and functioning of the European Public Prosecutor's Office.

References

Caianiello M (2013) The Proposal for a Regulation on the Establishment of an European Public Prosecutor's Office: Everything Changes, or Nothing Changes? European Journal of Crime, Criminal Law and Criminal Justice 21 (2013) 115–125

Commission (2013) Proposal for a Council Regulation on the establishment of the European Public Prosecutor's Office. COM(2013) 534 final

Corpus Juris (2000) *Corpus Juris* (Florence version); Appendix II (Guiding Principles of *Corpus Juris*) and Appendix III (*Corpus Juris* 2000). Available at https://ec.europa.eu/anti-fraud/sites/antifraud/files/docs/body/corpus_juris_en.pdf. Accessed March 2017

Council of Europe (2000) Committee of Ministers of the Council of Europe. The role of public prosecution in the criminal justice system, Recommendation Rec (2000)19. Available at https://rm.coe.int/CoERMPublicCommonSearchServices/DisplayDCTMContent?documentId=09000016804be55a. Accessed February 2017

EPPO partial general approach (2016) Doc. nr. 9799/16. Available at http://data.consilium.europa.eu/doc/document/ST-9799-2016-INIT/en/pdf. Accessed March 2017

Erkelens LH (2015) Introduction: Criminal Law Protection of the European Union's Financial Interests: A Shared Constitutional Responsibility of the EU and its Member States? In: Erkelens LH, Meij AWH, Pawlik M (eds) The European Public Prosecutor's Office: An Extended Arm or a Two-Headed Dragon? TMC Asser Press, The Hague

Erkelens LH, Meij AWH, Pawlik M (2015) The European Public Prosecutor's Office: An Extended Arm or a Two-Headed Dragon? TMC Asser Press, The Hague

European Court of Auditors (2015) Tackling intra-Community VAT fraud: More action needed (Special Report No. 24/2015). Available at http://www.eca.europa.eu/Lists/ECADocuments/SR15_24/SR_VAT_FRAUD_EN.pdf. Accessed January 2017

French/German Common Position (2013) Common Position of the Ministers of Justice of France and Germany on the European Public Prosecutor's Office (current as of 4 March 2013). Available at http://eppo-project.eu/design/eppodesign/pdf/converted/index.html?url=b0212eec88f918c78c4c6840e8ccf091.pdf&search=. Accessed March 2017

PIF Directive (2017) Proposal for a Directive of the European Parliament and of the Council on the protection of the Union's financial interests by means of criminal law. Doc. nr. 5434/17. Available at http://data.consilium.europa.eu/doc/document/ST-5434-2017-INIT/en/pdf. Accessed March 2017

Press Release 184/17 (2017) Press Release 184/17 of the Council of 3 April 2017. Available at http://www.consilium.europa.eu/en/press/press-releases/2017/04/03-eppo/. Accessed April 2017

Ritleng D (2016) Does the European Court of Justice take democracy seriously? Some thoughts about the Macro-Financial Assistance case. Common Market Law Review 2016, pp 11–33

TMC Asser Instituut (2013) Conference on the Commission Proposal on the Establishment of a European Public Prosecutor's Office (EPPO), Criminal law protection of the European Union's financial interests: a shared constitutional responsibility of the EU and its Member States? 6 September 2013. Available at http://www.asser.nl/upload/documents/20130604T113033-Flyer%20EPPO%20Conference.pdf. Accessed March 2017

TMC Asser Instituut, Leiden University (2016) Conference on the Establishment of the European Public Prosecutor's Office (EPPO) "State of Play and Perspectives". Programme available at http://www.asser.nl/media/2911/provisional-programme-eppo-2016-for-website.pdf. Accessed March 2017

Part I
General Perspectives on the EPPO: From the Outside and the Inside

Chapter 2
The European Public Prosecutor's Office (EPPO): Introductory Remarks

John A.E. Vervaele

Abstract These introductory remarks deal with the reasons why the EPPO is perceived by some as a controversial body. These reasons are mirrored with the problem identification and the causes thereof. The size of EU fraud and related corruption and money laundering, both at the income and expenditure side, is quite significant. There is also a strong enforcement deficit in the Member States, especially in the case of complex transnational VAT and customs fraud cases. Three fields of action are potentially of interest for the EPPO: VAT, customs and smuggling, and fraud and corruption within the EU institutions. This leads to the analysis of what the potential added value of the EPPO could be, both from a technical fraud perspective as from a political legitimacy perspective. Finally, the introduction deals with the ongoing negotiations on the EPPO proposal, taking into account the mandate and rationale of Article 86 TFEU in the framework of the Area of Freedom, Security and Justice.

Keywords Corpus Juris · Sovereignty · Area of Freedom, Security and Justice (AFSJ) · Financial Interests EU · Fraud · VAT Fraud · Customs Fraud · OLAF · European Public Prosecutor's Office

The author is full time professor of economic and European criminal law at Utrecht Law School and professor of European criminal law at the College of Europe in Bruges. He is also president of the world Association for Criminal Law, AIDP (Paris).

J.A.E. Vervaele (✉)
Faculty of Law, Economics, and Governance, Utrecht, 3512 BK Utrecht, The Netherlands
e-mail: j.a.e.vervaele@uu.nl

W. Geelhoed et al. (eds.), *Shifting Perspectives on the European Public Prosecutor's Office*, https://doi.org/10.1007/978-94-6265-216-3_2

Contents

2.1 The European Public Prosecutor's Office: A Controversial Body

Both the T.M.C. Asser Instituut and Leiden University deserve sincere congratulations for the organization of the event, as the choice of the topic and the timing could not have been better planned. At the end of the Dutch Presidency there is a first general draft of the Council, although quite some specific topics remain under debate and will be addressed by the incoming Slovak Presidency.

When one evaluates the scholarly work[1] on the topic—avoiding the very rich UK tabloid press—it is quite astonishing to see what words are used: the European Public Prosecutor's Office (EPPO) is a conundrum, it is an enigma, it is mysterious, it is a Trojan horse, it is a white elephant,[2] it is a two headed dragon,[3] and it can go on like that. This sounds appealing, but there is also something alarming, something threatening. At the tenth anniversary of the ECLAN network[4] in Brussels in April 2016, the Belgian Minister of Justice, Mr. Geens, labelled the EPPO draft design of the Council as follows: 'The baby is not a beauty, let's hope it has some brains'.[5]

So why is this topic so controversial? In fact, there are many reasons for that. The first reason is that it is a new supranational institution in the field of criminal law enforcement. Unlike Europol and Eurojust it would also be entrusted with autonomous operational investigative and prosecutorial powers. This means that Member States fear that their sovereign powers will be transferred to the supranational EU level.

The second reason is that this transfer of sovereignty is in fact a matter of 'shared sovereignty', or of what the Germans call '*Vergemeinschaftlichung*'. This means that at the national level, in this case the pre-trial investigation and prosecution, the European dimension is increasing. National authorities are increasingly bestowed with European functions. Transfer of sovereignty and shared sovereignty seems to

[1] Csúri 2016; Erkelens et al. 2015.

[2] Csúri 2016.

[3] Erkelens et al. 2015.

[4] ECLAN: European Criminal Law Academic Network.

[5] Conference programme available at: http://www.iee-ulb.eu/files/attachments/.1292/ECLAN_final_programme.pdf (accessed January 2017).

be contradictory, but that is only the case at first sight. In many areas of European regulation, and increasingly also with regard to European enforcement, European agencies, bodies and institutions have been created. However, they execute their powers in strong interaction with the national level, be it because they apply also national law or be it that they are acting in close cooperation with the national institutions. Verticalisation does not automatically mean that these powers are not embedded in the national legal orders. Mostly they are. This is for instance the case in the area of competence of the EU competition authority, the EU Central Bank (ECB) and the European financial regulatory and enforcement agencies, as for instance the European Securities and Markets Authority (ESMA). This would mean in our field that national prosecutors would investigate and prosecute offences under the direction and guidance of the EPPO. Both, transfer of powers and Europeanisation of domestic criminal justice at the operational level is for most Member States an uneasy scenario in the area of criminal justice. Member States are afraid that the EPPO will open the door for transferring powers to the EU level, but that this will also come back as a boomerang, harmonizing national procedures.

A third reason why the EPPO—just like the other European bodies—is so controversial is that it operates in a common space or area, comparable to the internal market and the monetary union: the policy Area of Freedom, Security and Justice (AFSJ). This entrusts it with the objective to protect common interests that go beyond the territories of every single state or jurisdiction. Member States do not like this combination of vertical institutions with transnational powers. By large, they do prefer horizontal and intergovernmental modes of cooperation. It comes to no surprise that some national parliaments stated that there is no need for the EPPO as the intergovernmental judicial cooperation could be further improved. Going beyond this would violate EU subsidiarity. During the negotiations in the EU Council, Member States have removed concepts as the 'single legal space'. They also have decentralized the functioning of the EPPO within their national jurisdictions, even to the extent that the EPPO would need mutual recognition instruments for transnational cooperation.

The fourth reason why a future EPPO is controversial, in my opinion, is related to the substantive competence (*ratione materiae*) of the EPPO. PIF-offences[6] look pretty much as a specialized and small area, but that is not really the case. They are related to corruption, organized crime, money laundering, tax offences, custom offences, etc. That could be a reason why the Member States are opposed to include VAT offences in the competence of the EPPO, although VAT carousel fraud is substantial and very transnational in nature. In addition to that, many Member States are concerned that the category of PIF-offences will very soon be broadened to other offences. These could be offences that are related to the EU interests, such as counterfeiting of the Euro, or tendering-fraud. Additionally, euro-offences could be added, as defined in under Article 83(1), including terrorism, trafficking in human beings, etc., and annex-offences harmonized under Article 83(2), such as

[6] PIF: French acronym: Protection des Intérêts Financiers (de l'Union européenne).

market abuse, serious violations of the environment, or VAT crimes *tout court*. Member States are afraid not to be able to lock the door, once it is opened.

The fifth reason, although not such a strong one, certainly is relevant as it is related to the institutional design of the EPPO as such. The EPPO that has been proposed is not identical to the public prosecutor's offices in the Member States. In many countries prosecutors do not investigate, they only prosecute, and the real investigation is in the hands of the police, or administrative bodies, with full or great autonomy. However, the EPPO that has been proposed will do both, investigate possible crimes and prosecute suspects, which for many Member States is a new model. Linked to that specific set of competences, the Commission proposed to have an independent prosecutor: independent from the executive branch of government both at the domestic and the Union level. To my opinion this is a very reasonable choice in view of the area EPPO has to work in. Its caseload will involve cases of corruption, not just in the private sector, but in the public sector as well. Therefore, the independence of the Office is a key factor in order for it to be successful. However, there are many Member States that do not have independent prosecutors, not just in Eastern Europe, but also in Western Europe.

Are these fears of the Member States new? I would not say so. If we take a look at the powers of European Anti-Fraud Office (OLAF),[7] a non-judicial body, we see that can investigate in the territory of Member States together with the law enforcement agencies or in very exceptional circumstances alone. Its administrative investigative powers have been laid down in EU regulations, but in practice Member States have tried to block it as much as possible. Member States do not like to transfer operational powers to law enforcement agencies. The same can be said about the reform of Eurojust. Member States were not willing to upgrade substantially the powers of the national members of Eurojust under the Amsterdam Treaty. Even in the actual reform—although the Lisbon Treaty provides for a legal basis to increase the powers of Eurojust—Member States prefer the *status quo*.

2.2 Problem Identification: Size of EU Fraud and Lack of Enforcement

The second question to be put forward relates to the problems at hand and the causes thereof. What is exactly the problem? The issue of criminal law protection of the EU budget and related corruption and money laundering offences is discussed now for over 30 years. Despite the magnitude of the cases and the large amount of money involved, few cases are prosecuted and very little money is collected (in case of income-fraud, like VAT) or recovered (in case of EU subsidy-fraud).[8] The

[7] OLAF: French acronym: Office européen de la Lutte Antifraude.

[8] See for example OLAF 2016: "In 2015, OLAF opened 219 new investigations. It concluded 304 investigations, which represents a new record for the Office." (p. 3).

judicial follow-up to OLAF reports is not impressive either. Nevertheless, still many national governments are trying to minimize the problems and do state that we can deal with it as it stands, namely through traditional horizontal cooperation between states.

In my opinion, despite 30 years of discussion there is still no clear picture of the phenomenon. Empirical research and empirical data are lacking in this area. One cannot just blame the Commission for that; also the Member States are to be held responsible. They are not willing to invest in independent academic investigation in this field of research.

Three fields of action are potentially of interest for the EPPO: VAT, customs and smuggling, and fraud and corruption within the EU institutions. Concerning VAT, fortunately one can rely on neutral sources. The European Court of Auditors (ECA) published in 2015 a special report on 'Tackling intra-community VAT fraud—more action needed'.[9] Despite the technicalities, this report is very readable and deserves to be consulted. Rather astonishingly, the report demonstrates that even for the European Court of Auditors it appears to be difficult to paint a clear picture of EU fraud. What is however clear to the Court is that the major players, who are the Member States, have no clue of the size and nature of the problem. Even if they have data, the data are not shared, not even at the national level, between judicial authorities and tax authorities. For certain, data on VAT fraud is not shared horizontally between Member States. Reasons for not doing so are both of a legal and practical nature.

Reading the report one really comes across the point that there is still only a very approximate idea of the features of the phenomenon. It is very difficult to come up with an evidence driven argumentation when the figures are not available. This does however not mean that the empirical problem is small, quite the contrary. The dark number is so big because of the lack of data and information flow between the enforcement authorities and the lack of judicial cooperation. Still, Member States are stating that they can deal with it at the national level. But let us not forget that VAT is an intra-community system. Even if most of the VAT income goes to the national budget, the system as such is very much transnational, as it is linked to the single area. Companies of all kind can run around with goods and services in the EU, deliberately avoiding VAT payments, and Member States do discover it in very few cases and prosecute only a handful of these offences.

In the field of customs we do have a completely unified EU customs code. However, the customs enforcement is fully national. At the national level, there is a very different set of authorities from one Member State to another. The division of labour between administrative and judicial authorities is also very different from one Member State to another. The cooperation within the states and the transnational horizontal cooperation remains fragmented too. The result is a harmonized EU customs code that is applied by a patchwork of national authorities with different powers. Moreover, the EU customs code did not harmonise the enforcement

[9] European Court of Auditors 2015, no. 24.

dimension, not even the administrative enforcement and administrative sanctioning. As an example of this, the EU internal market has historically shown to have a significant problem with counterfeited tobacco products and tobacco products that are smuggled to be sold on black markets in the EU. The result is of course that—apart from the health dimension—Member States and the EU lose significant amounts of tax revenue (VAT, excises, custom duties) due to illicit tobacco trade. In the last decade, there has been a strong increase in so-called 'white cheapies' that are illegally traded in the EU. They are legally produced in Belarus or Ukraine and then imported illegally in the EU through criminal networks operating for the black markets. Member States' enforcement is weak, certainly when they are only a transit-country. In some Member States, if illegal trade is discovered and the tobacco is seized, it is legally sold on the market by the customs authorities themselves.

The third field is related to fraud and corruption within the EU institutions, bodies and agencies. Thanks to OLAF internal investigations, to whistle blowers and also to national judicial investigations—mostly in Belgium—one can be sure that there were and are still are serious cases of fraud and corruption within the EU, which not only deserve disciplinary action, but also a criminal follow-up in the Member States. Since the coming into force of the new OLAF regulation in 2013, there is surely a better setting for cooperation between national judicial authorities and EU/OLAF. Belgian investigating magistrates can obtain from the OLAF director a waiver of immunity and receive access to the premises, without for instance a political decision of the College of the Commission. However, OLAF investigations are disciplinary and administrative only, and OLAF cannot impose any sanctions.

It can be deduced from these three fields of action that the magnitude of the phenomenon and the resulting problem should not be minimized. It is also a phenomenon that undermines both the budget and the legitimacy of the EU and the Member States together.

2.3 EPPO's Added Value

Notwithstanding the preceding critical comments, much can be asserted also on the possible added value of the EPPO. The discussion on the added value is partially a technical one and partially a political one. This means that the need and legitimacy of this choice cannot be based only on empirical evidence, but also on the objectives of EU integration, as laid down in Article 3 TEU and on the main objectives of the AFSJ.[10] What are the main arguments that have been mentioned in favour of the

[10] Article 3, para 2 TEU: The Union shall offer its citizens an area of freedom, security and justice without internal frontiers, in which the free movement of persons is ensured in conjunction with appropriate measures with respect to external border controls, asylum, immigration and the prevention and combating of crime.

setting up of the EPPO? They can be found in the *Corpus Juris* study of 1997,[11] the *Corpus Juris* study of 2000,[12] the green paper of the Commission of 2001,[13] the follow up on the green paper, and in the impact assessment done by the Commission prior to the EPPO proposal.[14] The main arguments can be summarised as follows. First, although over time the horizontal cooperation between Member States has been strengthened both in law and practice, there is still a serious problem of fragmentation in the European criminal law enforcement area that could be overcome with the EPPO.[15] Second, the horizontal cooperation model, even when it is based on mutual recognition, has its limits, as it depends on the action of the national authorities, which not always have the necessary oversight. Moreover, their criminal policy is generally not based on common EU interests, but on national priorities. Third, the judicial follow-up of the OLAF findings and reports by criminal proceedings in the Member States remains problematic. The EPPO could bring substantial change in this regard. Finally, EPPO could certainly contribute to more efficient and effective investigation and prosecution of fraud and corruption within the EU institutions, bodies and agencies.[16]

Even if an added value can be identified, the question remains for whom this actually is an added value. Obviously, the EPPO has added value for the Union itself, as it aims at the protection of essential interests of the EU and its functioning. Even if the substantive competence is limited to PIF offences, it is linked to common policies in the single legal area. One must not forget that for decades, national enforcement agencies, prosecutors and judges urge legislators to come up with more European solutions in order to deal with the problems they face. When this call is answered, it can also contribute to a greater legitimacy of the EU integration process. In addition to that, it is clear that the EPPO can offer added value to EU citizens. These citizens claim more transparency and an effective tackling of fraud and corruption. Taxpayers of course require value for money and demand effective investigations and prosecutions against illegal constructions in the area of customs fraud, VAT fraud and subsidy fraud. Finally, establishing an EPPO is also in the interest of suspects, as they would only have to face one authority and one set of rules, including procedural safeguards, instead of facing a multiplicity of potential investigations under different jurisdictions.

[11] Delmas-Marty 1997.

[12] Delmas-Marty and Vervaele 2001.

[13] Commission of the European Communities 2001.

[14] Commission staff working document impact assessment 2013.

[15] Ligeti and Simonato 2013.

[16] Weyembergh and Brière 2016.

2.4 Final Comments

Finally, it is necessary to make some comments on the ongoing negotiation process and on the legal basis in Article 86 TFEU, which is an astonishing article. In view of the ongoing crisis of the EU integration process, this article constitutes an important expression of shared sovereignty in the field of criminal justice. The fact that Member States (governments and parliaments) signed and ratified the Lisbon Treaty, including Article 86 TFEU, is of course not meaningless. Some think of a treaty as a box of toys—you can play with it depending on what you personally need. I cannot share this view at all. Article 86 TFEU is not only a legal basis for potential use. It is also related to duties under the treaties, related to the objectives of the AFSJ. The realization of the AFSJ is not an option, it is a duty under the Treaties. The legislative procedure according to which the EPPO regulation has to be adopted is based on the old-fashioned unanimity procedure (in which procedure each Member State has a veto right). At the same time, the Lisbon Treaty has also build in possibilities for enhanced cooperation, which allows the EU to introduce the EPPO within a subset of Member States. In any case, the European Parliament (EP) has to consent. Surely, the EPPO will not be establish using the qualified majority procedure including a trilogue. However, for the EP is it not a case of taking or leaving. The EP has followed the outcome of the Council negotiations closely and wants to influence certain points that (the majority of) its members define as critical. It is obvious that the negotiated EPPO must be able to solve most of the problems that have been mentioned. The outcome must also fit within article 86 TFEU. Article 86 TFEU is certainly not identical to Article 85 or Article 82, which means that the article must also have an added value compared to the classical horizontal cooperation and to the work of Eurojust. Without a sufficient added value compared to Articles 85 and 82, the negotiated EPPO cannot fit within the shoes of Article 86 TFEU. In that case it would be better to strengthen Eurojust under Article 86 TFEU.[17]

References

Commission of the European Communities (2001) Green Paper on criminal-law protection of the financial interests of the Community and the establishment of a European Prosecutor (presented by the Commission), COM (2001) 715 final. Available at: http://eur-lex.europa.eu/legal-content/EN/TXT/PDF/?uri=CELEX:52001DC0715&from=EN Accessed January 2017

Commission staff working document impact assessment (2013) Accompanying the Proposal for a Council Regulation on the establishment of the European Public Prosecutor's Office. SWD (2013) 274 final. Available at http://ec.europa.eu/justice/criminal/files/eppo_impact_assessment_en.pdf. Accessed January 2017

[17] See Weyembergh and Brière 2018.

Csúri A (2016) The Proposed European Public Prosecutor's Office - From a Trojan Horse to a White Elephant? In: Armstrong K et al (eds) Cambridge Yearbook of European Legal Studies. Cambridge University Press, Cambridge, Vol. 18, pp. 122–151

Delmas-Marty M (ed) (1997) *Corpus Juris* Introducing Penal Provisions for the Purpose of the Financial Interests of the European Union. Editions Economica, Paris

Delmas-Marty M, Vervaele JAE (eds) (2001) The Implementation of the *Corpus Juris* in the Member States: Penal Provisions for the Protection of European Finances, 4 Volumes. Intersentia, Antwerp

Erkelens LH, Meij AWH, Pawlik M (eds) (2015) The European Public Prosecutor's Office: An Extended Arm or a Two-Headed Dragon? TMC Asser Press, The Hague

European Court of Auditors (ECA) (2015) Tackling intra-Community VAT fraud: More action needed. http://www.eca.europa.eu/Lists/ECADocuments/SR15_24/SR_VAT_FRAUD_EN.pdf. Accessed January 2017

Ligeti K, Simonato M (2013) The European Public Prosecutor's Office: Towards a Truly European Prosecution Service? New Journal of European Criminal Law, Vol. 4, Issue 1–2, 2013

OLAF (2016) The OLAF report 2015. Sixteenth report of the European Anti-Fraud Office, 1 January to 31 December 2015. Available at http://ec.europa.eu/anti-fraud/sites/antifraud/files/olaf_report_2015_en.pdf. Accessed January 2017

Weyembergh A, Brière C (2016) Towards a European Public Prosecutor's Office (EPPO), Study for LIBE. European Parliament, PE 571.399

Weyembergh A, Brière C (2018) Relations between the EPPO and Eurojust – still a privileged partnership? In: Geelhoed W, Erkelens LH, Meij AWH (eds) Shifting Perspectives on the European Public Prosecutor's Office. TMC Asser Press, The Hague

Chapter 3
EPPO—Developments Under the Presidency of The Netherlands

Marnix J. Alink and Nicholas D.A. Franssen

Abstract This chapter provides a short overview of the progress made in the negotiations on the proposal for a Council Regulation on the establishment of the European Public Prosecutor's Office under the Netherlands Presidency of the EU during the first half of 2016.

Keywords European Public Prosecutor's Office · Netherlands Presidency of the Council · Relations with partners · Data protection · Simplified prosecution procedures · Enhanced cooperation

Contents

M.J. Alink (✉) · N.D.A. Franssen
Ministry of Security and Justice, The Hague, The Netherlands
e-mail: m.j.alink@minvenj.nl

N.D.A. Franssen
e-mail: n.franssen@minvenj.nl

W. Geelhoed et al. (eds.), *Shifting Perspectives on the European Public Prosecutor's Office*, https://doi.org/10.1007/978-94-6265-216-3_3

3.1 Introduction

Since the presentation of the Commission's proposal on the establishment of a European Public Prosecutor's Office (EPPO),[1] five consecutive Presidencies dealt with this file in the Council of the European Union. The Lithuanian, Greek, Latvian, Italian and Luxembourgish Presidency had all worked on the proposal for a Council Regulation on the establishment of the European Public Prosecutor's Office before the Netherlands took over the Presidency of the EU on 1 January 2016. Along the way, negotiations have been cumbersome as a result of the many complex issues involved. This contribution will provide a short overview of the progress made under the Netherlands Presidency of the EU during the first half of 2016.

The Netherlands Presidency picked up where the Luxembourgish Presidency left the file in December 2015. Following their successful work and that of other Presidencies on Articles 1–36—which, in short, cover the structure and competence of the European Public Prosecutor's Office—the objective of the Netherlands Presidency was to find agreement in the Council on as many of the remaining provisions of the draft Regulation as possible.

It looks as if the Netherlands Presidency succeeded in this, since it managed to present a considerable number of articles to the Justice and Home Affairs (JHA) Council at the end of its Presidency in June 2016.[2] Work was done on many different elements of the draft Regulation, ranging from the rules on the case management system and data protection, simplified prosecution procedures (in the Commission's proposal known as "transactions"),[3] general provisions and financial and staff provisions.

3.2 Relations with Partners

On the relations between EPPO and its partners, in particular Eurojust, Europol and OLAF, a model has been negotiated for the cooperation and relations between these bodies. This has, among other things, led to the introduction of new and specific articles on the relations with OLAF and Europol.

These relations turned out to be a complex matter. Many issues were to be solved, such as the exchange of data between the bodies and rules on the—indirect—access to information in the respective case management systems. The Council managed to find an approach, which guarantees that the bodies at stake will complement and not duplicate each other. Although intensive and effective cooperation between EPPO and its partners is key, their competences remain different and the establishment of the EPPO should create synergies and not duplications.

[1] European Commission 2013.

[2] Council 2016.

[3] European Commission 2013, Article 29.

OLAF, for instance, will continue to be responsible for administrative investigations into EU-fraud. Parallel investigations by the EPPO and OLAF into the same facts are to be avoided. However, EPPO will, as is now foreseen in the text, be able to request OLAF, within its mandate, to support or complement its prosecution activities. It can do this for instance by providing information, analyses and expertise.

As regards Eurojust, a solution has been found for the practical cooperation between the EPPO and Eurojust, where the EPPO may associate Eurojust with its activities concerning cross-border cases. The administrative relation between the EPPO and Eurojust, in terms of possible shared services, needed to be further discussed at a later stage of the negotiations. Apart from this, the draft Regulation on Eurojust, on which the Council reached a general approach in March 2015, will need to be re-examined in light of the outcome of the EPPO negotiations.[4] This holds in particular for Eurojust's mandate in relation to offences against the financial interests of the EU (so-called PIF crimes).[5]

3.3 Data Protection

Data protection opened entirely new territories for the criminal law experts dealing with the EPPO in the negotiations. It proved to be a rather complicated issue, as some Member States were concerned about possible conflicts between data protection rules for the EPPO on the one hand and provisions of national criminal procedural law on the other, especially as regards access to the case file and exchange of information.

There is now a "fully fledged own data protection regime" foreseen for the EPPO. Nevertheless, the provisions of this regime have been completely aligned with the so-called "Police Directive" of the recently adopted data protection package, and are thus coherent with the existing EU *acquis*.[6]

3.4 Simplified Prosecution Procedures

A compromise on a provision on simplified prosecution procedures (which was previously labeled 'transactions') could be reached only after lengthy discussions that commenced already at the start of the negotiations.[7] This compromise can be seen as a real achievement, brought about by all delegations, considering the

[4] Council of the European Union 2015.

[5] French acronym: Protection des Intérêts Financiers.

[6] European Parliament and Council 2016.

[7] *Supra* note 3.

difficulty to find a formula that would fit all the different national legal systems. Not all criminal law systems of the Member States include a system of transactions, but most Member States' legal systems provide for some kind of mechanism for out-of-court settlement, with various distinctive features.

On this point, it appeared to be impossible to take over the original Commission proposal for allowing the EPPO to conclude transactions. The proposal provided for a *sui generis* mechanism entailing a harmonisation of most of the procedural elements at the EU level. However, due to fundamental differences between Member States another solution had to be found.

The alternative, compromise solution was found in an approach that allows a degree of flexibility to adapt the EPPO mechanism to existing national mechanisms and enable it to resort to such systems. It is true that, as a result of relying on existing procedures under national law, suspects may be treated differently depending on which Member State they are located in. However, this applies to many types of measures and sanctions applied by the EPPO: the penalties are not fully harmonised, and neither are the terms of execution of penalties or conditions for arrest, to give a few examples.

The compromise achieved allows the European Delegated Prosecutor to propose to the central level of the EPPO (more specifically: to the Permanent Chamber), to make use of a simplified prosecution procedure if the applicable national law provides for one. This solution does have a real added value, as it enables the Permanent Chambers at the central level of the EPPO to supervise the use of the simplified mechanism in Member States. This may be qualified as quite an achievement, as for a long time it looked impossible to agree on any text on this topic at expert level.

3.5 Epilogue

The Netherlands Presidency also touched upon the topics of "judicial review", and the cooperation between the EPPO and third countries and non-participating Member States. However, these topics needed further discussion under the incoming new Presidency.

At the end of the Netherlands Presidency, a draft text of 80 articles could be delivered and presented to the JHA Council of June 2016. Nevertheless, it still looked as if the negotiations concerning this proposal would not only need to be continued under the Slovak Presidency but might possibly even extend to the Maltese Presidency, starting 1 January 2017.[8] Once the negotiations will have been

---

[8] Indeed, the Maltese Presidency dealt also with the EPPO and concluded that there was a lack of unanimity meaning that it cannot be approved by the Council of the EU. Malta EU 2017.

completed, the question will undoubtedly rise as to whether the final package to be submitted to Ministers will be sufficiently acceptable to all Member States involved. That question is obviously important in view of the unanimity required under Article 86 TFEU for the adoption of the Regulation.[9] Several Member States, including the Netherlands, have not taken up a final position on this issue. In fact, a number of these Member States are, for various reasons, inclined to refrain from taking part in the EPPO, among others because of existing parliamentary objections.

However, the absence of unanimity does not imply that the EPPO will not be set up at all. On the contrary, the Treaty foresees a specific procedure for that situation, including a role for the European Council. According to Article 86 TFEU, and in the absence of unanimity in the Council, a group of at least nine Member States may request that the draft Regulation be referred to the European Council. In that case, the procedure in the Council shall be suspended. After discussion, and in case of a consensus, the European Council shall, within four months of this suspension, refer the draft back to the Council for adoption. Within the same timeframe, in case of disagreement, and if at least nine Member States wish to establish enhanced cooperation on the basis of the draft regulation concerned, they shall notify the European Parliament, the Council and the Commission accordingly. In such a case, the authorisation to proceed with enhanced cooperation referred to in Article 20(2) of the Treaty on European Union and Article 329(1) of this Treaty shall be deemed to be granted and the provisions on enhanced cooperation shall apply. In other words, in this case, the EPPO will be set up for and by the Member States concerned.

It is important to note, though, that even in the case that the EPPO were to be set up on the basis of the procedure for enhanced cooperation described above, those Member States that choose not to participate in the EPPO may in practice still be confronted with requests for cooperation submitted by the EPPO. Conversely, non-participating Member States may equally well find themselves in a position having to seek some kind of assistance from the EPPO in investigations containing links to (suspects of) offences falling within the remit of their jurisdictions. After all, the EPPO will take over the role of the national authorities who are now competent to deal with EU fraud in the participating Member States. The legal arrangements for these forms of cooperation and their impact on non-participating Member States will need to become clearer in practice once the EPPO is up and running.

[9] On the basis of respectively the Protocols No. 21 and No. 22 to the Lisbon Treaty the UK and Ireland (No. 21) and Denmark (No. 22) are neither participating to the EPPO nor taking part in the voting procedure in the Council.

References

Council of the European Union (2015) Proposal for a Regulation on the European Union Agency for Criminal Justice Cooperation (Eurojust) [First reading] - General approach. Doc. 6643/15. Available at http://data.consilium.europa.eu/doc/document/ST-6643-2015-INIT/en/pdf. Accessed January 2017

Council of the European Union (2016) Proposal for a Regulation on the establishment of the European Public Prosecutor's Office - Partial general approach, Doc. 9799/16. Available at http://data.consilium.europa.eu/doc/document/ST-9799-2016-INIT/en/pdf. Accessed January 2017

European Commission (2013) Proposal for a Council regulation on the establishment of the European Public Prosecutor's Office, doc. COM (2013) 534 final. Available at http://data.consilium.europa.eu/doc/document/ST-12558-2013-INIT/en/pdf Accessed January 2017

European Parliament and Council (2016) Directive (EU) 2016/680 of the European Parliament and of the Council of 27 April 2016 on the protection of natural persons with regard to the processing of personal data by competent authorities for the purposes of the prevention, investigation, detection or prosecution of criminal offences or the execution of criminal penalties, and on the free movement of such data, and repealing Council Framework Decision 2008/977/JHA, *OJ* L 119/89, 4.5.2016

Malta EU 2017 (2017) Media Background Note Informal meeting of Justice and Home Affairs (26–27 January 2017). Available at https://www.eu2017.mt/Documents/Media%20Advisory%20Note/iJHA%20Media%20Background%20Note%2026-27JAN17.pdf. Accessed February 2017

Chapter 4
European Public Prosecutor's Office—A View on the State of Play and Perspectives from the European Parliament

Wouter van Ballegooij

Abstract During the discussions on the establishment of the European Public Prosecutor's Office ('EPPO'), the European Parliament had to make the best out of a role in which procedurally it could ultimately only say yes or no to the outcome of the negotiations between the Member States. It has done so by adopting a number of Interim Resolutions with Recommendations to the Council. In preparing its positions Parliament benefited from an in house Appraisal of the Impact Assessment accompanying the Commission Proposal. Parliament has insisted on the establishment of an effective EPPO which respects fundamental rights. Such an EPPO should also be efficient from a resources perspective creating the right synergies with Eurojust and OLAF, which will continue to play an important role in the fight against fraud, particularly now that the EPPO will be established under enhanced cooperation.

Keywords EU criminal law · European Public Prosecutor's Office · Better Regulation · Impact Assessment · European Parliament · Enhanced cooperation

---

The author is Policy Analyst for the Impact Assessment and European Added Value Directorate of the European Parliamentary Research Service, European Parliament.

The views expressed in this article are solely those of the author. They are without prejudice to the positions taken by Parliament on the matters discussed.

W. van Ballegooij (✉)
European Parliamentary Research Service, European Parliament, SQM 02Y095,
1047 Brussels, Belgium
e-mail: wouter.vanballegooij@europarl.europa.eu

W. Geelhoed et al. (eds.), *Shifting Perspectives on the European Public Prosecutor's Office*, https://doi.org/10.1007/978-94-6265-216-3_4

Contents

4.1 Introduction

This chapter provides a view on the state of play and perspectives on the establishment of the EPPO from the European Parliament. It will first outline the role of the European Parliament in the decision making procedure on the establishment of the EPPO. Second, it will summarize Parliament's Appraisal of the Impact Assessment accompanying the original Commission proposal. Then, it will discuss some of the points Parliament has highlighted in its Interim Resolutions on the EPPO. And, finally, it will describe the further negotiations on this file.

4.2 Role of the European Parliament in the Decision-Making Procedure

The ordinary legislative procedure does not apply to Article 86 TFEU, which is the legal basis for the establishment of the EPPO. Instead, unanimity is required in Council after obtaining consent of the European Parliament. In absence of unanimity the same article provides for a special procedure for enhanced cooperation. A group of nine or more Member States may request that the draft regulation by referred to the European Council. In case of consensus within the European Council the draft regulation will be referred back for adoption by the Council. In case of disagreement the said group of Member States is allowed to proceed after having notified the European Parliament, the Council and the Commission accordingly.[1] Parliament therefore had to make the best out of a role in which it could ultimately only say yes or no to the outcome of the negotiations. It has done so by adopting a

[1] This constitutes a sub-category of the so-called brake—accelerator mechanism (Piris 2010, p. 187); Drew 2015.

number of Interim Resolutions with Recommendations to the Council,[2] which will be discussed in more detail below.

However, one also needs to take into account that Parliament is or was involved on an equal footing on a number of related dossiers:

- Together with Council, Parliament decides on the Union's budget and verifies its correct implementation.[3] This will include the budget of the EPPO once adopted;
- Parliament was furthermore involved in accordance with the ordinary legislative procedure on the adoption of the Directive on the Fight against fraud to the Union's financial interests by means of criminal law;[4] and
- Finally, in accordance with Article 86 TFEU, the EPPO is to be established 'from Eurojust'. Eurojust itself is undergoing a substantial reform in a procedure in which Parliament equally has ordinary legislative powers.[5]

Parliament has sought to use these powers to increase its influence on the EPPO negotiations. This may be noticed by the explicit references in its Interim Resolutions to the costs to the EU budget of setting up the EPPO, the interaction with the scope of the Directive on the Fight against fraud to the Union's financial interests by means of criminal law and the relationship with Eurojust.[6] On Eurojust, Parliament's Committee on Civil Liberties has decided to wait with adopting its Report until the impact of the establishment of the EPPO on the role of Eurojust became clear.[7]

4.3 Parliament's Appraisal of the Impact Assessment Accompanying the Original Commission Proposal

As part of the Union's Better Law-making agenda,[8] Impact Assessments prepared by the Commission collect evidence to assess whether future legislative or non-legislative EU action is justified. The European Parliament also contributes to the Better Law-making agenda by drafting its own 'Appraisals' of these Impact

[2] European Parliament 2015, in accordance with Rule 99(3) of its Rules of Procedure.

[3] Articles 313, 314, 317, 318 TFEU.

[4] Directive (EU) 2017/1371 of the European Parliament and of the Council of 5 July 2017 on the fight against fraud to the Union's financial interests by means of criminal law, *OJ* L 198, 28.7.2017, p. 29-41.

[5] EU Agency for Criminal Justice Cooperation (Eurojust), 2013/0256(COD).

[6] See Sect. 4.4; European Parliament 2014, paras 4, 9–15; European Parliament 2015a, para 29; European Parliament 2016b, para 9.

[7] The setting up of the European External Action Service may serve as another example where Parliament sought to overcome a weak inter-institutional role under the Treaty of Lisbon, by *inter alia* leveraging its budgetary powers. See Erkelens and Blockmans 2012.

[8] Commission 2015; Renda 2015.

Assessments.[9] Parliament's Appraisal[10] of the Commission Impact Assessment on the EPPO has highlighted that the choice made by the Commission between the four policy options for the establishment of the EPPO required stronger evidence. These four options were:

- the creation of an EPPO Unit within Eurojust;
- a College-type EPPO;
- a decentralised EPPO, being the preferred option of the Commission; and
- a centralised EPPO.

The following reasons justified the urge for stronger evidence:

- First, the scale of the problem is difficult to quantify. The Commission estimates that the total value of offences against the EU's financial interest amounts to €3 billion.[11] However on this point the Impact Assessment admits that an exact estimate cannot be given due to weaknesses in the available data and the inherent difficulties in measuring the scale of undetected criminal activities.[12] This problem is exacerbated by the unresolved definitional issues surrounding fraud to the detriment of the Union's financial interests.
- Second, the actual costs of the various policy options for the Member States were probably underestimated. The Impact Assessment claims that the EPPO would to a large extent be able to rely on existing resources. It seems clear however that Member States are currently not devoting sufficient human and financial resources to overcome the lack of vigorous enforcement in the area of EU fraud.[13] Besides specific human resources for the EPPO one may also need to enhance the effectiveness of the judicial systems in a number of Member States more generally, for instance through the development of an annual European Union monitoring report on democracy, the rule of law and fundamental rights with country specific recommendations, as demanded by the European Parliament,[14] and by the further enhancement of judicial cooperation by means of training and coordination through EU agencies.[15]
- Third, the benefits of the preferred policy option were probably somewhat overestimated. Expecting a 300 million Euro reduction in annual fraud to the

[9] For further details see Collovà 2015.

[10] Davies 2013.

[11] Commission Impact Assessment Accompanying the Proposal for a Council Regulation on the establishment of the European Public Prosecutor's Office, SWD (2013) 274 ('Commission Impact Assessment'), p. 56.

[12] Commission Impact Assessment, p. 7.

[13] Instead of assuming the required staff is already there; Commission Impact Assessment, p. 36.

[14] European Parliament 2016c; Van Ballegooij and Evas 2016; Commission Impact Assessment, p. 16.

[15] Van Ballegooij and Zandstra 2016.

detriment of the EU budget is perhaps slightly optimistic. Another study conducted for the European Parliament on the Cost of Non-Europe in the area of organised crime and corruption estimates the damage rather around 200 million Euro.[16]

- Fourth, the fundamental rights impact of establishment of an EPPO were not sufficiently addressed in absence of common standards on investigation measures, the admissibility of evidence, and the rules applicable to the judicial review of acts by the EPPO in accordance with Article 86(3) TFEU.

The European Parliament requested a separate opinion covering these matters from the Fundamental Rights Agency ('FRA'), which was produced in February 2014. In this opinion the FRA *inter alia* insisted on more precise and prioritised criteria for the EPPO to follow when it makes a decision regarding the competent national jurisdiction, enabling individuals to foresee the consequences of such a decision, protect the principle of equality before the law and afford adequate protection against any arbitrary exercise of the EPPO's choice of jurisdiction. It also called for the specific framework within which the EPPO can undertake investigation measures to be sufficiently clear to ensure the proportionate use of investigation powers. The FRA called for defence rights to be explicitly and clearly guaranteed at all stages of investigations and prosecutions in order to ensure fundamental rights compliance. It deemed inadequate a general reference to EU secondary law in the area of defence rights or national law given the cross-border nature and intrusiveness of the EPPO regime. Specific safeguards should be considered including as regards access to legal representation and legal aid and the principle of *ne bis in idem*. Furthermore, the FRA called for the considerable limits imposed on the role of the CJEU by Article 36 of the proposed regulation to be re-considered to avoid violations of the right protected by Article 47 of the Charter and to ensure that any interferences with this right are proportionate and pursue a legitimate aim.[17]

Other weaknesses of the Impact Assessment identified in Parliament's Appraisal included the fact that the location of the future EPPO and the consequent costs involved, and the impact of the scenarios for enhanced cooperation, including specific measures for cooperation with Member States not participating, were not taken into consideration for the purpose of the cost-benefit analysis.[18]

---

[16] Van Ballegooij and Zandstra 2016, p. 9.

[17] European Union Agency for Fundamental Rights 2014.

[18] Commission Impact Assessment, p. 56.

4.4 Parliament's Interim Resolutions on the EPPO and the 'Response' by the Council

Parliament's political assessment of the Commission proposal and further negotiations in Council was made in a number of resolutions adopted in March 2014,[19] April 2015[20] and October 2016.[21]

This contribution will focus, first, on issues of effectiveness, and second, on protection of fundamental rights.

4.4.1 Effectiveness

Parliament has commented on the evolving structure of the EPPO. It has expressed its regret at the fact that Member States have moved towards a collegiate model for the EPPO instead of the hierarchical structure initially proposed by the Commission.[22] It sees this as a move which might unnecessarily slow down and complicate decision-making within the EPPO and hence weaken the efforts to overcome the current lack of follow up to OLAF recommendations.[23] Still, Parliament supports the EPPO in order to reduce the current fragmentation of national law enforcement efforts to protect the EU budget, thus strengthening the fight against fraud in the European Union.[24]

Parliament has also stressed the need for an unambiguous and clear set of competences for the EPPO based on the proposed Directive on the Fight against Fraud to the Union's financial interests by means of criminal law.[25] It has successfully called on the Council to include Value Added Tax ('VAT') fraud in the scope of this Directive.[26] In December 2016 a political agreement was reached with the Council by including serious cases of cross border VAT fraud (threshold of €10 million).[27]

As regards the procedural division of labour between the EPPO and the Member States, Parliament took the position that the EPPO should have been granted the occasion to first decide whether it has competence before national authorities

[19] European Parliament 2014.

[20] European Parliament 2015a.

[21] European Parliament 2016b.

[22] European Parliament 2015a, para 15.

[23] For a similar assessment see Commission Impact Assessment, p. 45/46.

[24] European Parliament 2016b, para 1.

[25] Also known as the 'PIF' Directive.

[26] European Parliament 2016b, para 2.

[27] Council 2016, with reference to the Directive as published in the OJ.

initiate their own investigations, in order to avoid parallel investigations.[28] It insisted that in the event of a disagreement between the EPPO and the national prosecution authorities regarding the question of competences, the final decision should be taken by an independent Court such as the Court of Justice of the European Union.[29] During the Council negotiations such demands proved too sensitive in terms of national sovereignty.[30]

Finally, Parliament has insisted on assurances for the EPPO to be given full independence from national governments and from EU institutions[31] and for it to be protected from any political pressure, even more so now that an extra governance layer has been introduced by the Council, a College consisting of the European Chief Prosecutor and one European Prosecutor per Member State.[32] Independence should be achieved through the selection and appointment procedures for the European Chief Prosecutor, his/her deputies, the European Prosecutors and the European Delegated Prosecutors.[33] Parliament has also called for its involvement in the appointment procedures of the European Prosecutors.[34] As regards the independence of the European Public Prosecutor's Office the Consolidated Council text[35] contains a number of safeguards as regards the appointment of the European Chief Prosecutor as well as dismissal procedures. Parliament however did not get a role in the appointment of European Prosecutors, except for the ability to appoint one member of the selection panel.[36] However, it does get a role in seeking their dismissal.[37]

4.4.2 Fundamental Rights

Parliament insisted that the investigative tools and investigation measures available to the EPPO should be uniform, precisely identified and compatible with the legal systems of the Member States where they are implemented. In addition, it requested

[28] European Parliament 2014, para 5(iii); European Parliament 2016b, para 2.

[29] European Parliament 2016b, para 3.

[30] Cf. Weyembergh and Brière 2016, Sect. 1.3, pp. 19–21.

[31] As defined in Article 13 TEU.

[32] European Parliament 2014, para 5(ii); Council text, Article 8.

[33] European Parliament 2015a, para 7.

[34] European Parliament 2015a, para 8.

[35] Council of the European Union, Proposal for a Regulation on the establishment of the European Public Prosecutor's Office—State of Play (consolidated text) Doc. 15760/16, 23 December 2016 ('Council text').

[36] Article 14(2) referring back to Article 13(3) Council text.

[37] Article 14(5) Council text.

that the criteria for the use of investigative measures be spelled out in more detail in order to ensure that 'forum shopping' is excluded.[38]

Article 25 of the Council text now spells out a number of specific investigation measures that European Delegated Prosecutors should be able to order or request. However the conditions for their use are still mostly left to national law. The lack of common standards for the use of investigation measures puts the individual subject to investigation at a significant disadvantage, particularly in sensitive areas such as the interception of electronic communications in accordance with Article 25(1) e.[39]

Parliament has called for cross-border investigations within the context of the EPPO to be based on the principle of mutual recognition as applied to evidence gathering measuring according to Directive 2014/41/EU regarding the European Investigation Order in criminal matters.[40] Article 26 of the Council text now contains a cooperation procedure between the European Delegated Prosecutor 'handling' the case and the one 'assisting' it in another Member State. It again relies extensively on national law, including as regards the determination whether a judicial authorisation is required. On the one hand this raises questions as regards the added value of this regime as opposed to the measures based on mutual recognition.[41] On the other hand not relying on existing mutual recognition measures once more creates legal uncertainty from a defence rights perspective, including as regards the applicability of (fundamental rights) conditions and exceptions.[42] Such uncertainty, which has hampered trust in judicial cooperation based on the European Arrest Warrant, and was addressed by co-legislators in the European Investigation Order[43] and the Court of Justice in the *Aranyosi* case,[44] should be avoided in the context of the EPPO.

Parliament urged the Council to clarify that the rules on investigative tools and admissibility of evidence need to comply with the Charter, the ECHR and constitutional traditions of the Member States.[45] Article 31(1) of the Council text and its accompanying recital 70 now seem to follow this line as well, even if it has been pointed out that national law and practices will continue to differ leading to 'a variable geometry affecting both the efficiency of EPPO's prosecutions and the effective protection of defendants' fundamental rights'.[46]

[38] European Parliament 2014, para 5(v).

[39] See Luchtman et al. 2015; European Union Agency for Fundamental Rights 2014 *supra* note 17.

[40] European Parliament 2014, para 5(vii); European Parliament 2015a, paras 24, 25; European Parliament 2016b, para 4.

[41] Cf. Weyembergh and Brière 2016, Sect. 3.2, pp. 30–33.

[42] For a more detailed comparison of the regime for cross border investigations foreseen by the Council text and the European Investigation Order see the contribution by Csúri.

[43] Cf. Van Ballegooij 2015, Sect. 5.2.2.1.

[44] Cf. Van Ballegooij and Bárd 2016.

[45] European Parliament 2014, paras 5(v), (vi); European Parliament 2015a, paras 20, 21.

[46] Weyembergh and Brière 2016, Sect. 3.2.2, p. 33.

The issue of judicial review was addressed in presentations by representatives of the Legal Services of the Council and the European Parliament during a hearing organised by Parliament's Committee on Civil Liberties, Justice and Home Affairs on 24 May 2016.[47] Parliament insisted that in order to ensure the effectiveness of judicial review in line with Article 47 of the Charter and the Treaties, any operational decision affecting third parties taken by the EPPO should be subject to judicial review before a competent national court. It also considered that for a number of decisions taken by the Permanent Chambers direct judicial review by the Court of Justice should be possible.[48] The Council text however still prevents judicial review by the Court of Justice as regards *inter alia* the choice and change of forum,[49] for which judicial review would have been possible, in addition to a general subsidiary mechanism for judicial review to the Court of Justice if the (initial) proposal by Germany and Italy on Article 36 would have been followed.[50]

As regards coherent legal protection for suspects or accused persons, Article 35 of Council text refers to the procedural rights measures including the Directive on Legal aid for suspects and accused persons in criminal proceedings published in the Official Journal in November 2016.[51] As has been pointed out by the FRA, lawyers' associations and academics, these measures are not sufficient in the context of supranational investigations conducted by the EPPO, as they were only adopted to support the application of the principle of mutual recognition between judicial authorities of Member States.[52] At least the Commission proposal provided further tailor-made safeguards.[53] This raises serious questions as regards the equality of arms between prosecution and defence.[54] Parliament insisted that EPPO suspects should have the right to legal aid, the right to information and access to case materials, and the right to present evidence and to ask the EPPO to collect evidence on behalf of them.[55]

[47] European Parliamentary Committee on Civil Liberties, Justice and Home Affairs (2016), Hearing, The European Public Prosecutor's Office (EPPO) and the European Union's Judicial cooperation Unit (EUROJUST), 24 May 2016.

[48] European Parliament 2016b, para 5; European Parliament 2015a, b, para 21.

[49] Council text, Articles 36, 22(4).

[50] German and Italian delegations (2016) Working Party on Judicial Cooperation in Criminal Matters (COPEN)—European Public Prosecutor Office (EPPO), WK 473/2016 INIT, 29 July 2016.

[51] Directive (EU) 2016/1919 of the European Parliament and of the Council of 26 October 2016 on legal aid for suspects and accused persons in criminal proceedings and for requested persons in European arrest warrant proceedings, *OJ* L 297, 4.11.2016, pp. 1–8.

[52] *Supra* n. 17; ECBA 2014; Luchtman and Vervaele 2014.

[53] Commission Proposal for a Council Regulation on the establishment of the European Public Prosecutor's Office, COM (2013) 534, Articles 32–35.

[54] See Meijers Committee 2015 for similar criticism.

[55] European Parliament 2016b, para 5.

4.5 Further Negotiations on This File

During the Council negotiations the structure of the EPPO has evolved from the hierarchical structure initially proposed by the Commission towards a collegiate model. In this context the European Parliament has insisted on safeguards for the EPPO to maintain its effectiveness, both from a material and procedural point of view.

The Slovak Presidency requested the Commission to come up with adjusted estimations of the budgetary implications of the collegiate structure within its cost and benefits analysis.[56] The Commission provided an update estimate of the human and financial resources needed to establish the EPPO in a revised legislative financial statement sent to Parliament on 21 September 2017. Parliament has stressed that it would also take this information into account before taking its final decision on whether to consent to the EPPO regulation or not.[57] In particular, it wanted to know the impact of the establishment of the EPPO on Eurojust's budget and the operational, organisational and administrative links between the two bodies.[58]

The EPPO will operate without common investigative tools, common rules on admissibility of evidence and common safeguards for suspects tailored to the EPPO. Certain safeguards have been built in, others were still desired by the European Parliament to uphold the equality of arms between prosecution and defence within the context of cross-border investigations by the EPPO. On 5 October 2017, Parliament followed the recommendation of its Rapporteur Barbara Matera (EPP/IT) to consent to the EPPO regulation agreed under enhanced cooperation, considering that the EP's concerns as regards the EPPO's competences, investigative powers, judicial review, procedural rights and relationships with other EU agencies and bodies as well as non-participating countries, have been largely addressed.[59]

References

Collovà C (2015) How does ex-ante Impact Assessment work in the EU? European Parliamentary Research Service, European Parliament, PE 528.809

Council (2016) Protection against fraud to the EU budget: Council agrees on its position. Available at http://www.consilium.europa.eu/en/press/press-releases/2016/12/08-jha-protection-against-fraud/. Accessed January 2017

[56] Agence Europe 09/07/2016, Slovak Presidency of EU Council requires cost-benefit analysis for European Prosecutor.

[57] European Parliament 2016b, para 8.

[58] European Parliament 2016a.

[59] http://www.europarl.europa.eu/sides/getDoc.do?pubRef=-//EP//TEXT+TA+P8-TA-2016-0376+0+DOC+XML+V0//EN.

Davies A (2013) Initial appraisal of a European Commission Impact Assessment European Commission proposal for a Council Regulation on the establishment of the European Public Prosecutor's Office. European Parliamentary Research Service, European Parliament, PE 514.087

Drew S (2015) How will the European Public Prosecutor's Office (EPPO) be born? In: Asp P (ed) The European Public Prosecutor's Office - Legal and Criminal Policy Perspectives. Stockholm University, Stockholm, pp 13–30

Erkelens LH, Blockmans S (2012) Setting up the External Action Service: An Act of Institutional Balance. European Constitutional Law Review, 8:246–279

European Commission (2015) European Commission website on Better Regulation. Available at http://ec.europa.eu/smart-regulation/index_en.htm. Accessed January 2017

European Criminal Bar Association (ECBA) (2014) Cornerstones for a draft regulation on the establishment of a European Public Prosecutor's Office. Available at http://www.ecba.org/extdocserv/201300207_ECBACORNERSTONESONEPPO.pdf. Accessed January 2017

European Parliament (2014) Resolution of 12 March 2014 on the proposal for a Council regulation on the establishment of the European Public Prosecutor's Office, P7_TA(2014)0234. Available at http://www.europarl.europa.eu/sides/getDoc.do?type=TA&reference=P7-TA-2014-0234&language=GA. Accessed January 2017

European Parliament (2015a) Resolution of 29 April 2015 on the proposal for a Council regulation on the establishment of the European Public Prosecutor's Office, P8_TA(2015)0173. Available at http://www.europarl.europa.eu/sides/getDoc.do?pubRef=-//EP//TEXT+TA+P8-TA-2015-0173+0+DOC+XML+V0//EN. Accessed January 2017

European Parliament (2015b) Rules of Procedure, September 2015. Available at http://www.europarl.europa.eu/sides/getDoc.do?pubRef=-//EP//TEXT+RULES-EP+20150909+TOC+DOC+XML+V0//EN&language=EN. Accessed January 2017

European Parliamentary Committee on Civil Liberties, Justice and Home Affairs (LIBE) (2016) Hearing, The European Public Prosecutor's Office (EPPO) and the European Union's Judicial Cooperation Unit (EUROJUST), 24 May 2016. Web stream available at http://www.europarl.europa.eu/ep-live/en/committees/video?event=20160524-1500-COMMITTEE-LIBE. Accessed January 2017

European Parliament (2016a) Oral Question O-000093/2016: European Public Prosecutor's Office and Eurojust. Available at http://www.europarl.europa.eu/sides/getDoc.do?pubRef=-//EP//TEXT+OQ+O-2016-000093+0+DOC+XML+V0//EN. Accessed January 2017

European Parliament (2016b) Resolution of 5 October 2016 on the European Public Prosecutor's Office and Eurojust, P8_TA (2016)0376. Available at http://www.europarl.europa.eu/sides/getDoc.do?pubRef=-//EP//TEXT+TA+P8-TA-2016-0376+0+DOC+XML+V0//EN. Accessed January 2017

European Parliament (2016c) Resolution of 25 October 2016 with recommendations to the Commission on the establishment of an EU mechanism on democracy, the rule of law and fundamental rights (2015/2254(INL)), P8_TA-PROV (2016) 0409. Available at http://www.europarl.europa.eu/sides/getDoc.do?pubRef=-//EP//TEXT+TA+P8-TA-2016-0409+0+DOC+XML+V0//EN. Accessed January 2017

European Union Agency for Fundamental Rights (2014) (FRA) Opinion on a proposal to establish a European Public Prosecutor's Office. Available at http://fra.europa.eu/sites/default/files/fra-2014-opinion-european-public-prosecutors-office_en.pdf. Accessed January 2017

Luchtman M, Ouwerkerk J, van Noorloos M, Geelhoed W, Rijpma J, Middelkoop L (2015) Fundamental Rights and the European Public Prosecutor's Office: An uncomfortable silence. EU law analysis, 10 April 2015. Available at http://eulawanalysis.blogspot.nl/2015/04/fundamental-rights-and-european-public.html. Accessed January 2017

Luchtman M, Vervaele J (2014) European Agencies for Criminal Justice and Shared Enforcement (Eurojust and the European Public Prosecutor's Office). Utrecht Law Review, 10:5, pp 132–150

Meijers Committee (2015) Gaps and inconsistencies in legal protection in EU criminal law, CM 1503, Legal Protection and the future European Public Prosecutor's Office. Available at https://

www.eerstekamer.nl/bijlage/20151030/cm1503_legal_protection_and_the/document3/f=/vjylev0k37v1.pdf Accessed January 2017
Piris JC (2010) The Lisbon Treaty: A Legal and Political Analysis. Cambridge University Press, Cambridge
Renda A (2015) Too good to be true. A quick assessment of the European Commission's new Better Regulation Package. CEPS special report, No 108. Available at https://www.ceps.eu/system/files/SR108AR_BetterRegulation.pdf. Accessed January 2017
Van Ballegooij W (2015) The Nature of Mutual Recognition in European Law. Re-examining the notion from an individual rights perspective with a view to its further development in the criminal justice area. Intersentia, Antwerp
Van Ballegooij W, Bárd P (2016) Mutual recognition and individual rights: did the Court get it right? New Journal of European Criminal Law, 7, Issue 4: pp 439–464
Van Ballegooij W, Evas T (2016) An EU Mechanism on Democracy, the Rule of Law and Fundamental Rights. European Added Value Assessment accompanying the Legislative initiative report (Rapporteur Sophie in 't Veld). European Parliamentary Research Service, European Parliament, PE.579.328
Van Ballegooij W, Zandstra T (2016) Organised Crime and Corruption. Cost of Non-Europe Report. European Parliamentary Research Service, European Parliament, PE 558.779
Weyembergh A, Brière C (2016) Towards a European Public Prosecutor's Office (EPPO). Study for the LIBE Committee. Directorate-General for Internal Policies, European Parliament, PE 571.399

Part II
Scholarly Perspectives on the EPPO: Constitutional, Regulatory and Institutional Issues

Chapter 5
The Establishment of a European Public Prosecutor's Office: Between 'Better Regulation' and Subsidiarity Concerns

Ester Herlin-Karnell

Abstract The chapter investigates the establishment of the European Public Prosecutor Office (EPPO) from the perspective of better regulation and subsidiarity. The chapter addresses the question as to what extent the idea for the creation of an EPPO represents 'Better Regulation' as well as to what extent the subsidiarity concerns expressed by the Member States are well founded when considering the EU financial crimes area as a whole. The chapter concludes by discussing the 'Better Regulation' criteria specifically with regard to subsidiarity concerns in EU criminal law.

Keywords EU · European Public Prosecutor's Office · Subsidiarity · Better Regulation · Criminal law · Financial crimes

Contents

The author is Professor of EU Constitutional Law and Justice and a University Research Chair at VU University Amsterdam.

E. Herlin-Karnell (✉)
1081 HV Amsterdam, The Netherlands
e-mail: e.herlinkarnell@vu.nl

W. Geelhoed et al. (eds.), *Shifting Perspectives on the European Public Prosecutor's Office*, https://doi.org/10.1007/978-94-6265-216-3_5

5.1 Introduction

The idea of the creation of a European Public Prosecutor's Office (EPPO) is one of the most contested EU criminal law topics in recent years. It emanates from the longstanding project of creating a comprehensive EU anti-fraud regime and has been extensively debated for over two decades, with the EPPO representing something of a jewel in the crown. As such the EPPO project represents a follow-up to the previous *Corpus Juris* venture.[1]

This chapter will focus on the legislative history and the European process for the creation of an EPPO. Specifically, I will discuss to what extent the proposal for a new regulation on the EPPO represents 'better' regulation. In doing so the paper will zoom in on some particularly sensitive questions from a constitutional perspective. The EPPO has, with regard to the original draft, triggered reasoned opinions or so called 'yellow cards', issued by 14 chambers of 11 different national Parliaments.[2] This has attracted a lot of attention and debate in academia and legal practice.[3] Therefore, it seems at present highly unclear whether unanimity can be achieved in the Council.[4] The only possibility for the EPPO project to survive would then be through the invocation of the enhanced cooperation mechanism, according to which some Member States (nine or more) could pursue flexible integration. This could be considered as a subsidiarity-friendly alternative as it allows for differentiation in the EU and thereby for divergence between the Member States. When discussing the concept of 'flexibility' in terms of differentiation, the starting point is often the enhanced cooperation mechanisms as the most clear-cut example of flexible integration.[5] In short, the classic notion of 'enhanced cooperation' means that some Member States go further on the path of integration than other States. The concept accepts that there is room for action outside the EU model and that not all Member States have to be in the same boat, while still respecting each other through the fundamental loyalty principle of the Article 4(3) TEU. However, from the perspective of the establishment of an EPPO through the notion of flexible integration, it also raises concerns about an office that seems to offer a half-baked solution. After all, it may be asked what the function of an EPPO is if not the whole of the EU is joining?

Let me briefly set out the relevant provisions of Article 86 TFEU. This article states that the Council may set up an EPPO in order to combat crimes affecting the financial interests of the Union, the EPPO shall be set up from Eurojust. Crucially, the provision reads that:

---

[1] Delmas-Marty and Vervaele 2000.

[2] Article 12(b) TEU provides for a competence of national Parliaments to see that the principle of subsidiarity is respected in accordance with Protocol No. 2.

[3] Erkelens et al. 2015; Fromage 2016.

[4] Fromage 2016, p. 24.

[5] E.g. Weatherill 1999, p. 21.

> In the absence of unanimity in the Council, a group of at least nine Member States may request that the draft regulation be referred to the European Council. In that case, the procedure in the Council shall be suspended. After discussion, and in case of a consensus, the European Council shall, within four months of this suspension, refer the draft back to the Council for adoption.
> Within the same timeframe, in case of disagreement, and if at least nine Member States wish to establish enhanced cooperation on the basis of the draft regulation concerned, they shall notify the European Parliament, the Council and the Commission accordingly. In such a case, the authorisation to proceed with enhanced cooperation referred to in Article 20(2) of the Treaty on European Union and Article 329(1) of this Treaty shall be deemed to be granted and the provisions on enhanced cooperation shall apply.

The enhanced cooperation procedure is similar to the well-known emergency brake provisions of Articles 82(2) and 83(1) and (2) TFEU, which stipulate in their common para 3 the possibility of applying a so-called 'emergency brake' if the proposed legal instrument in question would affect fundamental aspects of a Member State's criminal justice system. In these provisions, even a single Member State may request that the draft be referred to the European Council and in case of persisting disagreement, the enhanced cooperation mechanism applies to the remaining nine or more Member States, which can move further with their cooperation.

When discussing the possibilities of enhanced cooperation in the EPPO context, it is essential to understand the general climate in which this type of alternative integration takes place. Indeed, Member States, like the UK and Denmark already enjoy a major opt-out arrangement from the 'Area of Freedom, Security and Justice' (AFSJ) and with the UK leaving through its Brexit negotiations anyway, only Denmark is "out" of the mayor AFSJ scheme. Moreover, Member States like Sweden and The Netherlands have announced that they will not participate due to what they consider the far-reaching competences of the EPPO including the possibility of extending the competences of the EPPO to criminality not related to the EU budget.[6] It could also be pointed out that there has been a debate as to whether such prosecutor should have a wider criminal law mandate than the financial sphere

---

[6] The UK opt-out, Protocol No. 21 and Denmark position, Protocol No. 22 to the TEU and TFEU. As to Sweden's position on not joining the EPPO, see Council 2017, EPPO General Approach, point no. 11. On the Dutch position see NRC Handelsblad of 24 November 2016: "Nederland doet toch niet mee aan Europees OM" (available at: https://www.nrc.nl/nieuws/2016/11/23/nederland-doet-toch-niet-mee-aan-europees-openbaar-ministerie-a1533218 Accessed February 2017. "Prolonged negotiations on the [EPPO] proposal have spanned over three and a half years and every effort has been made to reach an agreement which is acceptable to all Member States. Despite these efforts, a meeting of EU Ambassadors (Committee of Permanent Representatives – COREPER II) on 19 January 2017 concluded that there is a lack of the necessary unanimity on the text, meaning that it cannot be approved by the Council of the EU." Malta EU 2017, informal ministers meeting on Justice and Home Affairs available at https://www.eu2017.mt/Documents/Media%20Advisory%20Note/iJHA%20Media%20Background%20Note%2026-27JAN17.pdf.

alone.[7] Indeed, Article 86(4) provides for the possibility of a future European Council to adopt a decision amending the competences of such a prosecutor to include serious crime with a cross-border dimension in a broader sense.

Despite the strong hostility in some Member States concerning the establishment of an EPPO, the Council has once again redrafted the Regulation so as to prevent this scenario of fragmentation taking place. In order to avoid too much overlap with other chapters in this volume, this contribution broadens the discussion and looks at the EPPO in the context of the financial crisis and the fight against financial crimes. There is a reason why the question of the fight against financial crimes has become a key issue for the EU legislator. It should be recalled that the fight against white-collar crime became a major priority in the aftermath of the immediate financial crisis and the regulatory responses that followed. At present, much of the thinking in the AFSJ is dominated by security concerns and the need for financial stability and the EU's obligation to ensure a high level of security within the Union and equal concerns of justice and freedom (as inherent in the EU policy area of "freedom, security and justice" mission). In this perspective, the EPPO would add a necessary element of infrastructure to facilitate the creation of EU criminal law and fight financial crimes more effectively.[8]

This chapter is structured as follows. Firstly, I will briefly discuss the background for the establishment of an EPPO and the context in which it will be operating. Secondly, I will discuss the idea of Better Regulation in the EU and I will zoom in on a couple of provisions of the proposed Regulation. Thirdly, I will look at the subsidiarity principle and discuss its importance in the AFSJ context and its effect on the establishment of an EPPO.

5.2 EU Financial Criminal Law and the EPPO Project

The EU has a strong interest to counter financial crimes and fraud against the EU budget as these crimes hamper the trust in the market and undermine consumer confidence to engage in internal market transactions.[9] A majority of the current instruments adopted by the EU in the area of the suppression of financial crimes have been agreed on the basis and justification that there is a need for increased regulatory response to financial crimes, thereby tackling the financial crises in the EU more effectively through getting tough in white-collar crime.[10]

Therefore, we need to understand the EPPO in context. Specifically, this chapter argues that we need to view the establishment of the EPPO against the backdrop of the EU current responses to the financial crisis. Hence, the discussion of the EU's

[7] Monar 2005, p. 226.

[8] On needed "infrastructure", see Willems 2017.

[9] Moloney 2014, Chapter 8.

[10] Ibid.

stance on financial crimes is closely connected to the larger debate on the reform of the EU financial system and the enhancement of the solidity of the euro. Recent examples of EU legislative activity in the area are the Market Abuse Directive (MAD)[11] and the Regulation to counter white-collar crime (MAR).[12] Moreover, the occurrence of financial crimes has (since the early days of the EU) constituted the main threat to the establishment of the internal market. With the global financial crisis in 2008, the fight against white-collar crime and fraud against the EU budget was again considered a main priority for the EU.[13] In addition, there is an overlap—or "hybridity"—in legal sources not only between EU internal market policies and the growing importance of the AFSJ, but also in relation to the external dimension of the EU. This is because a majority of the measures currently adopted to fight the financing of terrorism and financial crimes in the EU partially falls within the remit of international norms that are being adopted by the EU (e.g. the Financial Action Task Force).[14] Furthermore, the EU sanctions regime is built around the notion of regulatory powers involving different actors and processes and often through administrative sanctions rather than criminal law.[15] This is perhaps an indication of a move away from the "constitutionalized" picture where the rule of law and protection of human rights are the essential values, towards a more uncertain human rights framework based on effectiveness concerns in which agencies such as *Europol* and *Eurojust* play a pivotal role. While there have been many intriguing studies on the international impact of EU policies in the area of fisheries, and risk regulation/medicine in particular,[16] the regulatory consequences for the AFSJ remain largely unexplored.[17]

So the EU's fight against financial crimes takes place at multiple levels in the EU regulatory machinery: both within the framework and endeavour of the establishment of the AFSJ and within the EU internal market, with its need to ensure market integrity. While much has been said about the purpose of fighting financial crimes within the internal market,[18] much less has been said with regard to the impact of these findings on the operation of the crime-fighting project of the AFSJ. Recent examples of directives that illustrate this are the aforementioned MAD directive[19]

[11] Directive on criminal sanctions for insider dealing and market manipulation, Directive 2014/57/EU, L173/179, see Herlin-Karnell 2012a. On financial crimes in global context, see Ryder 2014.

[12] Regulation (EU) No. 596/2014, on market abuse (market abuse regulation) and repealing Directive 2003/6/EC of the European Parliament and of the Council and Commission Directives.

[13] Herlin-Karnell 2012a.

[14] Financial Action Task Force *Financial Action Task Force Recommendations* (Financial Action Task Force: Paris, 2012).

[15] Herlin-Karnell 2016, Chapter 11.

[16] Burgess et al. 2016.

[17] On regulatory regimes in administrative law, see e.g. Zumbansen 2013.

[18] See e.g. Stefanou and Xhanthaki 2005.

[19] See *supra* note 11.

and the related MAR regulation,[20] based on Article 83 TFEU and Article 114 TFEU respectively, as well as the Fourth Money Laundering Directive,[21] based on Article 114 TFEU. There is also a proposal for a so-called PIF Directive on countering Fraud against the EU budget,[22] on which the Council reached agreement in December 2016.[23] The EU's strategy to fight irregularities in the market should be seen in the light of the history of the debate on the market abuse regime and the question as to why the suppression of financial crimes is relevant in EU law.[24] The underlying objective of the EU's involvement in the fight against financial crime is to boost investor confidence and thereby contribute to the functioning of the internal market. Certainly, since the early days of the EU financial crimes together with organized crime have constituted the main criminal law threat to the establishment of the internal market and have formed the core of the EU's approach to criminal law until 9/11 when the fight against terrorism became a higher priority.[25] With the recent financial crisis in 2008, the EU has taken a tough approach on white-collar crime. Because of the pre-existing lack of competence in criminal law matters at the EU supranational level, the fight against financial crimes has traditionally taken place within the framework of the provisions of Article 114 TFEU purporting the establishment and functioning of the internal market. Should an EPPO be established (Article 86 TFEU), the involved prosecutor would receive far-reaching investigative powers in the area of financial crimes.[26] The prosecutor will be responsible for investigating, prosecuting and bringing to judgment, where appropriate in liaison with Europol, the perpetrators of and accomplices in offences against the Union's financial interests, as determined by the regulation provided for in Article 86 TFEU. The establishment of an EPPO has however met some serious opposition.[27] Considering the fact that 11 National Parliaments voted against the proposal in the yellow card procedure, one would have thought that the enhanced cooperation mechanism would have been triggered earlier. Instead, the Commission has maintained its proposal essentially intact, notwithstanding the fact that the yellow-card procedure has been used only for the second time since its inclusion in the Treaties.[28] The Member States have redrafted the regulation exactly so as to

---

[20] See *supra* note 12.

[21] Directive (EU) 2015/849 of the European Parliament and of the Council of 20 May 2015 on the prevention of the use of the financial system for the purposes of money laundering or terrorist financing, amending Regulation (EU) No. 648/2012 of the European Parliament and of the Council, *OJ* L 141/73, 5.6.2015.

[22] Commission PIF Directive 2012.

[23] Council Meeting December 2016, p. 4.

[24] On financial crimes in global context, see e.g. Ryder 2014.

[25] See e.g. Peers 2016.

[26] Commission EPPO Proposal 2013. See Erkelens et al. 2015; Vervaele 2013.

[27] See Ligeti 2012; Conway 2016; Wade 2013.

[28] Ibid.

avoid a scenario of fragmentation to take place. Nevertheless, these efforts could not prevent the scenario of enhanced cooperation from happening.[29]

While financial market regulation relies on a range of tools, anti-fraud rules remain imperative. Thus, in the EU context, the fight against fraud and related activities always sparks a complex debate as to the competences of the EU. Up until the entry into force of the Lisbon Treaty, the EU fought organized crime through the framework of the former 'third pillar', and also adopted a number of third pillar instruments on anti-fraud measures.[30] In the policy area of the AFSJ, Article 83 TFEU provides far-reaching powers in criminal law concerning cross-border criminality. But 'mainstream' internal market powers, such as Article 114 TFEU, are still crucially important in the context of the EU's fight against financial crimes. These powers are particularly significant with respect to the effect on the national arena, as Article 114 TFEU also allows for the adoption of regulations, thereby directly impacting citizens and Member State legislation. The Commission's Communication on reinforcing sanctioning regimes in the financial sector proves particularly intriguing in this context.[31] It states that efficient and sufficiently convergent sanctioning regimes amount to the necessary corollary to the new supervisory system and that '[s]upervision cannot be effective with weak, highly variant sanctioning regimes. It is essential that within the EU and elsewhere, all supervisors are able to deploy sanctioning regimes that are sufficiently convergent, strict, resulting in deterrence.'[32] Yet the Commission concludes that it would assess whether, and in which areas, the introduction of criminal sanctions and the establishment of minimum rules on the definition of criminal offences and sanctions may prove essential in order to ensure the effective implementation of EU financial services legislation.[33] Unfortunately, the EU's current response to financial crimes does not seem to reflect any such assessment, as will be shown below.

In short, most arguments against the initial proposal for an EPPO concerned the inaccuracy of the figures presented by the Commission as well as the lack of added value of EPPO investigations.[34] It was also argued that its establishment possibly had a detrimental impact on the existing actors in the area and their future cooperation with non-EPPO Member States.[35] On the contrary, could one now say that

---

[29] 17 Member States, in favour of establishing an enhanced cooperation among them, referred the EPPO Draft Regulation to the European Council (EC). The EC discussed the Draft at its meeting of 9 March 2017 (see Conclusions by the President of the European Council, p. 6).

[30] Treaty of Amsterdam Amending the Treaty on European Union, Articles 29–31, Oct. 11, 1997, 1997 *OJ* C (340) 1.

[31] Commission Communication 2010.

[32] *Id.* at 2.

[33] See *id.* at p. 11, where "The Commission holds the view that a legislative initiative is warranted to set some minimum common standards that Member States should respect in designing administrative sanctions for violations of financial services rules and when applying sanctions in this field.").

[34] Csúri 2016.

[35] Ibid.

the EPPO is a giant without powers?[36] Regardless the main argument as presented by the Commission, Eurojust and Europol only have a general mandate to facilitate the exchange of information and coordinate national criminal investigations and prosecutions, but lack the power to carry out acts of investigation or prosecution themselves.[37] According to the Commission, action by national judicial authorities remains often slow, average prosecution rates are low and the results obtained in the different Member States are unequal. Based on this track record, prosecution of EU fraud undertaken by Member States may currently not be considered as effective, equivalent and deterrent as is required under the Treaty. However, there is a fundamental flaw in the present proposal for a European Public Prosecutor's Office. It is difficult to separate on the one hand rules relating to investigations and prosecutions, at the EU level, and on the other hand, trials at Member State level. According to Peers, the Commission should have considered other possibilities of more limited measures to achieve the same objectives such as the harmonisation of the national prosecutions rules in this area.[38]

5.3 The Emergence of the EPPO

As noted above, the idea of an EPPO is not new but has been realized in practice in recent years. It had first publicly been developed by the so-called *Corpus Juris* group of academics and practitioners in the 1990s in response to a request by the Commission, with a model proposal in 1997, which was revised in 2000.[39] This *Corpus Juris* formed the basis for a *Commission Green Paper*,[40] which eventually led to Article 86 TFEU. Yet the question of enforcement of EU anti-fraud policies seems to have been largely left to the EU Court of Justice through its case law. According to the well-established case law starting with the Greek Maize case,[41] Member States have to protect EU interests the same way as they protect national interests and always honour EU rights. Specifically, the Greek Maize case concerned fraud against the EU where the Court held that, 'the Member States must ensure that infringements of EU law are penalised under conditions, both procedural and substantive, which are analogous to those applicable to infringements of

[36] See generally Gómez–Jara Díez 2015.

[37] COM(2011) 293 final "On the protection of the financial interests of the European Union by criminal law and by administrative investigations".

[38] Peers 2016, Chapter 6.

[39] Delmas-Marty and Vervaele 2000.

[40] European Commission, Green Paper on criminal law protection of the financial interests of the Community and the establishment of a European prosecutor, COM(2001) 715 final, Brussels, 11.12.2001.

[41] Case C-68/88 *Commission v Greece* [1989] ECR 1-2965, §24.

national law of a similar nature and importance and which, in any event, make the penalty effective, proportionate and dissuasive.'[42]

Moreover, as noted above, related to the adoption of an EPPO and the need to be more effective on the fight against financial crimes, the European Commission adopted in 2012 the Proposal for a Directive on the fight against fraud to the Union's financial interests by means of criminal law'.[43] The Commission proposal is based on Article 325 TFEU concerning the fight against fraud against the EU's budget. At first instance this appears to be a significant development in the evolution of the EU's counter fraud strategy. The scope of the proposed Directive is limited to fraud committed against the financial interests of the EU. The Commission states that the framework is complemented by general Union criminal law measures for the fight against certain illegal activities particularly harmful to the licit economy, such as money laundering and corruption which, although not specific to the protection of the Union's financial interests, also contribute to their protection.[44]

It could be argued that this division between the Union's financial interests and the Member States interests does not make much sense when viewed in the light of the EU's market regulation powers. Of course, Article 325 TFEU only empowers the EU to fight fraud against its own budget. However, the EU as is well known has largely transgressed the division of competence with regard to EU and Member States finances and fiscal powers, a story that has gone hand in hand with EU integration in general. In other words, the EU competences are largely functional and therefore difficult to fix once and for all.[45] Therefore, it is suggested that the limitation set in Article 325 TFEU entails a rather cosmetic rule since the overall approach adopted by the EU seems not to be limited to fight fraud against the EU but also sets out to regulate the Member States as a result of the financial crisis. In other words, the EU fight against financial crimes is an area that is also a regulatory case study of the division of competences between the EU and its Member States where less room is left for Member States' discretion than one would initially expect.

One could say that the recent judgment in the *Taricco* case implies a confirmation of this conclusion.[46] The EU Court of Justice held that national rules on prescription periods, which hinder prosecutions of VAT fraud against the national budget, infringe EU law. The Court stated that "The provisions of Article 325(1) and (2) TFEU therefore have the effect, in accordance with the principle of the precedence of EU law, in their relationship with the domestic law of the Member States, of rendering automatically inapplicable, merely by their entering into force,

[42] See for more on this Herlin-Karnell and Ryder 2017.

[43] Commission PIF Directive 2012.

[44] In addition, Regulation (EC, Euratom) No. 2988/95 sets out administrative rules for dealing with illegal activities at the expense of the Union's financial interests.

[45] See e.g. Weatherill 2011.

[46] Case C-105/14, *Taricco* delivered on 8 September 2015.

any conflicting provision of national law."[47] The Court also asserted that this approach was in line with the Charter of Fundamental Rights. Arguably, it should also be seen in the broader context as to why the EU considers the EPPO an important agent in order to maintain compliance with the EU financial rules.

5.4 What Is Better Regulation in this Context?

5.4.1 Better Regulation: Main Features

In the Better Regulation Agenda of 2016, entitled "Better Regulation: Delivering better results for a stronger Union", the Commission points out that where regulatory costs are found to be disproportionate to the goals pursued, alternative approaches to achieving the same goals will be explored.[48] Applying the principles of better regulation will ensure that measures are evidence-based, well-designed and deliver tangible and sustainable benefits for citizens, business and society as a whole. It could be argued that the very idea of "Better Regulation" is particularly important in EU criminal law as it can affect people's lives in a rather drastic way. Article 69 TFEU stresses the importance of subsidiarity in the AFSJ sphere as many of the subject matters in this policy (like criminal law, security and immigration law) area are closely related to national sovereignty.[49]

According to Commissioner Timmermans, responsible for the Better Regulation Agenda, '*We [the EU] will be ambitious where we must, and modest wherever we can. Citizens across Europe expect the European Union to change. ...We have culled many rules, we have improved many others, and we have put forward proposals that focus on the big issues such as migration, security, investment and climate change. We will continue on this path listening to and acting on people's concerns. And if the Parliament and the Council take up our proposals and adopt them, real change will be felt by citizens all around Europe soon.*'[50]

Indeed, there are various innovations in EU law such as the Regulatory Fitness and Performance Programme (REFIT), which is the Commission's programme for ensuring that EU legislation remains fit for purpose and delivers the results intended by EU lawmakers. These Commission guidelines are of course of relevance for the aptness of the EPPO, as the adoption of the EPPO should be seen in the context of EU law at large.

---

[47] Para 52.

[48] Better Regulation 2016.

[49] Article 69 TFEU: "National Parliaments ensure that the proposals and legislative initiatives submitted under Chapters 4 and 5 comply with the principle of subsidiarity, in accordance with the arrangements laid down by the Protocol on the application of the principles of subsidiarity and proportionality.".

[50] State of the Union 2016.

It could be argued that the very idea of Better Regulation is particularly important in EU criminal law and how it is implemented in the national arena. The recent Better Regulation Agenda urges Member States to avoid unjustified 'gold plating' or over-implementation of EU rules when transposing them into national law. While this may help achieving the legislation's objectives in the local context or aim to deliver greater benefits, it may also impose significant extra burdens. Member States should be invited to explain the reasons for any such gold plating. Over-implementation seems bad from the perspective of legitimacy of the EU regime and public support of the EU. Governments sometimes use EU law to justify their individual agenda and thereby 'over-implement'.[51]

The Commission's annual evaluation of its own approach to subsidiarity and proportionality is less enthusiastic albeit instructive: although things are becoming considerably more sophisticated in this field, the AFSJ sphere has merely been listed as an example of where attention was being paid to subsidiarity and proportionality in an impact assessment.[52] Yet, in its annual report on 2013 regarding subsidiarity and proportionality the Commission pointed out that, with regard to questions over nature and scope of the EPPO's competence, the crimes in question, including non-cross-border cases, have an intrinsic Union dimension. In particular, the Commission stated that a limitation of the scope would not only reduce EPPO's added value but also call into question the Union's competence in this matter.[53] According to the Commission, not granting the EPPO enough powers would be in breach of the subsidiarity test.

5.4.2 Does the EPPO Comply with the Idea of Better Regulation?

A key question is perhaps whether the EPPO represents "Better Regulation". As already mentioned, in its Better Regulation Agenda of 2016 the Commission points out that where regulatory costs are found to be disproportionate to the goals pursued, alternative approaches to achieving the same goals will be explored.[54] Applying the principles of Better Regulation will ensure that measures are evidence-based, well designed and deliver tangible and sustainable benefits for citizens, business and society as a whole.

In Article 5 of the proposed Regulation on "Basic principles of the activities" of the EPPO, the question of better regulation is addressed.[55] This article provides in para 3 (last sentence) that when a matter is governed by national law and this

[51] Herlin-Karnell 2012b.

[52] Commission Report on subsidiarity and proportionality 2010.

[53] Commission report on subsidiarity and proportionality 2014, p. 10.

[54] Better Regulation 2016.

[55] Council EPPO Draft Regulation 2017b.

Regulation, then the latter shall prevail. From EU law perspective this is like stating the obvious. This article also states that the EPPO shall be bound by the principles of the rule of law and proportionality. This is hugely important. This should apply without having to be specified but I believe it is important to have it as an extra assertion. And the same goes for the statement that the EPPO should be governed by the Charter of Fundamental Rights. Article 6 on "Independence and accountability" is also important as the lack of any clear criteria has been a main concern among academics.[56] However, this improvement may be weakened by the rules on judicial review. According to Article 36 of the Regulation only procedural matters can be challenged. Of course the Regulation also assures us again that it complies with Fundamental Rights and the EU directive on access to a lawyer.[57] However, in practice it may be difficult to limit objections to procedural questions. And yet, it might be in line with subsidiarity, at least on paper. Still, the EPPO proposal has far-reaching implications for the legal systems of the Member States in what is generally acknowledged to be the sovereignty-sensitive area of criminal law and procedure. Yet a key feature of the current proposal that the Commission identifies as catering to subsidiarity concerns, is that an EPPO would operate within existing national criminal procedures.[58] Thus, an EPPO would use standard national methods of investigation and prosecution. Yet, a uniform treatment of crime, which is one of the main reasons given for the adoption of the EPPO in the first place, is absent in the current version of the EPPO draft. It could be argued that too wide a discretion is left to the Member States. I am therefore far from sure whether this is in conformity with the "Better Regulation" requirements as established by the Commission.

As noted, the EPPO and the priorities to get it adopted seem closely connected to the reformation of the EU regulatory system for market regulation and as such in line with the recent Directives on Market abuse and money laundering and the new Fraud Directive and other measures. Moreover, the Better Regulation Agenda has become a lot more sophisticated in recent years: indeed, anyone who has followed the development of EU criminal law and the AFSJ will have noticed this.[59] But the EPPO's biggest challenge is not what happens in the EU's institutions but instead in what happens on the "field". It is the Member States and the Council who are to decide the fate of the EPPO with the consent of the European Parliament. Events such as Brexit and other national sentiments across Europe predict a difficult future ahead of the prospective establishment of an EPPO, despite the urgency of its establishment. The Member States must decide what it is they want the EU to achieve and what is best left at the local level. In these post-Brexit decision days, it is to be hoped that when it comes to the EPPO the Member States will understand

[56] Conway 2016.

[57] Directive on Access to Lawyer, 2013/48/EU.

[58] Conway 2012. The EPPO will not replace Eurojust, which will continue in its current role regarding all offences other than those against the financial interests of the EU.

[59] Herlin-Karnell 2012a, Chapter 5.

that joint business and freedoms also imply that it is necessary to embrace the full package of cooperation, including fully shaped defense rights and protection of the individual. As indicated above, in order for the EPPO project to be successful it is largely contingent on the willingness of the Member States and on the Commission's appraisal whether it considers the Draft EPPO Regulation—as amended by the Council—to comply sufficiently with its own Better Regulation standards.

5.5 Better Regulation in Relation to Subsidiarity

The notion of subsidiarity clearly is a context-dependent concept. It is also a concept that is not always in line with the idea of "Better Regulation". There are many advantages to doing things together on a smaller and more local scale than the supranational EU level.[60] For example, the fostering of a more intimate and more valued sense of community and shared identity, greater knowledge and expertise in collective decision-making, the spreading of the risks of bad government, a greater choice of location for mobile political 'consumers', and the scope for local experiment to weed out bad policy and refine good policy.[61]

Subsidiarity has of course been in the limelight for a long time and remained a contested concept in mainstream EU constitutional law due to its political nature. Protocol No. 2 on the Application of the Principles of Subsidiarity and Proportionality is attached to the Lisbon Treaty and is of crucial importance here. Briefly, this important protocol declares that the Commission must consult widely when proposing on legislation and that it must furnish reasons as to why an objective is better achieved at the EU level which are supported by qualitative and, wherever possible, quantitative indicators.[62]

For the purpose of discussing the concept of subsidiarity a number of 'better criteria' are available. This is reflected in the so-called efficiency check of proposed legislation, which requires a comparative evaluation of the costs and benefits of action at a Union and national level. This 'better criteria' analysis is commonly described as the comparative efficiency test,[63] according to which EU action must be, to put it simply, more effective than action at the national level. More specifically, the Union should act only if the action in question cannot be achieved by the individual Member States and the EU can better achieve the desired result because of its effects or scale.[64] A well-known difficulty is that the notion of effectiveness

[60] Walker 2015.

[61] Ibid.

[62] Moreover, the Commission must submit an annual report to the Council, the European Council and the EP.

[63] Craig 2012.

[64] Ibid.

suggests in itself various other criteria, such as whether a given level of government is in the best position to act from a geographical point of view or in terms of access to information.[65] However, part of the difficulty appears to be that there will be many areas in which the comparative efficiency test comes out in favour of EU action, as the very *raison d'être* of the EU will often demand supranational action to ensure the 'effectiveness' of EU law. In these times of a crisis-driven Union, the *raison d'être* is to maintain the EU values as proclaimed in the EU Charter and a sufficiently high human rights protection. But given the quest for EU effectiveness, it will always be possible to argue that EU action is necessary and that the efficiency test would favour the supranational level.

The principle of subsidiarity has been part of the EU constitutional landscape for some time now. However, it remains a contested concept due to its political nature. In addition, Protocol No. 1 on the Role of the National Parliaments in the European Union reaffirms the increased importance of subsidiarity if interpreting the Treaty literally. Indeed, one of the most important innovations in the Lisbon Treaty regarding subsidiarity is that the Treaty imposes an obligation on the Commission to send legislative initiatives to the national parliaments at the same time as to the EU institutions. Thereafter, the national parliaments have eight weeks to draft a statement of any objection as to why the proposed legislation does not comply with the subsidiarity principle. If the national parliaments expressing concern about non-compliance with the principle represent one-third of the votes—or one-quarter when it concerns a proposal in the AFSJ—allocated to these parliaments, the Commission is under a duty to review the proposal.

The question arises whether subsidiarity is to be conceived in a different manner in the present context as compared to EU law in general. Indeed, Article 69 TFEU emphasizes the importance of subsidiarity in Chaps. 4 and 5 of title V on the AFSJ concerning EU criminal law cooperation and police cooperation.[66] Does that mean that subsidiarity is not as important in the other policy fields of the AFSJ? The ordinary rules on subsidiarity monitoring including the Protocols No. 1 and 2 apply to all legislation. As noted above, and as discussed by other authors in this volume, the EPPO has triggered not only one yellow card but two. That is very unusual and it indicates the delicate nature of the matter.[67]

At the very least Article 69 TFEU singles out the need for subsidiarity in the areas of criminal law and police cooperation and thereby confirms the sensitive nature of EU action in these areas. The need for the containment of centralization, i.e., too much legislative action at the EU supranational level, appears particularly

[65] De Búrca 1999.

[66] See *supra* note 49 (text Article 69 TFEU).

[67] On 28 October 2013, the second yellow card ever was activated. Fromage 2016; Wieczorek 2016.

important in this field. After all, criminal law can be understood as having its own principle of subsidiarity embedded in the '*ultima ratio*' concept. Briefly, this means that criminal law should be the last resort as a means of control. According to this view, criminal law should be reserved for the most serious infringements of rules in society since less serious types of misconduct are more appropriately dealt with by civil law or by administrative regulation. So, when discussing criminalization, one has to ask whether it is justifiable to undertake criminal justice action at all: that is, whether the consequences of legislative action in the area in question are sufficiently clear, effective and precise. For this reason, it is impossible to understand the subsidiarity principle and the idea of Better Regulation in isolation from the principle of proportionality.[68] In the context of the EPPO, and given the extensive legislative framework to fight financial crimes it seems a genuinely proportionate measure for the EU to also focus on how to best enforce its policies.

5.6 Conclusion

The EPPO and the priorities to get it adopted seem closely connected to the reformation of the EU regulatory system for market regulation. As such, it is in line with the recent Directives on Market abuse and money laundering and the new Fraud Directive and other measures. Whereas the Better Regulation Agenda has become much more sophisticated in recent years, the EPPO's biggest challenge is not what happens in the EU's institutions but what happens on the 'field'. It is the Member States to decide the fate of the EPPO. Events such as the decision on Brexit, and national sentiments across Europe predict a difficult future ahead for the prospective establishment of an EPPO, despite the need for it. The Member States must decide what they want the EU to achieve and what is best left at the local level. In these post-Brexit decision days, it is to be hoped that when it comes to the EPPO the Member States will understand that joint business and freedoms also mean it is necessary to embrace the full package of cooperation, including fully shaped defence rights and protection of the individual. It might be a better solution to grant the EU more competences in order to establish an EPPO that constitutes a workable and effective institution, rather than establishing a half-baked solution of a prosecutor without true enforcement powers.

[68] Herlin-Karnell 2012b, Chapter 4.

References

Articles, Books, and Studies

Burgess A et al (2016) Routledge Handbook on Risk Research. Routledge

Conway G (2016) "The Future of a European Public Prosecutor" In: Fletcher M, Herlin-Karnell E, Matera C (eds) The European Union as an Area of Freedom, Security and Justice. Routledge, Chapter 7

Craig P (2012) EU Administrative Law. Oxford University Press, Oxford

Csúri A (2016) The Proposed European Public Prosecutor's Office – From a Trojan Horse to a White Elephant? Cambridge Yearbook of European Legal Studies, 1–30

De Búrca G (1999) "Reappraising Subsidiarity's significance after Amsterdam". Jean Monnet paper. New York Law School, New York

Delmas-Marty M, Vervaele J (eds) (2000) The Implementation of the *Corpus Juris* in the Member States. Intersentia, Antwerp

Erkelens LH, Meij AWH, Pawlik M (eds) (2015) The European Public Prosecutor's Office: An Extended Arm or a Two-Headed Dragon? TMC Asser Press, The Hague

Fromage D (2016) The Second Yellow Card on the EPPO Proposal: An Encouraging Development for Member State Parliaments? Yearbook of European Law, Vol. 35, No. 1 pp 5–27

Gómez–Jara Díez C (2015) Federal European Criminal Law. Intersentia, Antwerp

Herlin-Karnell E (2012a) White-Collar Crime and European Financial Crises: Getting Tough on EU Market Abuse. European Law Review 37

Herlin-Karnell E (2012b) The Constitutional Dimension of European Criminal Law. Hart Publishing

Herlin-Karnell E (2016) Is Administrative Law still relevant? How the battle of sanctions shaped EU Criminal law. In: Mitsilegas V, Bergstrom M, Konstadinides T (eds) Research Handbook on EU Criminal Law. Edward Elgar, Cheltenham

Herlin-Karnell E, Ryder N (2017) The Robustness of EU Financial Crimes Legislation: A Critical Review of the EU and UK Anti-Fraud and Money Laundering Scheme. European Business Law Review (forthcoming issue)

Ligeti K (ed) (2012) Toward a Prosecutor for the European Union, Volume 1. Hart Publishing

Moloney N (2014) EU Securities and Financial Markets Regulation. Oxford University Press, Oxford

Monar J (2005) Justice and Home Affairs in the EU Constitutional Treaty. What Added Value for the "Area of Freedom, Security and justice?" 1 EuConst Rev 226

Peers S (2016) EU Justice and Home Affairs, vol II. Oxford University Press, Oxford

Ryder N (2014) The Financial Crisis and White Collar Crime. Edward Elgar, Cheltenham

Stefanou C, Xhanthaki H (2005) Financial Crime in the EU. Kluwer Law International

Vervaele J (2013) European Territoriality and Jurisdiction: The Protection of the EU's Financial Interests in Its Horizontal and Vertical (EPPO) Dimension. In: Luchtman M (ed) Choice of Forum in Cooperation Against EU Financial Crime – Freedom, Security and Justice & the Protection of Specific EU-Interests. Eleven International Publishing, pp 167–184

Wade ML (2013) A European Public Prosecutor: Potential and Pitfalls. 59 Crime, Law & Social Change 439

Walker N (2015) Subsidiarity and the Deracination of Political Community: The EU and Beyond. Europa Working Paper No 2015/04, Edinburgh School of Law Research Paper Series

Weatherill S (1999) 'If I'd Wanted You to Understand I Would Have Explained it Better: What is the Purpose of the Provisions on Closer Co-operation Introduced by the Treaty of Amsterdam?' In: O'Keeffe D, Twomey P (eds) Legal Issues of the Amsterdam Treaty. Hart Publishing

Weatherill S (2011) The Limits of Legislative Harmonization Ten Years after Tobacco Advertising: How the Court's Case Law Has Become "Drafting Guide". 12 German Law Journal 827
Willems A (2017) Mutual trust as a core principle of EU criminal law. Conceptualising the principle with a view to facilitate mutual recognition in criminal justice matters. Unpublished PhD thesis, VUB/ULB
Wieczorek I (2016) The EPPO Draft Regulation Passes the First Subsidiarity Test: An Analysis and Interpretation of the European Commission's Hasty Approach to National Parliaments' Subsidiarity Arguments. German Law Journal 1248
Zumbansen P (2013) Administrative law's global dream: Navigating regulatory spaces between "national" and "international". International Journal of Constitutional Law 506

EU Documents and Other Sources

Better Regulation (2016) Communication from the Commission to the European Parliament, the European Council and the Council: Better Regulation: Delivering better results for a stronger Union. COM(2016) 615 final
Commission Report on subsidiarity and proportionality (2010) COM(2010) 547
Commission Communication (2010) Reinforcing Sanctioning Regimes in the Financial Services Sector, COM(2010) 716 final
Commission PIF Directive (2012) Proposal for a Directive of The European Parliament and of The Council on the fight against fraud to the Union's financial interests by means of criminal law, COM(2012) 363 final
Commission EPPO Proposal (2013) Proposal for a Council Regulation on the establishment of the European Public Prosecutor's Office; Doc. 2013/0255, 3 June 2016
Commission report on subsidiarity and proportionality (2014) COM(2014) 506 final
Council EPPO General Approach (2017a), Proposal for a Regulation on the establishment of the European Public Prosecutor's Office – General Approach, Doc. 5445/17, 31 January 2017
Council EPPO Draft Regulation (2017b), Proposal for a Regulation on the establishment of the European Public Prosecutor's Office – Draft Regulation, Doc. 5766/17, 31 January 2017
Council Meeting (December 2016) outcome of the council meeting (3508th Council meeting) Justice and Home Affairs, 8 and 9 December 2016
Directive of the European Parliament and of the Council on the right of access to a lawyer in criminal proceedings and in European arrest warrant proceedings, and on the right to have a third party informed upon deprivation of liberty and to communicate with third persons and with consular authorities while deprived of liberty, *OJ* L294/1, 6.11.2013
EPPO Proposal (2013) Proposal for a Council Regulation on the Establishment of the European Public Prosecutor's Office, COM(2013) 0534 final (July 7, 2013)
Malta EU 2017 (2017) Media Background Note Informal meeting of Justice and Home Affairs (26–27 January 2017). Available at https://www.eu2017.mt/Documents/Media%20Advisory%20Note/iJHA%20Media%20Background%20Note%2026-27JAN17.pdf. Accessed January 2017
Regulation (EU) No 596/2014, on market abuse (market abuse regulation) and repealing Directive 2003/6/EC of the European Parliament and of the Council and Commission Directives.
State of the Union (2016) European Commission - Press release State of the Union 2016: Commission presents results of Better Regulation approach. Available at http://europa.eu/rapid/press-release_IP-16-3014_en.htm. Accessed March 2017

Chapter 6
The European Public Prosecutor's Office and Human Rights

Valsamis Mitsilegas and Fabio Giuffrida

Abstract A system of prosecution at the European level poses multiple challenges. Among them, the adequate protection of the rights of the individuals involved in supranational investigations comes among the first. In the light of the forthcoming establishment of the European Public Prosecutor's Office (EPPO), this contribution deals with the place of human rights in the frame of the activities of such a body under four different perspectives. First, the application of the Charter of Fundamental Rights to the measures and acts of the EPPO is discussed. Second, the focus shifts to the provisions of the draft Regulation concerning the procedural safeguards. The third section analyses the debated issue of the judicial review of the acts of the Office. Finally, due attention is paid to the protection of human rights in the frame of cross-border investigations of the EPPO. The scenario emerging from the analysis is full of light and shade and it shows the complexity of one of the most relevant tensions underpinning the forthcoming establishment of this body, namely that between the perceived necessity to 'upgrade' the investigations on crimes affecting the financial interests of the EU at the European level and the concurrent need not to 'downgrade' the protection of human rights in the frame of supranational proceedings.

Keywords European Public Prosecutor's Office · Human rights · Directives on procedural rights · Judicial review · Cross-border investigations · Charter of Fundamental Rights

Valsamis Mitsilegas is Professor of European Criminal Law, Director of the Criminal Justice Centre and Head of the Department of Law at Queen Mary University of London.

Fabio Giuffrida is Ph.D. Candidate at Queen Mary University of London.

V. Mitsilegas (✉) · F. Giuffrida
Queen Mary University of London, London, UK
e-mail: v.mitsilegas@qmul.ac.uk

F. Giuffrida
e-mail: f.giuffrida@qmul.ac.uk

W. Geelhoed et al. (eds.), *Shifting Perspectives on the European Public Prosecutor's Office*, https://doi.org/10.1007/978-94-6265-216-3_6

Contents

6.1 Introduction

A system of prosecution at the European level poses multiple challenges. Among them, the adequate protection of the rights of the individuals involved in supranational investigations comes among the first. In the light of the forthcoming establishment of the European Public Prosecutor's Office (EPPO or the 'Office'), this contribution discusses the place of human rights in the frame of the activities of such a body. Since the Office has not been established yet, the following considerations are based on the last version publicly available of the draft Regulation on the EPPO ('draft Regulation'),[1] which is under negotiations in the Council since 2013.[2]

Against this backdrop, the possible impact of the Charter of Fundamental Rights (CFR or the 'Charter') on the activities of the EPPO is first discussed (Sect. 6.2). Second, the focus shifts to the analysis of the provisions of the draft Regulation concerning the procedural safeguards (Sect. 6.3). Third, further reflections are spent on the judicial review of the acts of the EPPO (Sect. 6.4). Finally, before drawing some conclusions (Sect. 6.6), the protection of human rights in the frame of cross-border investigations of the EPPO is dealt with (Sect. 6.5). The scenario emerging from the analysis is full of light and shade and it clearly mirrors one of the most relevant tensions underpinning the forthcoming establishment of the EPPO, namely that between the perceived necessity to 'upgrade' the investigations on crimes affecting the financial interests of the EU at the European level and the concurrent need not to 'downgrade' the protection of human rights in the frame of supranational proceedings.

---

[1] Proposal for a Regulation on the establishment of the European Public Prosecutor's Office—Preparation for a general approach, Council doc. 5154/17, 17 January 2017.

[2] The Proposal was tabled by the Commission in July 2013: Proposal for a Council Regulation on the establishment of the European Public Prosecutor's Office, COM(2013) 534 final, 17 July 2013 ('Commission's proposal').

6.2 The Applicability of the Charter of Fundamental Rights to the Proceedings of the EPPO

With the entry into force of the Treaty of Lisbon, the Charter has been recognised the same legal value as the Treaties.[3] Individuals can therefore rely on the rights therein enshrined and, when a conflict between national provisions and rights guaranteed by the Charter occurs, the competent national court is called to give full effect to the Charter, '*if necessary refusing of its own motion to apply any conflicting provision* of national legislation [...]'.[4]

This principle has been ruled in *Fransson*, where the Court also dealt with the debated issue of the interpretation of Article 51(1) CFR, which states that the Charter applies not only to 'the institutions, bodies, offices and agencies of the Union with due regard for the principle of subsidiarity', but also 'to the Member States only when they are *implementing Union law*' (emphasis added). Article 51 (1) CFR can be found among the final, horizontal provisions of the CFR, i.e. those regulating the relationship between the Charter and national law on the one hand, and the relationship between the Charter and other sources of human rights protection (including the European Convention on Human Rights) on the other.[5] The Court of Justice has thus far intervened on both aspects.

In the seminal ruling in *Melloni,* the Court found that EU law which is found to be in compliance with the Charter has *primacy* over national constitutional law which provides a higher level of protection.[6] While this ruling may be seen as lowering the protection of fundamental rights in certain jurisdictions, the Court has compensated for this potential outcome (which was explained by the need to ensure the primacy, unity and effectiveness of Union law) by adopting a broad interpretation of what constitutes the implementation of Union law which triggers the application of the Charter under Article 51(1) CFR. In the above-mentioned case of *Fransson*, the Court of Justice adopted a *broad interpretation* of the application of the Charter, including in cases where national legislation *does not implement expressly or directly* an EU criminal law instrument. The Court found that domestic law on VAT fraud does fall within EU law since there is a *direct link* between the collection of VAT revenue in compliance with the European Union law applicable

---

[3] Article 6(1) Treaty on European Union.

[4] Case C–617/10, *Åklagaren v Hans Åkerberg Fransson*, judgment of 26 February 2013, para 45, emphasis added. The disapplication envisaged by the Court should occur only when the Charter provides for a 'right', whereas this should not be the case when 'principles' come into consideration. Whereas the latter have to be 'observed' and have to be implemented both by EU institutions and bodies and by acts of Member States, 'rights' have to be 'respected' (see Article 51 CFR). See also the explanation to Article 51 CFR to be found in the Explanations relating to the Charter of Fundamental Rights, *OJ* C303/35, 14.12.2007.

[5] See in particular Articles 51–53 of the Charter. For commentaries see inter alia Lenaerts 2012, pp. 375–403; Hancox 2013, pp. 1411–1432; Sarmiento 2013, pp. 1267–1304; Fontanelli 2014, pp. 682–700.

[6] Case C-399/11, *Melloni*, judgment of 26 February 2013.

and the availability to the European Union budget of the corresponding VAT resources.[7]

The Court of Justice developed its approach on the applicability of the Charter in *Siragusa*,[8] where it ruled that the concept of 'implementing Union law', as referred to in Article 51 of the Charter, requires a certain degree of connection above and beyond the matters covered being closely related or one of those matters having an indirect impact on the other.[9]

The Court's approach has the effect of including a wide range of national legislation and measures related to national criminal justice systems within the scope of the Charter, even though those measures do not implement directly EU law. A key example is represented by national legislation concerning detention conditions.

This view is reinforced by the Court's finding in *Siragusa* that it is important to consider the objective of protecting fundamental rights in EU law, which is to ensure that those rights are not infringed in areas of EU activity, whether through action at EU level or through the implementation of EU law by the Member States.[10]

The interpretation of the vague reference to the implementation of EU law in Article 51(1) CFR has been discussed in a recent study of Eleanor Spaventa, who concludes that the Court shows 'a varied approach to the Charter, according to type of interest and area considered'.[11] In the light of the case-law on the applicability of the Charter, the author makes a distinction between those areas in which the intervention of the EU is meant to co-ordinate national legislation (e.g. asylum) and those in which there is a strong EU interest at stake (e.g. internal market or EU integration). Whereas in the former the Court is much more cautious to acknowledge the applicability of the CFR, in the latter 'the Charter is more likely to apply to national rules'.[12]

The EPPO and its activities lie somehow in between these two areas. On the one hand, the establishment of this body is intended to go beyond the mere co-ordination of national authorities in the fight against crimes affecting the financial interests of the EU and to introduce a sort of integration of the preliminary phase of criminal proceedings against these crimes. On the other hand, however, the current draft Regulation shows that the mechanism of co-ordination is still meant to play an extremely relevant role in the forthcoming investigations of the EPPO and that the expected aim of integration is only partially achieved.[13]

---

[7] Case C-617/10, *Fransson*, cit., para 26.

[8] Case C-206/13, *Siragusa*, judgment of 6 March 2014.

[9] Ibid., para 24.

[10] Ibid., para 31.

[11] Spaventa 2016, p. 24.

[12] Ibid., p. 14.

[13] For example, as far as the pre-trial arrest is concerned, the EPPO does not entail any step further with regard to the current scenario of judicial co-operation: if the person to be arrested is not in the

The application of the Charter to the activities of the EPPO is not contentious.[14] Even though, in practice, most of the acts and measures will be taken on the basis of national law by the European Delegated Prosecutors (EDPs), who will be national prosecutors carrying out the investigations in their Member States,[15] there is no doubt that this is a typical case where Member States are implementing Union law. Actually, it can even be argued that the Charter applies in the light of the first part of Article 51(1) CFR, since the latter states that the provisions of the Charter are addressed to 'institutions, *bodies*, *offices* and agencies of the Union', such as the EPPO indeed.

Even though strongly embedded in national systems, the EPPO remains an *EU body*. When the EDPs will carry out their investigations under the direction and the supervision of the 'central level'[16] of the EPPO, they will be to all intents and purposes *members of an EU body*. Thus, when the EDPs will act under the 'European hat',[17] the application of the Charter should be uncontested, independently of the legislation they will rely upon. It is true that the current Regulation sets out only the minimal rules of the forthcoming 'European investigations', whereas for most of the measures to be adopted it refers to the applicable national law.[18] Of course, if the application of the Charter is plain when the EDPs will act in

---

(Footnote 13 continued)

Member State in which the European Delegated Prosecutor is carrying out his (her) activities, the latter issues—or requests the competent authority of that State to issue—a European Arrest Warrant for the surrender of the suspect (Article 28 draft Regulation).

[14] See also Nieto Martín 2015, pp. 315ff.

[15] See Article 12 draft Regulation.

[16] Article 7(2) draft Regulation. The structure of the forthcoming Office shall be as follows: '2. The European Public Prosecutor's Office shall be organised at a central level and at a decentralised level. 3. The central level shall consist of a Central Office at the seat. The Central Office shall consist of the College, the Permanent Chambers, the European Chief Prosecutor, his/her deputies, the European Prosecutors and the Administrative Director. 4. The decentralised level shall consist of European Delegated Prosecutors who shall be located in the Member States' (Article 7(2), (3), and (4) draft Regulation).

[17] The expression 'double hat' is often used in works and studies concerning the EPPO, since it mirrors the peculiar status of the EDPs: they are national prosecutors who are and remain part of national prosecution services but, in the meanwhile, they are also part of an EU body. Therefore, when they conduct the investigations on crimes falling within the competence of the EPPO, they shall follow the instructions and directions coming from the central level of the EPPO. See, among the many, Spiezia 2013, p. 557; Satzger 2015, p. 74. However, the concept of 'two hats' had already been mentioned in the 2001 Green Paper on criminal-law protection of the financial interests of the Community and the establishment of a European Prosecutor, p. 29.

[18] For example, the investigations have to be initiated when, '*in accordance with national law*, there are reasonable grounds to believe that an offence' within the competence of the EPPO is being or has been committed (Article 22(1) draft Regulation, emphasis added); investigations are undertaken by the EDPs in accordance with the Regulation and 'with national law' (Article 23(1) draft Regulation); 'the procedures and the modalities for taking the [investigative] measures shall be governed by the applicable national law' (Article 25(3) draft Regulation); and so on.

accordance with the provisions of the Regulation,[19] there should be no difference in those cases when they will adopt investigative measures or take decisions on the basis of national law. In similar circumstances, even though the EDPs will be national prosecutors applying purely national law (as a code of criminal procedure code usually is), the applicability of the Charter should be uncontested in the light both of the *subjective link* between the EDP and the EPPO on the hand, and of the *objective link* between national law and the EU Regulation on the other (namely the multiple referrals made by the latter to domestic legislation). Those situations should therefore fall under the scope of the first part of Article 51(1) CFR.[20]

The matter becomes less straightforward when the focus shifts to the *trials* which will follow the investigations of the EPPO. Since the idea of the European Prosecutor was envisaged for the first time, it has been clear that no European Criminal Court would have been competent to adjudicate on crimes affecting the financial interests of the EU: an entirely domestic trial would have followed (and will follow) the investigations of the EPPO.[21] However, whereas the latter will be regulated—at least in their main features—at the EU level and will be conducted by members of an EU body, the subsequent trials will follow national rules, and the final decision will be taken, on their basis, by a national court. One of the parties to the proceedings could still have a relevant link with the EU, since the EDP who carries out the investigations should most probably represent the prosecution service during the trial and does not cease, at that stage, to be part of a European body pursuant to Article 51(1) CFR.[22] However, such a subjective link alone would probably not be sufficient to justify the application of the Charter, since the national courts which have to decide on the cases brought to judgment by the EPPO cannot be regarded as 'institutions, bodies, offices and agencies of the Union' according to Article 51(1) of the Charter.

Nevertheless, if *Fransson* is still good law, as it seems,[23] the fact that the trial will concern the crimes affecting the financial interests of the EU is already enough to guarantee the applicability of the Charter. Those crimes, moreover, will be defined by an EU piece of legislation, a forthcoming Directive, which will have to

[19] For instance, in the case of evocation of a case by the EPPO (see Article 22a draft Regulation).

[20] Likewise, it has been argued that '[a]s an EU body EPPO will be subject to the CFR' (Wasmeier 2015, p. 155). On the application of the Charter to any action of the EPPO, especially in the light of the *Fransson* case, see also Meij 2015, pp. 103–105.

[21] See Article 4 draft Regulation. Such a peculiar system of European investigations followed by national trials was already envisaged in the *Corpus Juris* (see Delmas-Marty 1997). For a further bibliography and considerations on the *Corpus Juris*, see Mitsilegas 2009, pp. 229ff.

[22] '[…] the European Public Prosecutor's Office shall undertake investigations, and carry out acts of prosecution and *exercise the functions of prosecutor in the competent courts of the Member States*, until the case has been finally disposed of' (Article 4 draft Regulation, emphasis added).

[23] However, commenting on the above-mentioned *Siragusa* case, Spaventa cautiously submits that '[i]t is not clear whether Case C-617/10 *Åkerberg Fransson* […] would have passed the *Siragusa* test' (Spaventa 2016, p. 21).

be implemented by Member States ('PIF Directive').[24] Also from this perspective, therefore, the applicability of the Charter to the activities of the EPPO and to the ensuing trial should be beyond doubt.

After all, the duty for the Member States to counter fraud and any other illegal activities affecting the financial interests of the Union is provided at the level of EU primary law, and namely in Article 325 of the Treaty on the Functioning of the European Union (TFEU). In the recent *Taricco* case,[25] moreover, the link between VAT revenues and the EU budget has been restated and the Court has even recognised direct effect to Article 325 TFEU, with the consequence that domestic legislation on the statute of limitation of crimes (a typical national matter) has to be disapplied if this is necessary to fight effectively against crimes to the detriment of the EU budget.[26] In this judgment, the Court does not deal with the applicability of the Charter, but it confirms once more the central place of the protection of the Union's financial interests in the EU legal system.

Therefore, it seems uncontested that during the whole proceedings concerning crimes affecting the EU finances—from the investigations to the trial—the Charter shall apply.

Looking at the current draft Regulation, the Charter is mentioned twice (excluding the Preamble). First, Article 5(1) draft Regulation points to the respect of the rights enshrined in the Charter as the first of the *basic principles* underpinning the activities of the EPPO. Second, the provision concerning the *procedural safeguards* restates that such activities shall be carried out in full compliance with the rights of suspects and accused persons enshrined in the Charter, 'including the right to a fair trial and the rights of defence'.[27] The latter issue is discussed in more detail in Sect. 6.3.1.

With regard to Article 5(1) draft Regulation, which seems mostly a symbolic provision, Marta Pawlik and André Klip have noted that a reference also to the European Convention on Human Rights (ECHR) would have been appropriate, especially 'in the light of anticipated proximity of EU's accession to the ECHR'.[28] The case law of the European Court of Human Rights (ECtHR) touches upon many

---

[24] Article 17(1) draft Regulation states that the EPPO will be competent for the crimes provided for by the forthcoming Directive on the fight against fraud to the Union's financial interests by means of criminal law ('PIF Directive'). The proposal for the Directive was issued by the Commission in 2012 (see Proposal for a Directive of the European Parliament and of the Council on the fight against fraud to the Union's financial interests by means of criminal law, COM(2012) 363 final, 17 July 2012) and negotiations are not over yet. At the time of writing, however, a preliminary agreement has been found in Coreper (see Proposal for a Directive of the European Parliament and of the Council on the fight against fraud to the Union's financial interests by means of criminal law (Second reading) – Analysis of the final compromise text with a view to agreement, Council doc. 14902/16, 2 December 2016).

[25] Case C-105/14, *Taricco and others*, judgment of 8 September 2015. On this judgment see, among the many, Billis 2016, pp. 20–38; Caianiello 2016, pp. 1–17; Giuffrida 2016, pp. 100–112.

[26] Case C-105/14, *Taricco*, cit., paras 49ff.

[27] Article 35(1) draft Regulation.

[28] Pawlik and Klip 2015, p. 188.

sensitive issues concerning criminal investigations and prosecutions and it is increasingly recalled by the Court of Justice.[29] It is known that, according to Article 52(3) CFR, in so far as the Charter contains rights which correspond to rights guaranteed by the ECHR, 'the meaning and scope of those rights shall be the same as those laid down by the said Convention'; however, also symbolically, an explicit reference to the ECHR would have been welcome.

To sum up, the Charter will apply in the framework of the activities of the EPPO, even though they will depend on national law for most of their part. During the trial, which will take place before national courts, the Charter shall likewise apply in the light of the broad interpretation of Article 51(1) CFR espoused by the Court of Justice in the *Fransson* case.

6.3 Procedural Safeguards

A chapter of the draft Regulation is devoted to the procedural safeguards of the persons involved in the proceedings of the EPPO.[30] It is composed of two Articles, which deal with strictly interlinked matters, namely the scope of the rights of the suspects and accused persons and the judicial review of the acts of the EPPO. The latter issue is further discussed in Sect. 6.4, whereas the former is analysed in Sect. 6.3.1, which is followed by some considerations regarding more in detail the matter of evidence and its relations with human rights.

6.3.1 Rights of Suspects and Accused Persons

Current Article 35 draft Regulation provides three different levels of protection of the rights of the persons involved in the proceedings of the EPPO.

First, in the light of the peculiar embedment of the EPPO in national systems, it is stated that suspects and accused persons shall have the procedural rights available to them under the *applicable national law*. The same provision extends a similar guarantee to the other persons involved in the proceedings of the EPPO. Such a regulation of defence rights on the basis of domestic law is in line with the hybrid nature of the EPPO, a body which will be partially European and partially based on national criminal justice systems. As argued by Maria Kaiafa-Gbandi, however, if such a complementarity of domestic law can be 'practically favorable for rights', the envisaged system

[29] See, for example, the *Covaci* judgment mentioned in the following section.

[30] For a recent analysis on the provisions of the draft Regulation concerning the procedural safeguards see Weyembergh and Brière 2016, pp. 34ff.

> may become extremely dysfunctional and ineffective for individuals concerned, due to its high complexity brought forth not only by the combination of EU and national law, but also by the *multitude of applicable national provisions*. Moreover, it does not ensure legal certainty or foreseeability for suspects and defendants in order to enable effective defense patterns, neither does it avert the risk of patchwork proceedings that allow the subsistence of different levels of protection within the same criminal procedure, even when it refers to the same right [...].[31]

In order to temper similar consequences, the draft Regulation provides for two further levels of protection—on the EU plane—of the rights of the persons involved in the activities of the EPPO.

First, the draft Regulation contains an express reference to the *Directives on the rights of the individuals in criminal procedure* adopted on the basis of Article 82(2) TFEU.[32] More precisely, Article 35(2) draft Regulation refers to the Directive on the right to interpretation and translation;[33] the Directive on the right to information and access to the case materials;[34] the Directive on the right to access to a lawyer;[35] the Directive on the right to remain silent and the right to be presumed innocent;[36] and the Directive on legal aid.[37] The draft Regulation requires that the rights enshrined in these Directives shall be granted, 'as a minimum',[38] to the suspects and accused persons in the criminal proceedings of the EPPO.

The adoption of EU measures harmonising national law on the rights of the individual in criminal proceedings has a *transformative effect*.[39] It signals a paradigm shift from a system focused primarily—if not solely—on promoting the interests of the state and of law enforcement under rules of quasi-automatic mutual recognition to a system where the rights of individuals affected by such rules are brought into the fore, protected by and enforced in EU law. This becomes even more important in the frame of the activities of the EPPO, which itself entails another paradigm shift, i.e. that from judicial co-operation to European-driven prosecution. In this frame, there is a strong need for homogenous and effective

[31] Kaiafa-Gbandi 2015, pp. 245–246.

[32] For broader considerations on these Directives, see Tinsley 2013, pp. 461–480.

[33] Directive 2010/64/EU on the right to interpretation and translation in criminal proceedings, *OJ* L280/1, 26.10.2010.

[34] Directive 2012/13/EU on the right to information in criminal proceedings, *OJ* L142/1, 1.6.2012.

[35] Directive 2013/48/EU on the right of access to a lawyer in criminal proceedings and in European arrest warrant proceedings, and on the right to have a third party informed upon deprivation of liberty and to communicate with third persons and with consular authorities while deprived of liberty, *OJ* L294/1, 6.11.2013.

[36] Directive (EU) 2016/343 of the European Parliament and of the Council of 9 March 2016 on the strengthening of certain aspects of the presumption of innocence and of the right to be present at the trial in criminal proceedings, *OJ* L65/1, 11.3.2016.

[37] Directive (EU) 2016/1919 of the European Parliament and of the Council of 26 October 2016 on legal aid for suspects and accused persons in criminal proceedings and for requested persons in European arrest warrant proceedings, *OJ* L297/1, 4.11.2016.

[38] Article 35(2) draft Regulation.

[39] Mitsilegas 2016c.

protection of the procedural safeguards of persons who are involved in the proceedings of the EPPO.

There are *four main ways* in which the Directives on procedural rights in criminal procedure will enhance the protection of fundamental rights in EU Member States in general, and in the course of the proceedings of the EPPO in particular. First of all, a number of key provisions conferring rights in the Directives have *direct effect*. This means that individuals can evoke and claim rights directly before their national courts if the EU Directives have not been implemented or have been inadequately implemented. Direct effect means in practice that a suspect or accused person can derive a number of key rights—such as the right to an interpreter or the right to access to a lawyer—directly from EU law if national legislation has not made appropriate provision in conformity with EU law. The possibility for the suspects or accused persons to rely on the Directives is especially relevant with regard to the activities of the EPPO, since the rules of such activities will be laid down by a Regulation, which shall be 'directly applicable in all Member States'[40] taking part in the establishment of the EPPO. Therefore, the direct effect of those Directives will help to reduce the imbalance between the direct applicability of EU law as far as the prosecution side is concerned and the absence of a directly applicable EU legislation on the defence rights.

Secondly, this avenue of decentralised enforcement is coupled with the high level of centralised enforcement of EU criminal law which has been 'normalised' after the entry into force of the Lisbon Treaty. The European Commission now has full powers to monitor the implementation of these Directives by Member States and has the power to introduce infringement proceedings before the Court of Justice when it considers that the Directives have not been implemented adequately.[41] In view of the above-mentioned Court's approach regarding the applicability of the Charter and of the broad objectives of the procedural rights Directives, the scope of the Commission's monitoring exercises is broader than to check merely the provisions of national legislation adopted to implement specifically the EU Directives in question. The Commission is also entitled to monitor national criminal procedure systems more broadly to ensure that effective implementation has taken place, as well as to ensure that rights are applied in practice and not only in the books. The requirement to comply with the Charter in these terms mandates an intensive and far-reaching monitoring of Member States' implementation of both mutual

[40] Article 288 TFEU.

[41] All the above-mentioned Directives provide for the obligation both of the Member States to transmit to the Commission the text of the measures adopted to comply with the Directives and of the Commission to submit a report to the Parliament and to the Council assessing the extent to which the Member States have taken the necessary measures in order to implement the Directives: see Articles 9(2) and 10 Directive 2010/64/EU; Articles 11(2) and 12 Directive 2012/13/EU; Articles 15(3) and 16 Directive 2013/48/EU; Articles 11 and 12 Directive (EU) 2016/343; and Articles 10 and 12 Directive (EU) 2016/1919. In addition, the Court of Justice has now full jurisdiction to rule on infringement proceedings in criminal matters, pursuant to Articles 258–260 TFEU.

recognition and procedural rights instruments, including on the ground assessment of the day-to-day functioning of aspects of domestic criminal justices including detention conditions, length of pre-trial detention and duration of judicial proceedings.[42] The need for a careful supervision by the Commission becomes even stronger if the failure of the State to comply with the Directives could endanger the rights of individuals who are subject to the supranational investigations of the EPPO.

Thirdly, national criminal procedural law must be applied and interpreted in compliance and conformity with the Directives.[43] The procedural standards set out in the Directives will have an impact on a wide range of acts under national criminal procedure, which will still be important in the frame of the activities of the EPPO. Finally, the implementation of the Directives must take place in compliance with the Charter of Fundamental Rights. In light of the broad interpretation of the application of the Charter ruled in *Fransson*, the Charter will apply not only to national legislation which specifically implements the EU Directives on procedural rights, but also to all other elements of domestic criminal procedure which have a connection with EU law on procedural rights in criminal proceedings. In the case of the Directives on procedural rights, there are a number of elements in domestic criminal procedures which, although not implementing specifically the Directives, meet the degree of connection required by the Court's case-law and thus trigger the applicability of the Charter.[44]

The transformative effect of the Directives is enhanced by the potential for a number of key concepts included therein to be interpreted by the Court of Justice in an autonomous manner.[45] These can be concepts determining both the *scope* (who is a 'suspect' or an 'accused' person) and the *applicability* of the defence rights (in which proceedings and when are the rights triggered), as well as the interpretation of the *content* of the rights granted (for instance, what is the meaning of granting rights 'promptly' or 'without undue delay'). Autonomous concepts go beyond harmonisation in introducing in intra-EU criminal justice cooperation a degree of uniformity, which is highly desirable when the criminal investigations are carried out by an EU body on the basis of a Regulation directly applicable in the participating Member States. Apart from the much needed contribution to build an autonomous and homogenous corpus of rules that should apply in the Member States taking part in the EPPO, autonomous concepts also become a mechanism of enforcement of EU law which has significant impact on domestic criminal justice systems and legal cultures, in changing both perceptions and practice in national

[42] Mitsilegas 2016b, p. 123.

[43] See Opinion of AG Bot, Case C-216/14, *Criminal Proceedings against Gavril Covaci*, 7 May 2015, in particular paras 105–106.

[44] See more in Mitsilegas 2016a, pp. 175–176.

[45] Mitsilegas 2016d, pp. 125–160.

criminal justice systems.[46] Changes in domestic legal cultures which lead to the enhancement of fundamental rights in the criminal justice process may also serve to address the consequences of the perceived moral distance inherent in the system of mutual recognition in criminal matters.[47]

If the reference to the Directives is positive for the reasons mentioned above, it must be noted that most of their provisions represent a complex *compromise* among the Member States. Therefore, the content of the rights provided therein can be sometimes quite broad and vague, with the consequence that the impact of the Directives on national legal systems risks being all in all quite limited: this means that 'suspects and accused will continue to be subject to different standards depending on the applicable national law'.[48]

For example, notwithstanding the importance of the right to a lawyer and the fact that such a right is inextricably linked with the right to a fair trial, which all EU Member States are under the obligation to respect within the framework of both the ECHR and the CFR, negotiations on the Directive on access to a lawyer have proven to be complex. The need to find compromises in order to reach agreement between the Council and the European Parliament in the post-Lisbon co-decision era has led to the adoption of a text accompanied by a lengthy Preamble consisting of no less than 59 recitals. As has been noted, the greater emphasis on the preambular provisions reflects a strategy whereby areas where no agreement on the imposition of express obligations can be reached in negotiations are moved to the Preamble.[49] A number of compromises had also to be reached within the main body of the Directive, which includes a number of provisions on exceptions and derogations.

The challenges which even minimum harmonisation of the right to access to a lawyer was perceived to pose for the integrity of national criminal justice systems and policies have led to the watering down of harmonisation in four main respects:

[46] On the concept of legal culture as one encompassing these elements, see Nelken 2012, pp. 1–51. On a view of legal culture as embracing the participants' experience, see Cotterrell 2008, pp. 709–737.

[47] The problem of 'moral distance' has been defined as the frequent remoteness or separation of law's normative expectations from many of those that are current and familiar in the fields of social interaction that it purports to regulate (Cotterrell 1995, pp. 304–305). In a system of mutual recognition based on automaticity, the problem of moral distance may appear particularly acute in the executing Member State, where a judicial authority is required to recognise and execute a decision which is the outcome of the legal system of another Member State on the basis of almost blind trust. Key questions in this context are whether mutual trust can justify the recognition of judgments which may have a detrimental effect on the protection of the fundamental rights of the defendant and whether mutual recognition on the basis of mutual trust can operate without a parallel degree of harmonisation of criminal procedural standards in Member States (see Mitsilegas 2016a, p. 129). The harmonisation of such standards by means of the Directives can therefore reduce the problems linked with the issue of 'moral distance' and prepare the field for the creation of a common European system of investigations and prosecutions under the aegis of the EPPO.

[48] Weyembergh and Brière 2016, p. 35.

[49] Nowell-Smith 2012. On the application of this approach to the access to a lawyer Directive, see also Cras 2014.

in limiting the reach of the application of the Directive by attempting to exclude minor offences from its scope; in introducing temporary derogations to rights; in attempting to reach a compromise in the provision on confidentiality of communications between lawyers and defendants; and in excluding from the scope of this instrument provisions on legal aid, which have been included in a separate Directive.

Nevertheless, the Directive on the right of access to a lawyer constitutes a decisive step towards strengthening procedure rights by translating into concrete secondary law the principles emanating from Strasbourg case-law and at times developing these principles further and providing for more extensive protection.

Therefore, it emerges a scenario full of light and shade, as submitted also by Lorena Bachmaier Winter, who has highlighted that, on the one hand, the Directive at stake represents 'a step forward' since it 'has added value with regard to the present situation'.[50] However, on the other hand, she argues that 'there are certain shortcomings that render [the Directive] clearly insufficient to the aim of protecting [...] the rights of suspects and defendants facing a criminal procedure led by the EPPO'.[51] Among the other critical elements that lead the author to such a conclusion, the lack of any provision on legal aid can be mentioned.

However, the latter issue has finally been regulated by the Directive (EU) 2016/1919, which probably represents the most controversial Directive adopted by the EU in the field. Given the sensitivity of the topic, the Directive only introduces general and broad duties for the Member States, such as that to 'ensure that suspects and accused persons who lack sufficient resources to pay for the assistance of a lawyer have the right to legal aid when the interests of justice so require'.[52] Likewise, it is provided that the legal aid system should be of adequate quality.[53] In other words, Member States still enjoy a relevant margin of discretion in the implementation of the Directive, so that it needs to be evaluated, once the EPPO will begin its activities, whether the regime provided for by the Directive is actually effective enough to protect the rights of the suspects or accused persons.

More in general, it seems that a relevant practical problem that the investigations of the EPPO will pose is that of the *costs of the defence*. If a person is requested to exercise its right of defence with regard to investigations carried out in various countries, it can be easily understood that this issue will probably raise several concerns in the near future and it seems unlikely that an adequate solution can be found in the general provisions of the Directive on legal aid.[54]

---

[50] Bachmaier Winter 2013, p. 530.

[51] Ibid., Likewise, Suominen submits that the Directives 'are positive improvements for the suspect, but perhaps do not solve all nor the bigger problems in relation to deficits in European criminal proceedings' (Suominen 2014, p. 21).

[52] Article 4(1) Directive (EU) 2016/1919.

[53] Article 7 Directive (EU) 2016/1919.

[54] On the practical problems linked with the expectedly high costs of the defence in the frame of the activities of the EPPO, see Council of Bars and Law Societies of Europe 2013, p. 6; European Criminal Bar Association 2013, pp. 195–196; Mazza 2013, p. 493.

Finally, in addition to the Directives and to applicable national law, the third level of protection of human rights is represented by the Charter, expressly referred to in Article 35(1) draft Regulation,[55] which recalls also the right to a fair trial and the rights of defence. Since the applicability of the Charter to the activities of the EPPO has been discussed in the previous section, it can now be added that, by and large, the rights provided for by the Charter that could be relevant in the frame of the activities of the EPPO can be divided in two categories: the rights specifically concerning the field of (criminal) justice and the other rights, which bear some kind of connection with that field.

As far as the first category is concerned, the title of the Charter devoted to Justice (title VI) comes into consideration. It is composed of four provisions, which shall be taken into account during the investigations of the EPPO. Some of the rights listed in those four Articles have been regulated more in depth by means of the above-mentioned Directives. This is the case of the rights to legal aid (Article 47 CFR) and to the presumption of innocence (Article 48 CFR). In this context, the Charter could add value in providing an interpretative tool to the secondary law provisions in the relevant instruments. It may serve as a tool for clarifying the meaning of certain provisions and for addressing possible shortcomings in the wording of secondary law.

For the rest, Article 47 CFR lists also the rights to an effective remedy and to a fair trial, whereas Article 48 CFR concerns also the more general right of defence:[56] all of them could definitely be called to play a role in the activities of the EPPO, even though only practice will show whether these broad rights will cover aspects which are not already regulated either by the EU Directives or by the applicable national law. In that regard, it can be noted that the Court of Justice has already clarified that the right to a fair trial encompasses *vary basic and general principles*. Recalling the ECtHR, the Court has for example stated that 'compliance with the requirements relating to a fair trial merely ensures that the accused person knows what is being alleged against him and can defend himself, and does not necessitate a written translation of all items of written evidence or official documents in the procedure (European Court of Human Rights, *Kamasinski v. Austria*, 19 December 1989, § 74, Series A no. 168)'.[57]

Nevertheless, an autonomous—although limited—role for the Charter has been envisaged with regard to the right to a fair trial. Commenting on the original version of the Commission's proposal, some authors argued that such a right 'requires that in all the stages of the criminal procedure, including pre-trial proceedings, the *applicable law is foreseeable*'.[58] The matter seems to be regulated in a more

[55] See Sect. 6.2 of this contribution.

[56] As mentioned, the right to a fair trial and the rights of defence are expressly recalled in Article 35(1) draft Regulation.

[57] Case C-216/14, *Covaci*, judgment of 15 October 2015, para 39.

[58] Ligeti and Weyembergh 2015, p. 67 (emphasis added). See also, among the many, Luchtman et al. 2015.

detailed way in the recent drafts, even though it is debatable that satisfactory clarity has actually been reached. In fact, when identifying the European Delegated Prosecutor competent to carry out the investigations, Article 22(4) draft Regulation uses some vague notions such as 'focus of the criminal activity' and 'bulk of the offences' (in cases of several connected offences).[59] Moreover, the same provision allows the competent Permanent Chamber to instruct the European Delegated Prosecutor of *another* Member State to initiate the investigations, on the basis of some criteria hierarchically listed therein. Therefore, it is questionable whether the suspect or accused persons are actually able to know from the beginning in which country the investigations will take place and, consequently, which will be the applicable national law.

The choice of the Member State where the *investigations* have to be initiated is also relevant for the ensuing *trial*, since the Permanent Chamber 'shall in principle decide to bring the case to prosecution in the Member State of the European Delegated Prosecutor handling the case'.[60] Such an uncertainty on the applicable law is extremely problematic under a human rights perspective, because '[a]s early as possible, the accused person must have clarity as to the Member State and the national law he will be accountable to. This is the only way to ensure effective defence in pre-trial investigations'.[61]

Going back to the Charter, Article 49 CFR deals with the principles of legality and proportionality of criminal offences and penalties, so that it could come into consideration especially in the implementation by national legislators of the forthcoming PIF Directive.[62] Therefore, as far as the activities of the EPPO are concerned, Article 49 CFR seems less relevant than the other provisions of the Title VI of the Charter, as it also emerges from the current version of the Preamble of the draft Regulation: it recalls the Title VI of the Charter and, more in detail, (only) Articles 47, 48, and 50 CFR.[63]

Article 50 CFR enshrines the right to *ne bis in idem*, which can be easily endangered in the frame of the forthcoming investigations of the EPPO. Already without a European system of prosecution, the case-law of the Court of Justice (as well as that of the ECtHR) shows that risks of double jeopardy can arise both in

---

[59] 'A case shall as a rule be initiated and handled by a European Delegated Prosecutor from the Member State where the focus of the criminal activity is or, if several connected offences within the competences of the Office have been committed, the Member State where the bulk of the offences has been committed. [...]' (Article 22(4) draft Regulation).

[60] Article 30(2) draft Regulation.

[61] German Federal Bar and German Bar Association 2012, p. 4. On the issue of the choice of forum and applicable law in the frame of the proceedings of the EPPO see, among the many, Zimmermann 2015, pp. 156–177.

[62] For instance, one could imagine a national legislation which introduces penalties that go far beyond those requested in the PIF Directive, with a possible violation of the principle of proportionality.

[63] See, respectively, Recitals Nos. 70 and 73 of the Preamble of the draft Regulation. Article 49 Charter is instead recalled in the Preamble of the draft PIF Directive (see Recital No. 25).

cases of transnational crimes, when more than one Member State has jurisdiction,[64] and in cases of concurring national administrative and criminal proceedings on the same facts.[65]

Once the EPPO is established, there could also be a risk of double prosecution at the national and the supranational level. Therefore, the draft Regulation provides that if the EPPO 'decides to exercise its competence, the competent national authorities shall not exercise their own competence in respect of the same criminal conduct'.[66] Likewise, the draft Regulation also prohibits OLAF to 'open any parallel administrative investigation into the same facts' where the EPPO decides to open a case.[67]

With regard to rights which are not directly regulated in the Title of the Charter concerning Justice, during the investigations of the EPPO, as well as during any national investigation, many different human rights can be endangered by the activities of public officials (privacy in case of wiretapping, liberty in case of pre-trial detention measures, etc.); therefore the Charter could play a relevant role also in similar cases.[68] In that regard, the current version of the Preamble of the draft Regulation also mentions Article 8 CFR on the protection of personal data and Article 42 CFR on the right of access to documents.[69] In this contribution we do not focus on such issues, but it can be reminded that a whole raft of provisions of the draft Regulation are devoted to data protection,[70] and that most of them replicate the content of the recently adopted Directive on the matter.[71]

[64] Since Joined Cases C-187/01 and C-385/01, *Gözütok and Brügge*, judgment of 11 February 2003, the issue of transnational *ne bis in idem* has been dealt with in many decisions of the Court of Justice. For a recent overview of the matter see, among the many, Mitsilegas 2016a, pp. 84ff.

[65] See Case C-489/10, *Bonda*, judgment of 5 June 2012, and Case C-617/10, *Fransson*, cit.

[66] Article 20(1) draft Regulation.

[67] Article 57a (2) draft Regulation.

[68] On this issue, see for instance Balsamo 2013, pp. 432ff.

[69] See, respectively, Recitals Nos. 93 and 108 of the Preamble of the draft Regulation.

[70] See the more than 40 Articles of the Chapter VI of the current draft Regulation.

[71] Directive (EU) 2016/680 of the European Parliament and of the Council of 27 April 2016 on the protection of natural persons with regard to the processing of personal data by competent authorities for the purposes of the prevention, investigation, detection or prosecution of criminal offences or the execution of criminal penalties, and on the free movement of such data, and repealing Council Framework Decision 2008/977/JHA, *OJ* L119/89, 4.5.2016. This Directive represents *lex specialis* (limited to the field of criminal justice) to the General Data Protection Regulation which has been adopted on the same date (see Regulation (EU) 2016/679 of the European Parliament and of the Council of 27 April 2016 on the protection of natural persons with regard to the processing of personal data and on the free movement of such data, and repealing Directive 95/46/EC (General Data Protection Regulation), *OJ* L119/1, 4.5.2016).

6.3.2 *Rights and Evidence*

Within the analysis of the protection afforded to the rights of the persons involved in the proceedings of the EPPO, another element needs to be addressed, namely that of evidence.

From the perspective of the suspects and accused persons, the issue at stake is as clear as contentious: should they and their lawyers be allowed to gather evidence in the frame of the investigations carried out by the EPPO? The application of the principle of equality of arms, which underpins the right to a fair trial, should lead to a positive answer. However, the matter is extremely sensitive under a legal and political point of view, since the right of the defence to gather evidence is provided only in some Member States.

In the original proposal, it was stated that, in accordance with national law, the suspect and accused person should have the right both to *present evidence* to the consideration of the EPPO and to *request the EPPO* to gather any evidence relevant to the investigation, 'including appointing experts and hearing witnesses'.[72] Such a provision was removed during the negotiations in the Council but eventually it has been included again in the text, even though partially reworded.[73] Article 35(3) draft Regulation indeed states that

> [w]ithout prejudice to the rights provided in this Chapter, suspects and accused persons as well as other persons involved in the proceedings of the European Public Prosecutor's Office shall have all the procedural rights available to them under the applicable national law, including the *possibility to present evidence*, *to request the appointment of experts* or expert examination and *hearing of witnesses*, and *to request* the European Public Prosecutor's Office to obtain such measures on behalf of the defence.[74]

Commenting on the similar provision of the Commission's proposal, Michiel Luchtman and John Vervaele underlined that 'the proposal only mentions a "right to request", implying implicitly a certain degree of discretion for the EPPO not to grant the request, or not to specify the reasons for that decision'.[75] Nevertheless, other authors welcomed the rule at stake, since a proactive role of the suspects and

---

[72] Article 35(2) Commission's proposal.

[73] Also the European Parliament had shed light on the issue, since in its last Resolution on the draft Regulation it stated that 'the regulation should provide for additional rights of defence for EPPO suspects, in particular [...] the right to present evidence and to ask the EPPO to collect evidence on behalf of the suspect' (European Parliament 2016, p. 3).

[74] Article 35(3) draft Regulation (emphasis added). This provision recalls Recital No. 55, according to which the EPPO has the obligation to seek all types of evidence 'inculpatory as well as exculpatory, either *motu proprio* or *on request of the defence*' (emphasis added). The duty of the EPPO to conduct the investigations in an impartial manner and to seek all relevant evidence, whether inculpatory or exculpatory, is also enshrined in Article 5(4) draft Regulation.

[75] Luchtman and Vervaele 2014, p. 148.

accused persons and of their lawyers was envisaged, because they could at least *present evidence* to the consideration of the EPPO.[76]

Similar considerations are still valid, but what is to be noted is that, on the one hand, the breadth of the right at stake seems now more limited than it was in the Commission's proposal. Whereas the latter referred to the right 'to gather *any evidence* relevant to the investigation, *including* appointing experts and hearing witnesses',[77] the draft Regulation *only* refers to the right to request the appointment of experts or expert examination and hearing of witnesses.

On the other hand, in line with the Commission's proposal, the right at issue can be exercised *only if provided by national law*, as the wording of Article 35(3) suggests.[78] Therefore, the draft Regulation does not harmonise this peculiar aspect of national criminal justice systems, since the right at issue cannot be exercised in those countries where it does not already exist according to domestic legislation. As a consequence, individuals involved in the proceedings of the EPPO will enjoy a different degree of protection according to the applicable national law.

Until the adoption of the current version of the draft Regulation, the issue of evidence in the frame of the activities of the EPPO was linked with human rights under a further perspective. After stating that evidence shall not be denied admission just because it has been collected in a different country, Article 31(1) of the *previous* version of the draft Regulation added that '[w]here the law of the Member State of the trial Court requires that the latter examines the *admissibility of evidence*, it shall ensure it is satisfied that its admission would not be incompatible with Member States obligations to respect the *fairness of the procedure*, the *rights of defence*, or *other rights* as enshrined in the Charter, in accordance with Article 6 TEU'.[79]

[76] Allegrezza 2013, p. 485. The need to allow the defendant to carry out investigations and gather evidence in the frame of the activities of the EPPO has been underlined by Council of Bars and Law Societies of Europe 2013, p. 4; European Criminal Bar Association 2013, p. 197; Comi 2014, p. 197.

[77] Article 35(2) Commission's proposal (emphasis added).

[78] '[...] suspects and accused persons [...] shall have all the procedural rights available to them *under the applicable national law*, *including* the possibility to present evidence [...]' (Article 35(3) draft Regulation, emphasis added). Likewise, Article 35 of the Commission's proposal was phrased as follows: '1. The suspect and accused person shall have, *in accordance with national law*, the right to present evidence to the consideration of the European Public Prosecutor's Office. 2. The suspect and accused person shall have, *in accordance with national law*, the right to request the European Public Prosecutor's Office to gather any evidence relevant to the investigation, including appointing experts and hearing witnesses' (emphasis added).

[79] Article 31(1) of the previous version of the draft Regulation (Proposal for a Regulation on the establishment of the European Public Prosecutor's Office—Completed text, Council doc. 12774/2/16, 12 October 2016) (emphasis added).

The previous version of Article 31(1) draft Regulation was also different from the text of the Commission's proposal.[80] The latter provided that evidence presented by the EPPO to the trial court *should have been admitted* in the trial 'without any validation or similar legal process',[81] even if the national law of the Member State provided for different rules on the collection or presentation of evidence. The only condition for such a 'free circulation of evidence'[82] was that the trial court had to consider that the admission of evidence would have not adversely affected the fairness of the procedure or the rights of defence as enshrined in Articles 47 and 48 CFR.

On the contrary, the previous version of Article 31(1) draft Regulation did not guarantee such an (almost) automatic 'presumption of admissibility of evidence'.[83] In fact, it seemed to imply that, *if* national law required for a scrutiny on evidence, such a scrutiny should have taken into account the respect of the *fairness of the procedure*, of the *rights of defence* and of *other rights* as enshrined in the Charter. The violation of one of them should have been sufficient to exclude the collected evidence from the trial. It was evident, however, that the national judge would have been required to undertake an evaluation based on too vague concepts ('fairness of the procedure', 'rights of defence', etc.), which are usually meant to encompass different principles and rules. The power conferred to national authorities with regard to the admissibility of evidence was deemed to be, all in all, too discretionary and risks of 'legal uncertainty'[84] were quite obvious.

However, the ambiguous provision at stake has been eventually removed from the current draft Regulation, whose Article 31 only provides, on the one hand, that evidence shall not be denied admission just because it has been collected in a different Member State, and, on the other hand, that the Regulation will not affect the power of the *trial court* to freely assess evidence presented by the defendant or by the EPPO.[85] With regard to the admissibility of evidence, therefore, it seems that the EU legislator has decided to take a step backwards and to leave the burning issue in the hands of national courts.

[80] For further reflections on the provisions concerning the admissibility of evidence in the Commission's proposal and in the previous version of the draft Regulation see Weyembergh and Brière 2016, pp. 33–34.

[81] Article 30(1) Commission's proposal. For some critical views on this provision see Zerbes 2015, pp 221ff.

[82] Caianiello 2013, p. 122. See also Spiezia 2013, p. 568.

[83] Helenius 2015, p. 191.

[84] Ibid., p. 201.

[85] See, respectively, Article 31(1) and (2) of the current draft Regulation.

6.4 Judicial Review of the Acts of the EPPO

Notwithstanding the establishment of the EPPO as a European Union body operating within a single legal area,[86] the *Commission's proposal* excluded the judicial review of EPPO acts at EU level. Article 36 of the Commission's draft states clearly that when adopting procedural measures in the performance of its functions, the European Public Prosecutor's Office is to be considered as a *national* authority for the purpose of judicial review.[87] It is further added that where provisions of national law are rendered applicable by the Regulation, such provisions will not be considered as provisions of Union law for the purpose of Article 267 of the Treaty.[88] Shielding the EPPO from EU judicial scrutiny is also confirmed elsewhere in the Commission's proposal where judicial review of certain EPPO decisions is excluded in general.[89]

The Commission justified the exclusion of EU judicial review on three main grounds: on the perceived specificity and difference of the EPPO from all other Union bodies and agencies which requires special rules on judicial review;[90] the strong link between the operations of the EPPO and the legal orders of the Member States;[91] and the need to respect the principle of subsidiarity.[92] The Commission's approach towards the limited judicial review of the EPPO at EU level was encapsulated in the Preamble to its proposal as follows:

> Article 86(2) of the Treaty requires that the European Public Prosecutor's Office exercise its functions of prosecutor in the *competent courts* of the Member States. Acts undertaken by the European Public Prosecutor's Office in the course of its investigations are closely related to the prosecution which may result therefrom and have effects in the legal order of the Member States. In most cases they will be carried out by national law enforcement authorities acting under the instructions of European Public Prosecutor's Office, sometimes after having obtained the authorisation of a national court. It is therefore appropriate to consider the European Public Prosecutor's Office as a national authority for the purpose of the judicial review of its acts of investigation and prosecution. As a result, *national courts* should be entrusted with the judicial review of all acts of investigation and prosecution of the European Public Prosecutor's Office which may be challenged, and the Court of Justice of the European Union should not be directly competent with regard to those acts pursuant to Articles 263, 265 and 268 of the Treaty, since such acts should *not be considered as acts of a body of the Union for the purpose of judicial review*.

---

[86] The concept of 'single European area' is mentioned in Article 25(1) of the Commission's proposal. For some considerations on this issue see Damaskou 2015, p. 147. See also Sect. 6.5 of this contribution.

[87] Article 36(1) Commission's proposal.

[88] Article 36(2) Commission's proposal.

[89] This applied to the decision to dismiss a case following a transaction (Article 29(4) Commission's proposal).

[90] Explanatory Memorandum to the Commission's proposal, para 3.3.5.

[91] Ibid.,

[92] Ibid., p. 5.

> In accordance with Article 267 of the Treaty, national courts are able or, in certain circumstances, bound to refer to the Court of Justice questions for preliminary rulings on the interpretation or the validity of provisions of Union law, including this Regulation, which are relevant for the judicial review of the acts of investigation and prosecution of the European Public Prosecutor's Office. National courts should not be able to refer questions on the validity of the acts of the European Public Prosecutor's Office to the Court of Justice, since those acts should not be considered acts of a body of the Union for the purpose of judicial review.
>
> It should also be clarified that issues concerning the interpretation of provisions of national law which are rendered applicable by this Regulation should be dealt with by national courts alone. In consequence, those courts may not refer questions to the Court of Justice relating to the interpretation of national law to which this Regulation refers.[93]

The Commission's treatment of the EPPO as a national body for the purposes of judicial review was strikingly at odds with its overall vision of the EPPO as a centralised body establishing a system of vertical cooperation in the field of investigation and prosecution in the European Union. The Commission emphasised the links of the EPPO with national legal orders, yet disregarded the fact that EPPO acts and decisions are acts adopted by an EU agency—with the Commission's draft effectively creating a European agency lying outside European judicial control.[94] The Commission further justified this exclusion on the basis of the special nature of the EPPO. However, if anything, the specificity of the EPPO in relation to other EU agencies—which consists of the fact that the EPPO is an operational body whose action has the potential to affect significantly fundamental rights across the EU—should render EU judicial review even more imperative.

Moreover, the possibilities allowed by the Treaty of Lisbon for specific rules concerning judicial review of EU agencies in general[95] and the EPPO in particular (Article 86(3) TFEU) do not mean that these rules can entail the total exclusion of EU judicial review for EU agencies, including the EPPO.[96] The exclusion of such review—at least the total exclusion—would be a direct attack to the rule of law in the European Union and would challenge the obligation of the EU to uphold fundamental rights as enshrined in the ECHR and the Charter. A total exclusion of EU judicial review of the EPPO would in particular be hard to reconcile with the *right to effective judicial protection* (Article 47 CFR), which has assumed a central role in EU constitutional law in recent years.[97]

Finally, the Commission's approach to the judicial review of the EPPO rested on a wrong understanding of the application of the principle of subsidiarity. The

[93] Preamble of the Commission's proposal, Recitals Nos. 37–39 (emphasis added).

[94] In this context, see also the established Luxembourg case-law according to which national courts have no jurisdiction themselves to declare the invalidity of measures taken by EU institutions (e.g. Case 314/85, *Foto-Frost*, judgment of 22 October 1987).

[95] Article 263, fifth paragraph TFEU.

[96] For similar considerations see Meij 2015, pp. 115–117.

[97] See for instance the Court's rulings in the *Kadi* litigation, and in particular the Court's findings in *Kadi II* (Joined Cases C-584/10 P, C-593/10 P. and C-595/10 P, *European Commission v Kadi*, judgment of 18 July 2013).

subsidiarity test to be met is whether the European Union level is the right level of legislative action with regard to the establishment of the EPPO in order to achieve the stated legislative objectives.[98] The question of judicial review is a meta-question concerning the functioning of the EPPO, which should arise after the decision on whether the establishment of an EPPO *per se* meets the requirements of the subsidiarity test.[99]

It comes as no surprise, therefore, that the provision at stake has been one of the most contested. In the debate it triggered, three different perspectives had been put forward on the matter.[100]

Firstly, one could have thought of a distinction between acts and decisions of the EPPO in its centralised functions on the one hand and under its decentralised formations on the other.[101] It is true that the centralised/decentralised distinction is increasingly harder to make, in particular after the additional layers in the EPPO structure introduced in the Greek Presidency's draft (European Chief Prosecutor, European Prosecutors, College, Permanent Chambers, and European Delegated Prosecutors). Moreover, it is also clear that acts and decisions of the EPPO both in its centralised and its decentralised incarnations constitute acts taken by an EU body which should thus in principle be subject to EU judicial review within the constitutional parameters of the Treaties. However, in the light of the peculiar multi-level nature of the forthcoming Office, it seems that this perspective could represent a reasonable compromise. On the one hand, decisions adopted by the Permanent Chambers, which represent the beating European heart of the EPPO, should be revised at the EU level: they concern the key moments of the proceedings of the EPPO,[102] so that an EU check seems necessary. On the other hand, decisions taken on the national plane (e.g. adoption of a specific investigative measure)—still in the frame of the EPPO though—could be left to the review of national authorities.

The second perspective was to distinguish between judicial review of the *types of act* adopted by the EPPO: pre-prosecution acts (e.g. investigation acts enumerated in Article 26 of the Commission's proposal, now Article 25 draft Regulation) could have been left to national courts to deal with, while decisions on prosecution could have been subject to EU judicial review. However, this distinction disregards the fact that both investigation and prosecution decisions are taken by the same, EU body whose acts should in principle be subject to EU judicial review. More importantly, it would be contrary to the rule of law and a challenge to effective

---

[98] For a detailed and negative subsidiarity assessment of the Commission's draft EPPO Regulation, see House of Lords European Union Committee 2013.

[99] On the EPPO and the principle of subsidiarity, see Fromage 2015, pp. 1–23; Wieczorek 2015, pp. 1247–1270; Mitsilegas 2016a, pp. 40ff.

[100] See more in Mitsilegas 2016a, pp. 115–116.

[101] See above, footnote 16.

[102] For instance, pursuant to Article 9(3) draft Regulation it is for the Permanent Chamber to decide to bring a case to judgment, to dismiss a case, to apply a simplified procedure, and to reopen an investigation.

judicial protection if acts of an EU body which may have profound consequences for fundamental rights—such as investigation acts and decisions adopted by the EPPO—were shielded from EU judicial scrutiny.

The third perspective was to distinguish in terms of applicable law, with EPPO acts and decisions to which EU law applies being subject to EU judicial scrutiny and acts and decisions to which national law applies being subject only to national judicial review. However, this perspective would also disregard the European Union nature of the EPPO and the acts and decisions adopted by this body, and could result in serious adverse consequences with regard to legal certainty as to which acts or decisions would qualify as 'national' for the purposes of judicial review.

In other words, a judicial review at the EU level, applying as extensively as possible to the acts and decisions of the EPPO, was advocated.[103]

However, the current text provides for a partially different solution, which sits in between the first and the second of the above-mentioned perspectives.[104] Article 36 (1) draft Regulation reaffirms the competence of *national courts* to rule on the 'procedural acts of the European Public Prosecutor's Office which are intended to produce legal effects vis-à-vis third parties'. The same applies when the EPPO has *failed* to adopt procedural acts 'which are intended to produce legal effects vis-à-vis third parties and which it was legally required to adopt'[105] under the Regulation. However, the negotiations have not neglected the European nature of the EPPO and have enhanced the role of the Court of Justice, mainly in two directions.[106]

First, the Court of Justice has been expressly recognised the power to give *preliminary rulings* concerning: (i) the *validity* of *procedural acts* of the EPPO, 'insofar as such question of validity is raised before any court or tribunal of a Member State directly on the basis of Union law';[107] (ii) 'the interpretation or the validity of *provisions of Union law*',[108] including the Regulation; and (iii) the interpretation of the Articles of the Regulation which delimit the material competence of the EPPO.[109]

---

[103] Mitsilegas 2015, pp. 76ff.

[104] On the issue of the judicial review of the acts of the EPPO see, among the many, Đurđević 2012, pp. 986–1010; Giudicelli-Delage et al. 2015.

[105] Article 36(1) draft Regulation.

[106] This contribution focuses only on the judicial review of the procedural acts of the EPPO. However, it can be reminded that the Court of Justice is also competent in any dispute concerning: (i) compensation for damage caused by the EPPO; (ii) arbitration clauses contained in contracts concluded by the EPPO; and (iii) staff-related matters (respectively, Article 36(4), (5), and (6) draft Regulation). The Court of Justice has jurisdiction on the dismissal of the European Chief Prosecutor or European Prosecutors, too (Article 36(7) draft Regulation). Finally, pursuant to the fourth paragraph of Article 263 TFEU, the Court is competent to review the decisions of the EPPO which are not procedural acts, such as those dismissing the EDPs or concerning data protection (Article 36(8) draft Regulation).

[107] Article 36(2)(a) draft Regulation.

[108] Article 36(2)(b) draft Regulation (emphasis added).

[109] Article 36(2)(c) draft Regulation.

Second, pursuant to the fourth paragraph of Article 263 TFEU, the Court of Luxembourg shall be competent to review the decisions of the EPPO to *dismiss* a case, 'in so far as they are contested directly *on the basis of Union law*'.[110] As known, Article 263 TFEU regulates the judicial review of Union measures, and its fourth paragraph concerns the so-called 'non-privileged applicants',[111] i.e. the natural or legal persons who intend to institute proceedings against an act addressed to them or which is of direct and individual concern to them. The conditions to trigger the right of the natural and legal persons to ask the Court of Justice to review some EU measures have been abundantly discussed in the literature and better clarified by the Court of Luxembourg.[112]

Even though the draft Regulation takes the Commission's proposal a step forward in the direction of EU scrutiny of the decisions and acts of the EPPO, a closer look shows that this development is all in all quite limited.

In fact, the competence of the Court of Justice to give preliminary rulings on the interpretation or validity of the Regulation, including its Articles on the material competence of the EPPO, was already uncontested on the basis of EU law. Since the Regulation will be an act of the Council, the competence of the Court of Justice to rule on its interpretation or validity comes from Article 267(1)(b) TFEU, rather than from the provisions of the EPPO Regulation. This was not excluded from the Commission's draft, which only excluded from the scope of application of Article 267 TFEU *national law* which is rendered applicable by the Regulation.

On the contrary, preliminary rulings on the validity of the procedural acts of the EPPO were forbidden by the original proposal. Such a competence of the Court of Justice comes into consideration only when the question of validity is raised *on the basis of Union law*. Therefore, this seems to imply that, for example, a procedural act of the EPPO can be subject to a preliminary reference when a national tribunal has reason to believe that this act violates general principles of the EU, fundamental rights, the Treaties, or even the Regulation itself. However, since the investigations will be mostly regulated by national legislation, the latter case does not seem to be able to lead to numerous decisions of the Court.

Moreover, as mentioned, the Council has decided to raise at the EU level the scrutiny on the decisions of the EPPO to *dismiss* the case, 'insofar as they are contested directly on the basis of Union law'.[113] Once again, the consequence is that those decisions can be contested when they are thought to violate general principles of the EU, fundamental rights, the Treaties, or the Regulation. The Regulation lists some grounds to dismiss the case, which justify the closure of the investigations if the prosecution has become impossible 'pursuant to the law of the

[110] Article 36(3) draft Regulation (emphasis added).

[111] Chalmers et al. 2014, p. 444.

[112] Ibid., pp. 444–455.

[113] For further considerations on the judicial review of the EPPO's dismissal decisions, see Göhler 2015, pp. 102–125.

Member State of the European Delegated Prosecutor handling the case'.[114] In other words, the Regulation lists the reasons why a case shall be closed, but it is for the domestic legislators to better regulate them and the procedures thereof. One could imagine, therefore, that the judicial review of the decisions at stake could be triggered because the case has been closed on the basis of a ground which is not provided for by the Regulation.

It is not clear whether the power of the Court to review the decision to close the case excludes the possible scrutiny of national authorities who could also be empowered to carry out such an evaluation, or whether this is an additional guarantee against an unfounded dismissal. The relevant provision begins with '[b]y way of exception to paragraph 1',[115] i.e. the paragraph on the competence of *national* courts to rule on the procedural acts of the EPPO. Therefore, such an exception could mean that the decision on the dismissal of a case is subject *only* to the judicial review of the Court of Justice.[116]

The power of the Court of Justice to review the decisions to dismiss a case is consistent with the current envisaged structure of the EPPO: such a decision is taken at the EU level by the Permanent Chamber, so that it is reasonable to make it subject to the control of the Court of Luxembourg. For the very same reason, it is regrettable that such a scrutiny has not been extended to the decisions to bring the case to judgment, which are to be taken by the Permanent Chambers too. It is true that the EPPO is meant to overcome the current deficiencies in the fight against crimes affecting the EU finances, so that the decision not to launch the prosecution has to be revised at the EU level in order to avoid that cases are unreasonably dropped. Nevertheless, also the decisions to bring a case to judgment should be subject to an EU scrutiny: once the EPPO is conceived as a multi-level body, it would be logical that decisions taken at the EU level (including those to launch a prosecution) are revised by a judicial authority of the same level.

In that regard, it can be interesting to remind that a similar problem arose at the times of the *Corpus Juris*, which provided that the decision of the European Delegated Prosecutor to bring a case to judgment had to be 'verified' by a *national* judicial authority, the so-called 'judge of freedoms'.[117] However, such a solution was regarded as unsatisfactory and the option to set-up a *European pre-trial chamber* was discussed: 'This chamber could either exercise all the functions of a judge of freedoms at the level of the European Judicial Spacc and could *fully*

[114] Article 33(1) draft Regulation.

[115] Article 36(3) draft Regulation.

[116] It can also be reminded that, pursuant to Article 5(3) draft Regulation, 'The investigations and prosecutions on behalf of the European Public Prosecutor's Office shall be governed by this Regulation. National law shall apply to the extent that a matter is not regulated by this Regulation. [...] Where a matter is governed by national law and this Regulation, *the latter shall prevail*' (emphasis added).

[117] See Articles 21(3), *Corpus Juris* 2000 (Delmas-Marty and Vervaele 2000, pp. 187ff).

control the preparatory stage and the decision to bring a case to court [...]'.[118] In short, the need of guaranteeing a 'European check' on the decisions to be adopted at the end of the investigations was envisaged.

One of the members of the study group which drafted the *Corpus Juris*, however, suggested a more limited role for such a pre-trial chamber, namely that to choose the Member State where the case had to be brought to judgment:

> This Preliminary Chamber would oversee the choice of the forum. In my view, this would be a *nihil ostat* procedure rather than a *fiat* procedure: only if one of the parties wanted to challenge the forum choice of the prosecutor (Eurojust or European Public Prosecutor) would there be a decision of the court. [...] I believe that a European Preliminary Chamber is a necessary complement to concurrent jurisdiction in the European legal area and, as such, is a minimum requirement for judicial integration in a Union that will soon consist of twenty-five Member States or more.[119]

The issue of the *choice of forum* remains problematic also in the light of the current draft Regulation.

As briefly mentioned above,[120] the EDP who shall begin the investigations is in principle the one from 'the Member State where the focus of the criminal activity is or, if several connected offences within the competence of the Office have been committed, the Member State where the bulk of the offences has been committed'.[121] However, the Permanent Chamber can decide to reallocate the case to a European Delegated Prosecutor 'in another Member State',[122] taking into account the criteria laid down in the Regulation.

Usually, the Member State of the EDP who has conducted the *investigations* is also the one in which the *trial* will take place,[123] but once again the Permanent Chamber may 'decide to bring the case to prosecution in a *different* Member State'.[124]

None of the two mentioned decisions of the Permanent Chamber is subject to judicial review. The Court of Justice has only been empowered to give *preliminary rulings* concerning the interpretation of the Articles of the Regulation on the material competence of the EPPO[125] and the Regulation makes it clear that the role of the Court of Luxembourg cannot go beyond the boundaries of Article 267 in this field:

---

[118] Delmas-Marty 2000, p. 53 (emphasis added). Eventually, the pre-trial chamber was not included in the text of the *Corpus Juris* 2000.

[119] Van den Wyngaert 2004, pp. 238–239.

[120] See Sect. 6.3.1 of this contribution.

[121] Article 22(4) draft Regulation.

[122] Article 22(5)(a) draft Regulation.

[123] Article 30(2) draft Regulation.

[124] Article 30(2) draft Regulation (emphasis added).

[125] Article 36(2)(c) draft Regulation.

> [i]n case of *disagreement* between the European Public Prosecutor's Office and the *national* prosecution authorities over the question of whether the criminal conduct falls within the scope of Articles 17(1a), 17(2), 20(2) or 20(3) the *national authorities* competent to decide on the attribution of competences concerning prosecution at national level shall decide who is to be competent for the investigation of the case. [...].[126]

However, it seems that the draft Regulation refers to those cases in which, within the *same domestic system*, a conflict between a European Delegated Prosecutor and another national prosecutor arises; in similar circumstances, the disagreement concerns whether the case has to be dealt with by the EPPO or by ordinary national prosecution services. Therefore, the EDP is treated as a national prosecutor to all intents and purposes, so that the decision on the possible conflicts is in the hands of a *national* court, whereas the role of the Court of Justice is limited to issue preliminary rulings on the relevant rules of the Regulation.

Nothing is said, on the contrary, on those cases in which the conflicts concern *different* Member States: what if, for instance, the Italian EDP believes to be competent on the case, as well as the Greek one? As noted above, if they cannot find an agreement, the Permanent Chamber is called to decide on the issue. Since the EPPO will mainly function on the basis of national laws, the choice of the Member State where the *investigations* are carried out is of fundamental importance, not least because in that same Member State the *trial* will take place. Therefore, it is striking the choice of forum is not subject to any form of scrutiny at the European level during the proceedings of the EPPO.[127]

EU legislation does not provide for any binding rule concerning the conflicts of jurisdiction, but the current institutional scenario only features a system of judicial cooperation among national authorities. On the contrary, when the EPPO will be established there will an EU body exercising direct powers vis-à-vis individuals in the field of criminal law, so that it is unacceptable that such a sensitive matter is regulated in a vague way and without any form of control at the EU level.

In conclusion, the EU legislator is called to strike a very delicate balance with regard to the judicial review of the EPPO decisions. As the Parliament states in its last resolution on the EPPO, 'in order to ensure the effectiveness of judicial review in line with Article 47 of the Charter of Fundamental Rights of the European Union and with the Treaties, any operational decision affecting third parties taken by the EPPO should be subject to judicial review before a *competent national court*';[128] however, it also adds that 'direct judicial review by the European Court of Justice should be possible'.[129]

In other words, on the one hand the uniform application of EU rules concerning European investigations and the right to effective judicial protection would call for

---

[126] Article 20(5) draft Regulation (emphasis added).

[127] For similar views on the need of an EU scrutiny on the matter see, among the many, Vervaele 2010, p. 192; Candi 2013, pp. 629–630; Lohse 2015, p. 181.

[128] European Parliament 2016, p. 3 (emphasis added).

[129] Ibid. See Giuffrida 2017, pp. 32–34.

the scrutiny of the Court of Justice. It would be quite odd, under a legal and constitutional point of view, to establish an EU body which is not accountable to the Court of Luxembourg. On the other hand, however, the very same right to an effective remedy could lead to the opposite conclusion, since it could also be argued that, in practice, the European review of the acts of the EPPO—at least of all of them—could be less convenient for the parties to the proceedings. One could think, for example, that the costs of a procedure before the Court of Justice are higher than those of the proceedings before national courts. If this is a realistic scenario when the defendant lives in the same country where the measure or the act of the EPPO to appeal is adopted, it can be not necessarily true with regard to a person living in Member State A who wants to challenge a decision taken in Member State B.

Moreover, should the Court be overwhelmed by many requests concerning the activities of the EPPO (in addition to its regular workload), longer times could be necessary for the Court to adopt its decisions, with obvious negative consequences both on the investigations of the EPPO and on the rights of the suspects or accused persons. Nevertheless, it seems that the current legal framework of the EU allows for different solutions which could meet the need for a swift European scrutiny of the acts of the EPPO.

For instance, Article 257 TFEU allows the European Parliament and the Council to establish *specialised courts* attached to the General Court to hear and determine certain classes of action or proceeding brought in specific areas. If a ground-breaking body as the EPPO will be set up, it would be reasonable to envisage the establishment of a specialised court with *ad hoc* competences on the matter: it will not be a European Criminal Court, but rather a Court which would guarantee the control, at the EU level, of the activities of an EU body operating in the specific area of criminal law. However, this does not seem very realistic for the time being, especially in the light of the recent reform of the General Court: in order to face its enormous workload, the number of its judges has been doubled, but no specialised courts have been created.[130] Nevertheless, it cannot be excluded that the enlarged General Court will provide for specialised chambers with expedited procedures.[131]

Moreover, the Court has developed different procedures over the years, in order to reduce delays and speed up the decision mechanism. Should the Court be made finally competent for the review of the acts of the EPPO, the resort to such procedures seems appropriate. In particular, the *urgent preliminary ruling procedure* (PPU) has been introduced in 2008 with regard to references for preliminary rulings raising questions on issues concerning the Area of Freedom, Security and Justice.

[130] According to Article 48 of the latest version of the Statute of the Court of Justice of the European Union, as from 1 September 2019 the General Court shall consist of two judges per Member State.

[131] Expedited procedures of the General Court are regulated by Chapter 16, Title III of the Rules of Procedure of the General Court of 4 March 2015 (*OJ* L105/1, 23.4.2015), as amended on 13 July 2016 (*OJ* L217/71, 12.8.2016). On the establishment of specialised chambers within the General Court, see Sarmiento 2015.

Now regulated in Articles 107ff. of the Rules of Procedure of the Court,[132] this procedure is also mentioned in Article 267, fourth paragraph TFEU, where it is stated that if a 'question is raised in a case pending before a court or tribunal of a Member State with regard to a person in custody, the Court of Justice of the European Union shall act with the minimum of delay'. Likewise, the Rules of Procedure also provides for an expedited preliminary ruling procedure and for an expedited procedure in cases of direct actions.[133] It can be added that the Court of Justice is also empowered to adopt interim measures, which could turn out to be useful in the framework of possible procedures concerning the review of the acts of the EPPO.[134]

6.5 Mutual Recognition in the Framework of the EPPO: Cross-Border Investigations and Human Rights

Finally, the overview of the interrelations between the EPPO and human rights needs to take into account the regulation of cross-border investigations.

As briefly reminded above, the Commission's draft provided that, for the purpose of investigations and prosecutions conducted by the EPPO, the territory of the Union's Member States should have been considered a 'single legal area'.[135] The Commission's proposal thus mirrored the approach taken by the *Corpus Juris*. The Guiding Principles of *Corpus Juris* introduced the principle of European territoriality by stating that for the purposes of investigation, prosecution, trial and execution of sentences concerning the *Corpus Juris* offences, the territory of the Member States of the EU constituted a single area and that the competence *ratione loci* of the European Public Prosecutor and of national prosecutors to issue warrants and judgments pursuant to the *Corpus Juris* extended to the *entire* European judicial area.

This was somehow restated in the Commission's draft, whose Article 26(7) provided that the EPPO 'may request from the competent judicial authority the arrest or pre-trial detention of the suspected person in accordance with national law'. In the view of the Commission, the EPPO should function as a unique body in a unique area, without the need to resort to instruments of mutual recognition. As

[132] Rules of Procedure of the Court of Justice of 25 September 2012 (*OJ* L265/1, 29.9.2012), as amended on 18 June 2013 (*OJ* L173/65, 26.6.2013) and on 19 July 2016 (*OJ* L217/69, 12.8.2016).

[133] Respectively, Articles 105–106 and 133ff. Rules of Procedure of the Court. For an overview of the accelerated procedures before the Court of Justice see Wathelet 2014, pp. 33–45, who also briefly discusses the priority treatment pursuant to Article 53(3) Rules of Procedure of the Court ('The President may in special circumstances decide that a case be given priority over others'). However, former Advocate General Jacobs warned that the accelerated procedures 'must be used sparingly because they lead to greater delays in other cases' (Jacobs 2013, p. 53).

[134] See Articles 160ff. Rules of Procedure of the Court.

[135] Article 25(1) Commission's proposal.

argued by Mireille Delmas-Marty, indeed, '[*l*]*e principe de territorialité européenne est différent du principe de reconnaissance mutuelle* […], *parce qu'il implique une véritable intégration normative et institutionelle*'.[136]

The concept of 'single legal area'—ruled out during the negotiations—had implications also on cross-border investigations of the EPPO. In the Commission's draft, indeed, it is provided that the European Delegated Prosecutor who conducts the investigations (the 'EDP handling the case') has to 'act in close consultation'[137] with the EDP of the other Member State where an investigative measure has to be carried out. Thus, a close consultation between the EDPs should have been sufficient to lead to the adoption of investigative measures in different Member States, as one would expect in the frame of a single office working in a single legal area.

This scenario has significantly changed and the current text regulates the issue of cross-border investigations in a perspective clearly recalling that of *mutual recognition*, i.e. the perspective that should be abandoned (or at least reduced to the minimum) in the light of a forthcoming EU-centered prosecution. The issue is extremely sensitive under a political point of view: if the EPPO replicates to a considerable extent the existing system of judicial cooperation, what is the added value of establishing such a body?

The dynamics of mutual recognition emerge from Article 26 draft Regulation. It states that, when the EDP handling the case needs to take a measure in another Member State, (s)he *assigns* the measure to an EDP located in that Member State (the 'assisting EDP').[138] Article 26 draft Regulation makes clear that the rules on the *judicial authorisation* of the investigative measures provided by national legislations have to apply. Therefore, if the assigned measure needs a judicial authorisation in the Member State where it has to be carried out, the assisting EDP shall obtain it; if the authorisation is refused, the EDP handling the case shall withdraw the assignment. However, if the authorisation is needed in the Member State of the latter, (s)he will have to obtain it and to submit it together with the assignment.[139]

Articles 26 draft Regulation also lists some reasons that could be defined as *grounds for refusal of the execution* of the assigned measure. Actually, the text does not expressly say that the measure can be refused, but it makes clear that—when one of those situations occur (see immediately *infra*)—the matter shall be referred to the competent Permanent Chamber, which will decide 'whether and by when the assigned measure needed, or a substitute measure, shall be undertaken by the assisting European Delegated Prosecutor'.[140] Therefore, such a procedure suggests that these are cases when the assisting EDP basically *refuses* the execution of the measure assigned by the EDP handling the case, or at least (s)he cannot promptly execute it.

136 Delmas-Marty 2010, p. 167.

137 Article 18(2) Commission's proposal.

138 Article 26(1) draft Regulation.

139 Article 26(3) draft Regulation.

140 Article 26(7) draft Regulation.

The reasons which trigger the procedure above are four: (i) the assignment is incomplete or contains a manifest relevant error; (ii) the measure cannot be undertaken within the time limit set out in the assignment for justified and objective reasons; (iii) an alternative but less intrusive measure would achieve the same results as the measure assigned; and (iv) the assigned measure does not exist or would not be available in a similar domestic case under the law of his or her Member State.[141]

It is evident, therefore, that the EU legislator has not been willing to give up on the principle of mutual recognition, with the consequence of watering down the original proposal. The above-mentioned regulation of cross-border investigations recalls the recent Directive on the European Investigation Order (EIO),[142] although during the negotiations an 'alignment of the EPPO provision with those of the EIO was [...] rejected in favour of a *sui generis* regime for the EPPO'.[143] The EIO is a judicial decision issued by national judicial authorities of a Member State to have one or more specific investigative measure(s) carried out in another Member State, with the aim to obtain evidence.[144] As the European Arrest Warrant, in practical terms the EIO is a form to be completed by a national competent authority, who will send it to the executing State where the needed evidence can be found. Once the EIO is executed, the executing authority shall, without undue delay, transfer the evidence obtained or already in its possession to the issuing State.[145]

The EIO Directive modernises the system of judicial cooperation at the EU level and the corresponding provisions of the three traditional conventions in the field will be replaced as of 22 May 2017, i.e. from the date by which the Member States bound by the Directive are required to implement it.[146] In the panorama of mutual recognition, the EIO Directive is characterised by some interesting features that show a clear intent to balance the needs of the investigations with an adequate protection of human rights.

In particular, the Directive expressly includes *non-compliance with fundamental rights* as a ground of non-recognition or non-execution of the EIO.[147] Following

---

[141] Article 26(5) draft Regulation.

[142] Directive 2014/41/EU of the European Parliament and of the Council of 3 April 2014 regarding the European Investigation Order in criminal matters, *OJ* L130/1, 1.5.2014. See Giuffrida 2017, pp. 21–25.

[143] Weyembergh and Brière 2016, p. 31.

[144] Article 1 Directive 2014/41/EU.

[145] Article 13(1) Directive 2014/41/EU.

[146] Articles 34(1) and 36(1) Directive 2014/41/EU. The conventions replaced are: (a) the 1959 Convention on Mutual Assistance in Criminal Matters of the Council of Europe and its two additional protocols, as well as the bilateral agreements concluded pursuant to Article 26 thereof; (b) the Convention implementing the Schengen Agreement; and (c) the Convention on Mutual Assistance in Criminal Matters between the Member States of the European Union and its protocol. As we can read in Recitals Nos. 43–45 of the Preamble of the Directive, the United Kingdom is bound by the Directive, whereas Ireland and Denmark are not. At the time of writing, the effects of the referendum on the exit of the UK from the EU are not known and the UK has not yet notified its intention to withdraw from the Union pursuant to Article 50 TEU.

[147] Article 11(1)(f) Directive 2014/41/EU.

case-law by the Strasbourg and Luxembourg Courts in the field of asylum law, the Preamble of the Directive affirms that the presumption of compliance by Member States with fundamental rights is rebuttable.[148] Quite curiously, however, such a ground for refusal is not provided for in the draft Regulation on the EPPO. This choice of the legislator is quite debatable: it is true that the draft Regulation does not formally provide for a system of mutual recognition, but in practice the rationale behind the rules on cross-border investigations seems the same as that underpinning the EIO Directive. Therefore, the silence of the draft Regulation cannot be easily justified: if the concept of 'single legal area' is abandoned and national authorities remain the kingpins of the investigations carried out by the EPPO, human rights cannot be paid less attention than in case of ordinary cooperation among judicial domestic bodies.

Notwithstanding this silence of the draft Regulation, the protection of human rights is guaranteed in the light of two further provisions. First, Article 27 draft Regulation provides that the formalities and procedures expressly indicated by the European Delegated Prosecutor handling the case shall be complied with, unless they are contrary to the '*fundamental principles of law* of the Member State of the assisting European Delegated Prosecutor'.[149] A broad expression such as 'fundamental principles of law' could probably be understood as going beyond the field of criminal procedural law and it could also refer to the constitutional traditions of the EU Member States, which encompass the protection of fundamental rights.

Second, in the frame of cross-border investigations the protection of human rights can also be guaranteed by means of the 'proportionality check' required by the Regulation. It should be remembered that, in general, proportionality is emerging as a limit to mutual recognition. Proportionality concerns have been raised by governments and defendants alike and stem from the fear that mutual recognition instruments, and European Arrest Warrants in particular, will be issued for offences which are deemed to be minor or trivial in the executing state. Calls for the introduction of a proportionality check in the operation of the principle of mutual recognition in criminal matters have been put forward in order to ensure that pressure on criminal justice systems of executing Member States, and disproportionate results for the requested individuals, are avoided.[150] The debate on proportionality as a limit to mutual recognition has arisen prominently regarding the

[148] Recital No. 10 of the Preamble of Directive 2014/41/EU reads as follows: 'The creation of an area of freedom, security and justice within the Union is based on mutual confidence and a presumption of compliance by other Member States with Union law and, in particular, with fundamental rights. However, that *presumption is rebuttable*. Consequently, if there are substantial grounds for believing that the execution of an investigative measure indicated in the EIO would result in a breach of a fundamental right of the person concerned and that the executing State would disregard its obligations concerning the protection of fundamental rights recognised in the Charter, the execution of the EIO should be refused' (emphasis added).

[149] Article 27 draft Regulation (emphasis added).

[150] For a discussion, see Baker 2011, paras 5.120–5.155; Joint Committee on Human Rights 2011, pp. 40–43.

issue of European Arrest Warrants by the Polish authorities, which has been viewed as disproportionate by a number of executing states, including in particular the United Kingdom.[151]

Viewed from the perspective of the affected individual, demands for proportionality checks appear to be reasonable in ensuring checks and balances to automatic mutual recognition. However, the legal reality is much more complex. It is necessary first of all to pin down and specify which concept of proportionality is applicable to the discussion on mutual recognition in criminal matters. It is then essential to focus on determining in which way proportionality can enter the system of mutual recognition in criminal matters: by secondary law, or case-law? In the issuing state, in the executing state, or in both? The matter cannot be dealt with in depth in the present contribution, but it can be reminded that, as far as the EAW is concerned, the prevailing view has thus far been for proportionality to be dealt with in the *issuing* and not in the executing Member State.[152] Nevertheless, in the United Kingdom the non-compliance with proportionality is regarded a ground of refusal to execute an EAW, on the basis of the latest version of the Extradition Act 2003.

As far as the EIO Directive is concerned, it introduces a proportionality check in the *issuing State*: the issuing authority may only issue an EIO when this is necessary and proportionate and when the investigative measures indicated in the EIO could have been ordered under the same conditions in a similar domestic case.[153] The Directive thus links proportionality with the requirement to avoid abuse of law via the undertaking of 'fishing expeditions' by the authorities of the issuing State. Moreover, the EIO Directive also provides that the executing authority may 'have recourse to an investigative measure other than that indicated in the EIO where the investigative measure selected by the executing authority would achieve the same result by *less intrusive means* than the investigative measure indicated in the EIO'.[154]

Likewise, according to the EPPO draft Regulation, the assisting EDP can 'refuse' the execution of the assigned measure also when 'an alternative but *less intrusive* measure would achieve the same results as the measure assigned'.[155] It can be noted that these provisions do not raise the above-mentioned typical risks of vagueness linked with the application of the principle of proportionality, since the assisting EDP (or the executing authority in the case of the EIO) shall usually indicate which is the other, less intrusive, measure available. One would expect that, if the EDP handling the case (or the issuing authority, with regard to the EIO) believes that such a measure can really lead to the same results, (s)he shall not object to its adoption. Therefore, in the evaluation of the proportionality of the

[151] For an overview of the debate, see Ostropolski 2014, pp. 167–191.

[152] For a broader analysis on proportionality and mutual recognition, see Mitsilegas 2016a, pp. 142ff.

[153] See Article 6(1) Directive 2014/41/EUEU.

[154] Article 10(3) Directive 2014/41/EU (emphasis added).

[155] Article 26(5)(c) draft Regulation (emphasis added).

assigned measures, the protection of human rights of the persons concerned by those measures shall be carefully taken into account, by resorting to less intrusive measures when they are available.

Finally, it can be reminded that also in the frame of cross-border investigations of the EPPO the Charter does apply, with the consequences already pointed out in the previous sections.

In conclusion, the current regulation of cross-border investigations of the EPPO is quite different from the original one: the concept and the implications of a 'single legal area' have been abandoned, and a system which recalls that of mutual recognition has been introduced. In this frame, in addition to the application of the Charter, the human rights of the persons potentially involved are protected either by the national courts which shall give the necessary *authorisations* for the investigative measures or by the assisting EDP who carries out a check on the *proportionality* of those measures and on their compatibility with the fundamental principles of law of the Member State where they have to be adopted.

6.6 Conclusion

The relations between human rights and the forthcoming EPPO have been discussed under four different perspectives. First, we have focused on the Charter of Fundamental Rights, which shall apply in the frame of the activities of the EPPO, at least because of the broad interpretation of Article 51(1) CFR espoused by the Court of Justice. However, it also seems that the Charter can come into consideration already because all the acts of the EPPO, even though adopted on the basis of national law, have to be considered to all intents and purposes acts and decisions of an EU body.

Second, the analysis has shifted to the provisions of the draft Regulation dealing with the procedural safeguards. In this frame, the reference to the Directives concerning the procedural rights of the individuals has been discussed. Those legal instruments represent an important achievement for the protection of the rights of suspects and accused persons, also in the light of their direct effect, but it remains to be evaluated whether their practical implementation will actually enhance the rights of people who will be concerned by the investigations of the EPPO.

Among the rights mentioned in the draft Regulation, moreover, due attention has been paid to those concerning evidence. The right of the defendant to present evidence and to request the EPPO to obtain some measures has been eventually reintroduced in the text, even though it can be exercised only when it is provided for by the applicable national law. On the contrary, the check on the admissibility of evidence based on admittedly vague and ambiguous criteria linked with the respect of human rights has been finally removed from the current draft Regulation.

Third, the issue of the judicial review of the acts of the EPPO has been addressed. In comparison with the original proposal, the current text has enhanced the European control on the activities of the EPPO, especially providing for the competence of the Court of Justice to review the decisions of the EPPO to dismiss the case pursuant to the fourth paragraph of Article 263 TFEU. However, it seems that a significant part of the acts and measures of the Office will not be subject to any judicial control at the European level, including the decision to launch a prosecution at the end of the investigations. This choice is strikingly at odds with the European nature of the forthcoming body and it does not take into account that such a decision, as well as that on the dismissal of the case, is taken at the central level of the Office by the Permanent Chamber; as a consequence, the judicial review should be placed on the same level. Also the lack of any judicial control on the choice of forum seems worrying, since it could lead to unacceptable cases of forum shopping and to serious violations of the defendant's rights.

Finally, it has been noted that in the frame of cross-border investigations, in addition to the application of the Charter, the human rights of the persons potentially involved are protected either by the national courts which shall give the necessary authorisations for the investigative measures or by the assisting EDP who carries out a check on the proportionality of those measures and on their compatibility with the fundamental principles of law of the Member State where they have to be adopted. The system recalls that of the Directive on the EIO, even though nothing similar to the provision of the Directive expressly recognising the violation of human rights as one of the grounds for refusal of the EIO can be found in the current version of the Regulation.

References

Articles, Books, and Studies

Allegrezza S (2013) Pubblico Ministero europeo e posizione della difesa: nuovi scenari per la tutela delle garanzie della persona sottoposta alle indagini. Le questioni in gioco. In: Grasso G, Illuminati G, Sicurella R, Allegrezza S (eds) Le sfide dell'attuazione di una Procura europea: definizione di regole comuni e loro impatto sugli ordinamenti interni. Giuffrè, Milan, pp 461–489

Bachmaier Winter L (2013) The establishment of a European Public Prosecutor's Office and the right to defence: critical approaches to the EU Directive of access to a lawyer. In: Grasso G, Illuminati G, Sicurella R, Allegrezza S (eds) Le sfide dell'attuazione di una Procura europea: definizione di regole comuni e loro impatto sugli ordinamenti interni. Giuffrè, Milan, pp 505–531

Bachmaier Winter L (2015) The Potential Contribution of a European Public Prosecutor in Light of the Proposal for a Regulation of 17 July 2013. European Journal of Crime, Criminal Law and Criminal Justice 23:101–120

Baker S (2011) A Review of the United Kingdom's Extradition Arrangements, presented to the Home Secretary on 30 September 2011

Balsamo A (2013) Le regole di procedura della Procura europea tra disciplina delle indagini e formazione della prova. In: Grasso G, Illuminati G, Sicurella R, Allegrezza S (eds) Le sfide dell'attuazione di una Procura europea: definizione di regole comuni e loro impatto sugli ordinamenti interni. Giuffrè, Milan, pp 419–449

Billis E (2016) The European Court of Justice: A "Quasi-Constitutional Court" in Criminal Matters? The *Taricco* Judgment and Its Shortcomings. New Journal of European Criminal Law 7:20–38

Caianiello M (2013) The Proposal for a Regulation on the Establishment of an European Public Prosecutor's Office: Everything Changes, or Nothing Changes? European Journal of Crime, Criminal Law and Criminal Justice 21:115–125

Caianiello M (2016) *Dum Romae (et Brucsellae) Consulitur*... Some Considerations on the *Taricco* Judgment and Its Consequences at National and European Level. European Journal of Crime, Criminal Law and Criminal Justice 24:1–17

Candi A (2013) La struttura della Procura europea e i rapporti con gli organi d'indagine nazionali. In: Grasso G, Illuminati G, Sicurella R, Allegrezza S (eds) Le sfide dell'attuazione di una Procura europea: definizione di regole comuni e loro impatto sugli ordinamenti interni. Giuffrè, Milan, pp 623–637

Chalmers D, Davies G, Monti G (2014) European Union Law. Cambridge University Press, Cambridge

Comi V (2014) The establishment of a European Public Prosecutor's Office. The commitment of lawyers for professional training that ensures effective and competent defence. In: Bazzocchi V (ed) Protecting Fundamental and Procedural Rights. From the Investigation of OLAF to the Future EPPO. Fondazione Basso, Rome, pp 190–201

Cotterrell R (1995) Law's Community. Legal Theory in Sociological Perspective. Clarendon Press, Oxford

Cotterrell R (2008) Comparative Law and Legal Culture. In: Reimann M, Zimmermann R (eds) The Oxford Handbook of Comparative Law. Oxford University Press, Oxford, pp 709–737

Council of Bars and Law Societies of Europe (2013) A European Public Prosecutor's Office (EPPO). http://www.ccbe.eu/fileadmin/speciality_distribution/public/documents/CRIMINAL_LAW/CRM_Position_papers/EN_CRM_20130207_A-European-Public-Prosecutor-s-Office-EPPO.pdf. Accessed 1 February 2017

Cras S (2014) The Directive on the Right of Access to a Lawyer in Criminal Proceedings and in European Arrest Warrant Proceedings. Eucrim 1:32–44

Damaskou A (2015) The European Public Prosecutor's Office. A Ground-Breaking New Institution of the EU Legal Order. New Journal of European Criminal Law 6:126–153

Delmas-Marty M (ed) (1997) *Corpus Juris* introducing penal provisions for the purpose of the financial interests of the European Union. Economica, Paris

Delmas-Marty M (2000) Necessity, legitimacy and feasibility of the *Corpus Juris*. In: Delmas-Marty M, Vervaele J (eds) The Implementation of the *Corpus Juris* in the Member States. Intersentia, Antwerp/Groningen/Oxford, pp 11–104

Delmas-Marty M (2010) La genèse du projet du procureur européen. In: Ghaleh Marzban P (ed) Quelles perspectives pour un Ministère Public Européen. Protéger les intérêts financiers et fondamentaux de l'Union. Dalloz, Paris, pp 163–169

Delmas-Marty M, Vervaele J (eds) (2000) The Implementation of the *Corpus Juris* in the Member States. Intersentia, Antwerp/Groningen/Oxford

Đurđević Z (2012) Judicial Control in Pre-Trial Criminal Procedure Conducted by the European Public Prosecutor's Office. In: Ligeti K (ed) Toward a Prosecutor for the European Union, vol 1. Hart, Oxford/Portland, pp 986–1010

European Criminal Bar Association (2013) Cornerstones for a Draft Regulation on the Establishment of a European Public Prosecutor's Office ("EPPO") in Accordance with Article 86 Par. 1–3 TFEU. New Journal of European Criminal Law 4:185–198

Fontanelli F (2014) Implementation of EU Law through Domestic Measures after Fransson: the Court of Justice Buys Time and 'Non-Preclusion' Troubles Loom Large. European Law Review 39:682–700

Fromage D (2015) The Second Yellow Card on the EPPO Proposal: An Encouraging Development for Member State Parliaments? Yearbook of European Law, doi: 10.1093/yel/yev024, pp 1–23. Accessed 15 November 2016

German Federal Bar and German Bar Association (2012) Joint position on the creation of a European Public Prosecutor's Office. http://www.eppo-project.eu/index.php/Home/News/German-Federal-Bar-Bundesrechtsanwaltskammer-and-German-Bar-Association-Deutscher-Anwaltverein-on-the-creation-of-a-EPPO. Accessed 5 October 2017

Giudicelli-Delage G, Manacorda S, Tricot J (eds) (2015) Le contrôle judiciaire du parquet européen. Nécessité, modéles, enjeux. Société de législation comparée, Paris

Giuffrida F (2016) The Limitation Period of Crimes: Same Old Italian Story, New Intriguing European Answers–Case note on C-105/14, *Taricco*. New Journal of European Criminal Law 7: 100–112

Giuffrida F (2017) The European Public Prosecutor's Office: King without kingdom? CEPS Research Report No 2017/03. https://www.ceps.eu/publications/european-public-prosecutor%E2%80%99s-office-king-without-kingdom. Accessed 5 October 2017

Göhler J (2015) To Continue or Not. Who Shall Be in Control of the European Public Prosecutor's Dismissal Decisions? New Journal of European Criminal Law 6:102–125

Hancox E (2013) The meaning of "implementing" EU law under Article 51(1) of the Charter: *Åkerberg Fransson*. Common Market Law Review 50:1411–1432

Helenius D (2015) Admissibility of Evidence and the European Public Prosecutor's Office. In: Asp P (ed) The European Public Prosecutor's Office – Legal and Criminal Policy Perspectives. Stiftelsen Skrifter utgivna av Juridiska fakulteten vid Stockholms universitet, Stockholm, pp 178–209

House of Lords European Union Committee (2013) Subsidiarity Assessment: The European Public Prosecutor's Office, 3rd Report, session 2013-14, HL Paper 65

Jacobs FG (2013) The Court of Justice in the Twenty-First Century: Challenges Ahead for the Judicial System? In: Court of Justice of the European Union (eds) The Court of Justice and the Construction of Europe: Analyses and Perspectives on Sixty Years of Case-law. TMC Asser Press, The Hague, pp 49–59

Joint Committee on Human Rights (2011) The Human Rights Implications of UK Extradition Policy, Fifteenth Report, session 2010–2012. http://www.publications.parliament.uk/pa/jt201012/jtselect/jtrights/156/156.pdf. Accessed 1 February 2017

Kaiafa-Gbandi M (2015) The Establishment of an EPPO and the Rights of Suspects and Defendants: Reflections upon the Commission's 2013 Proposal and the Council's Amendments. In: Asp P (ed) The European Public Prosecutor's Office – Legal and Criminal Policy Perspectives. Stiftelsen Skrifter utgivna av Juridiska fakulteten vid Stockholms universitet, Stockholm, pp 234–254

Lenaerts K (2012) Exploring the Limits of the EU Charter of Fundamental Rights. European Constitutional Law Review 8:375–403

Ligeti K, Weyembergh A (2015) The European Public Prosecutor's Office: Certain Constitutional Issues. In: Erkelens LH, Meij AWH, Pawlik M (eds) The European Public Prosecutor's Office. An Extended Arm or a Two-Headed Dragon? TMC Asser Press, The Hague, pp 53–77

Lohse KM (2015) The European Public Prosecutor: Issues of Conferral, Subsidiarity and Proportionality. In: Erkelens LH, Meij AWH, Pawlik M (eds) The European Public Prosecutor's Office. An Extended Arm or a Two-Headed Dragon? TMC Asser Press, The Hague, pp 165–182

Luchtman M, Vervaele J (2014) European Agencies for Criminal Justice and Shared Enforcement (Eurojust and the European Public Prosecutor's Office). Utrecht Law Review 10:132–150

Luchtman M, Ouwerkerk J, van Noorloos M, Geelhoed P, Rijpma J, Middelkoop L (2015) Fundamental Rights and the European Public Prosecutor's Office: An uncomfortable silence. http://eulawanalysis.blogspot.co.uk/2015/04/fundamental-rights-and-european-public.html. Accessed 1 February 2017

Mazza O (2013) Procura europea e regole comuni in materia di garanzie procedurali e posizione della difesa. In: Grasso G, Illuminati G, Sicurella R, Allegrezza S (eds) Le sfide dell'attuazione di una Procura europea: definizione di regole comuni e loro impatto sugli ordinamenti interni. Giuffrè, Milan, pp 491–497

Meij AWH (2015) Some Explorations into the EPPO's Administrative Structure and Judicial Review. In: Erkelens LH, Meij AWH, Pawlik M (eds) The European Public Prosecutor's Office. An Extended Arm or a Two-Headed Dragon? TMC Asser Press, The Hague, pp 101–119
Meijers Committee (2013) Note on the proposed Council Regulation on the establishment of the European Public Prosecutor's Office (COM(2013) 534 final. http://www.eppo-project.eu/index.php/Home/News/Utrecht-Note-of-Meijers-Committee-on-the-proposed-regulation-on-the-EPPO. Accessed 5 October 2017
Mitsilegas V (2009) EU Criminal Law. Hart, Oxford/Portland
Mitsilegas V (2015) The European Public Prosecutor before the Court of Justice. The challenge of effective judicial protection. In: Giudicelli-Delage G, Manacorda S, Tricot J (eds) Le contrôle judiciaire du parquet européen. Nécessité, modéles, enjeux. Société de législation comparée, Paris, pp 67–85
Mitsilegas V (2016a) EU Criminal Law after Lisbon. Rights, Trust and the Transformation of Justice in Europe. Hart, Oxford/Portland
Mitsilegas V (2016b) Justice and Trust in the European Legal Order. The Copernicus Lectures (Grandi C (ed)). Jovene, Naples
Mitsilegas V (2016c) Legislating for Human Rights After Lisbon: The Transformative Effect of EU Measures on the Rights of the Individual in Criminal Procedure. In: Fletcher M, Herlin-Karnell E, Matera C (eds) The European Union as an Area of Freedom, Security and Justice. Routledge, London
Mitsilegas V (2016d) Managing Legal Diversity in Europe's Area of Criminal Justice: The Role of Autonomous Concepts. In: Colson R, Field S (eds) EU Criminal Justice and the Challenges of Legal Diversity. Towards A Socio-Legal Approach to EU Criminal Policy. Cambridge University Press, Cambridge, pp 125–160
Nelken D (2012) Using Legal Culture: Purposes and Problems. In: Nelken D (ed) Using Legal Culture. Wildy, Simmonds and Hill, London, pp 1–51
Nieto Martín A (2015) Le parquet européen et l'organisation judiciaire au sein de l'Union. In: Giudicelli-Delage G, Manacorda S, Tricot J (eds) Le contrôle judiciaire du parquet européen. Nécessité, modéles, enjeux. Société de législation comparée, Paris, pp 311–322
Nowell-Smith H (2012) Behind the Scenes in the Negotiations of EU Criminal Justice Legislation. New Journal of European Criminal Law 3:381–393
Ostropolski T (2014) The Principle of Proportionality under the European Arrest Warrant – with an excursus on Poland. New Journal of European Criminal Law 5:167–191
Pawlik M, Klip A (2015) A Disappointing First Draft for a European Public Prosecutor's Office. In: Erkelens LH, Meij AWH, Pawlik M (eds) The European Public Prosecutor's Office. An Extended Arm or a Two-Headed Dragon? TMC Asser Press, The Hague, pp 183–192
Sarmiento D (2013) Who's Afraid of the Charter? The Court of Justice, National Courts and the New Framework of Fundamental Rights Protection in Europe. Common Market Law Review 50:1267–1304
Sarmiento D (2015) The reform of the General Court. Unleashing the forces of change. http://eulawanalysis.blogspot.co.uk/2015/12/the-reform-of-general-court-unleashing.html. Accessed 1 February 2017
Satzger H (2015) The Future European Public Prosecutor and the National Prosecution: Potential Conflicts and How They Could be Avoided. In: Asp P (ed) The European Public Prosecutor's Office – Legal and Criminal Policy Perspectives. Stiftelsen Skrifter utgivna av Juridiska fakulteten vid Stockholms universitet, Stockholm, pp 69–87
Spaventa E (2016) The interpretation of Article 51 of the EU Charter of Fundamental Rights: the dilemma of stricter or broader application of the Charter to national measures. Study for the PETI Committee
Spiezia F (2013) Gli scenari di struttura per l'istituzione del Procuratore europeo alla luce del Trattato di Lisbona. Le questioni in gioco. In: Grasso G, Illuminati G, Sicurella R, Allegrezza S (eds) Le sfide dell'attuazione di una Procura europea: definizione di regole comuni e loro impatto sugli ordinamenti interni. Giuffrè, Milan, pp 537–580

Suominen A (2014) What Role for Legal Certainty in Criminal Law Within the Area of Freedom, Security and Justice in the EU? Bergen Journal of Criminal Law and Criminal Justice 2:1–31

Tinsley A (2013) Protecting Criminal Defence Rights Through EU Law: Opportunities and Challenges. New Journal of European Criminal Law 4:461–480

Van den Wyngaert C (2004) Eurojust and the European Public Prosecutor in the *Corpus Juris* Model: Water and Fire? In: Walker N (ed) Europe's Area of Freedom, Security and Justice. Oxford University Press, Oxford, pp 201–240

Vervaele J (2010) Quel statut pour le ministère public? European Enforcement Agencies in the Area of Freedom, Security and Justice: the Eurojust-European Public Prosecutor binomial. In: Ghaleh Marzban P (ed) Quelles perspectives pour un Ministère Public Européen. Protéger les intérêts financiers et fondamentaux de l'Union. Dalloz, Paris, pp 171–200

Wasmeier M (2015) The Choice of Forum by the European Public Prosecutor. In: Erkelens LH, Meij AWH, Pawlik M (eds) The European Public Prosecutor's Office. An Extended Arm or a Two-Headed Dragon? TMC Asser Press, The Hague, pp 139–161

Wathelet (2014) Accelerated Procedures before the European Court of Justice. In: Bradley K, Travers N, Whelan A (eds) Of Courts and Constitutions. Liber Amicorum in Honour of Nial Fennelly. Hart, Oxford/Portland, pp 33–45

Weyembergh A, Brière C (2016) Towards a European Public Prosecutor's Office (EPPO). Study for the LIBE Committee

Wieczorek I (2015) The EPPO Draft Regulation Passes the First Subsidiarity Test: An Analysis and Interpretation of the European Commission's Hasty Approach to National Parliaments' Subsidiarity Arguments. German Law Journal 16:1247–1270

Zerbes I (2015) Collecting and Using Evidence: A Patchwork of Legal Orders. In: Asp P (ed) The European Public Prosecutor's Office – Legal and Criminal Policy Perspectives. Stiftelsen Skrifter utgivna av Juridiska fakulteten vid Stockholms universitet, Stockholm, pp 210–233

Zimmermann F (2015) Choice of Forum and Choice of Law under the Future Regulation on the Establishment of a European Public Prosecutor's Office. In: Asp P (ed) The European Public Prosecutor's Office – Legal and Criminal Policy Perspectives. Stiftelsen Skrifter utgivna av Juridiska fakulteten vid Stockholms universitet, Stockholm, pp 156–177

EU Case Law

Åklagaren v Hans Åkerberg Fransson (Case C–617/10) judgment of 26 February 2013

Bonda (Case C-489/10) judgment of 5 June 2012

Covaci (Case C-216/14) judgment of 15 October 2015

Criminal Proceedings against Gavril Covaci (Case C-216/14) Opinion of AG Bot, 7 May 2015

European Commission v Kadi (Joined Cases C–584/10 P, C–593/10 P and C–595/10 P) judgment of 18 July 2013

Foto-Frost (Case 314/85) judgment of 22 October 1987 [1987] ECR 04199

Gözütok and Brügge (Joined cases C-187/01 and C-385/01) judgment of 11 February 2003 [2003] ECR I-1345

Melloni (Case C-399/11) judgment of 26 February 2013

Siragusa (Case C-206/13) judgment of 6 March 2014

Taricco and others (Case C-105/14) judgment of 8 September 2015

EU and Council of Europe Legislation

Convention implementing the Schengen Agreement of 14 June 1985 between the Governments of the States of the Benelux Economic Union, the Federal Republic of Germany and the French Republic on the gradual abolition of checks at their common borders, *OJ* L239/19, 22.9.2000

Council Act of 29 May 2000 establishing in accordance with Article 34 of the Treaty on European Union the Convention on Mutual Assistance in Criminal Matters between the Member States of the European Union, *OJ* C197/1, 12.7.2000

Directive 2010/64/EU on the right to interpretation and translation in criminal proceedings, *OJ* L280/1, 26.10.2010

Directive 2012/13/EU on the right to information in criminal proceedings, *OJ* L142/1, 1.6.2012

Directive 2013/48/EU on the right of access to a lawyer in criminal proceedings and in European arrest warrant proceedings, and on the right to have a third party informed upon deprivation of liberty and to communicate with third persons and with consular authorities while deprived of liberty, *OJ* L294/1, 6.11.2013

Directive 2014/41/EU of the European Parliament and of the Council of 3 April 2014 regarding the European Investigation Order in criminal matters, *OJ* L130/1, 1.5.2014

Directive (EU) 2016/343 of the European Parliament and of the Council of 9 March 2016 on the strengthening of certain aspects of the presumption of innocence and of the right to be present at the trial in criminal proceedings, *OJ* L65/1, 11.3.2016

Directive (EU) 2016/680 of the European Parliament and of the Council of 27 April 2016 on the protection of natural persons with regard to the processing of personal data by competent authorities for the purposes of the prevention, investigation, detection or prosecution of criminal offences or the execution of criminal penalties, and on the free movement of such data, and repealing Council Framework Decision 2008/977/JHA, *OJ* L119/89, 4.5.2016

Directive (EU) 2016/1919 of the European Parliament and of the Council of 26 October 2016 on legal aid for suspects and accused persons in criminal proceedings and for requested persons in European arrest warrant proceedings, *OJ* L297/1, 4.11.2016

European Convention on Mutual Assistance in Criminal Matters, ETS No 030, Strasbourg, 20 April 1959

European Parliament (2016) Resolution of 5 October 2016 on the European Public Prosecutor's Office and Eurojust (2016/2750(RSP))

Explanations relating to the Charter of Fundamental Rights, *OJ* C303/17, 14.12.2007

Green Paper on criminal-law protection of the financial interests of the Community and the establishment of a European Prosecutor, COM(2001) 715 final, 11 December 2001

Proposal for a Council Regulation on the establishment of the European Public Prosecutor's Office, COM(2013) 534 final, 17 July 2013

Proposal for a Directive of the European Parliament and of the Council on the fight against fraud to the Union's financial interests by means of criminal law, COM(2012) 363 final, 17 July 2012

Proposal for a Directive of the European Parliament and of the Council on the fight against fraud to the Union's financial interests by means of criminal law (Second reading) – Analysis of the final compromise text with a view to agreement, Council doc. 14902/16, 2 December 2016

Proposal for a Regulation on the establishment of the European Public Prosecutor's Office – Completed text, Council doc. 12774/2/16, 12 October 2016

Proposal for a Regulation on the establishment of the European Public Prosecutor's Office – Preparation for a general approach, Council doc. 5154/17, 17 January 2017

Regulation (EU) 2016/679 of the European Parliament and of the Council of 27 April 2016 on the protection of natural persons with regard to the processing of personal data and on the free movement of such data, and repealing Directive 95/46/EC (General Data Protection Regulation), *OJ* L119/1, 4.5.2016

Rules of Procedure of the Court of Justice of 25 September 2012 (OJ L265, 29.9.2012), as amended on 18 June 2013 (*OJ* L173/65, 26.6.2013) and on 19 July 2016 (*OJ* L217/69, 12.8.2016)

Rules of Procedure of the General Court of 4 March 2015 (OJ L105/1, 23.4.2015), as amended on 13 July 2016 (*OJ* L217/71-73, 12.8.2016)

Chapter 7
A Blunt Weapon for the EPPO? Taking the Edge Off the Proposed PIF Directive

Rosaria Sicurella

Abstract This chapter focuses on the progressive watering down of the proposal for a Directive on the fight against fraud to the Union's financial interests by means of criminal law (PIF directive). The result of negotiations, reflected in the (draft) directive as agreed by the Council and the European Parliament, is seen as quite unsatisfactory. The ECJ judgment in the *Taricco* case constitutes a decisive contribution to the negotiations. In particular, one of the most crucial issues of the case concerns the reasoning of the ECJ defining the legal context of the case and the reference made to Article 325(1) and (2) TFEU as the legal basis for obligations of the Member States in the field of PIF crimes. The ECJ thus sent a clear message to the Member States, inducing them to abandon their opposition to the formal recognition of VAT-related fraud as a PIF crime and thereby a crime within the material scope of the EPPO. The judgment also confers problematic obligations on the national judge, who is confronted with the incompatibility of national provisions with EU law in case these provisions inadequately protect EU interests. Furthermore, the impact of such an outcome on the legality principle as conceived in the Italian system, which was concerned in the *Taricco* case, is discussed. In conclusion, the unsatisfactory legal framework, combining provisions in the PIF directive with provisions in the EPPO regulation defining the conditions for exercising its competences, constitutes a substantial risk for the effectiveness of the EPPO.

Keywords Article 325 TFEU · Protection of Financial Interests of the EU · EU budget · Taricco case · EPPO material competence · Criminal Law Directives · Obligation to Establish Criminal Sanctions

Prof. Dr. Rosaria Sicurella is full professor at the University of Catania, LLM College of Europe, Brugge, vice-President of the *Centro di Diritto Penale Europeo*, Catania.

R. Sicurella (✉)
University of Catania – Law Department, Via Gallo, 24, 95124 Catania, Italy
e-mail: rsicurella@lex.unict.it

W. Geelhoed et al. (eds.), *Shifting Perspectives on the European Public Prosecutor's Office*, https://doi.org/10.1007/978-94-6265-216-3_7

Contents

7.1 Introductory Remarks

Defining the scope of competence of the European Public Prosecutor's Office (EPPO) has proven to be a controversial issue… The proposal for a regulation on the basis of Article 86 TFEU establishing the EPPO presented by the Commission on the 17th July 2013,[1] stated in Article 12 that the EPPO would be competent for "the criminal offences affecting the financial interests of the Union as provided for by the Directive",[2] thus referring to the future PIF Directive, for which the Commission adopted a proposal the year before.[3] The EPPO's scope of competence, according to the proposal, should depend not directly on the PIF directive, but on the directive as "implemented by national law". The issue came into the spotlight when negotiations in the Council on the proposal for a PIF directive ended up on 6 June 2013 with a General Approach significantly amending the text proposed by the Commission.[4] The General Approach amended the proposal with respect both to the contents and to the sensitive issue of the legal basis. The Council proposed to change the legal basis for the PIF Directive from Article 325 TFEU into Article 83 TFEU.

[1] COM(2013) 534.

[2] In addition to the competence of the EPPO especially devoted to PIF offences, the Commission's proposal, in its Article 13, also provided for an "ancillary competence", aiming at satisfying "the interest of a good administration" that could require joined investigations and prosecutions with respect to any other criminal offence whenever "inextricably linked" with any of the PIF offences, provided that it is "based on identical facts" and that PIF offences are "preponderant". Both these types of competence are now dealt with in Article 17 of the draft Regulation establishing the EPPO of 31 January 2017 (Council document 5766/17), which also includes the competence of the EPPO for "offences regarding participation in a criminal organization as defined in Framework Decision 2008/841/JHA as implemented in national law" if the focus of the criminal activity of such a criminal organisation is to commit PIF offences. This contribution only deals with the direct competence established in Article 17(1). On the ancillary competence, see Sitbon's contribution in Chap. 8.

[3] COM(2012) 363/2.

[4] Council document 10729/13 of 10 June 2013.

The Commission's choice to define the scope of competence of the future EPPO by referring to the PIF Directive implies a decision to stick to the basic mandate of EPPO as referred to in Article 86(1) TFEU. In particular, this choice excludes the option of an EPPO that would be competent, from the start of its creation, for any "serious crime having cross-border dimension".[5] Furthermore, this line of action shows the refusal of a more courageous solution aiming at defining the material scope of the EPPO in the regulation establishing it. Such a solution would have required that this regulation would at least give a definition of the expression "crimes affecting the financial interests of the Union" employed in Article 86(1) TFEU when referring to the scope of competence of the EPPO. This would have been in line with the wording of Article 86(2) TFEU which refers to the "[…] offences against the Union's financial interests *as determined by the regulation in par.1*". According to some scholars, this wording would even have allowed the European legislator to determine offences directly applicable to individuals, as is in the nature of provisions in regulations.[6] That would imply that the EU enjoys full competence to adopt criminal law provisions in the PIF sector, in the sense of EU criminal law offences directly applicable to individuals by the courts of the Member States. However, such a reading does not seem to be supported by the wording of Article 86(3) TFEU. That provision, indicating the contents of the regulation establishing the EPPO, does not mention the definitions of situations and behaviours constituting criminal offences falling within the material scope of the EPPO. As such, it appears to comply with the basic choice of the Treaty to restrict the legal instruments of EU competence in criminal matters to the adoption of directives.[7] However, at least one could have expected a definition of such crimes in the regulation by singling out the concrete facts to be considered as "affecting the financial interests of the Union", following the example of Article 2 of the EAW Framework Decision. In particular, such an approach would clarify whether the competence of the EPPO is limited to crimes which *harm* the Union's financial interests or, on the contrary, covers any crime involving these interests and that *can be detrimental* to them even *indirectly*. This alternative is well-known in the history of the protection of the financial interests of the Union, and was widely discussed among experts involved in the *Corpus juris* studies.[8] The choice between these two alternatives is unequivocally a crucial political point, since it implies very

---

[5] This conclusion is confirmed by Article 17 of the 31 January 2017 draft of the EPPO regulation (Council document 5766/17), since the offence of participating in a criminal organization only falls into the material scope of the EPPO "if the focus of the criminal activity of such a criminal organization is to commit offences referred to in paragraph 1", that is to say offences provided for by the PIF directive. An extension of the EPPO scope of competence should be provided for only after evaluation of its functioning during a certain period of time, according to Klip 2012, pp. 370–371.

[6] Picotti 2005, pp. 76–79; Vervaele 2014, p. 92.

[7] Sicurella 2011, footnote 56; Sicurella 2013a, p. 894.

[8] Delmas-Marty 1997; Delmas-Marty and Vervaele 2000. Further references to this document are related to the second version ('*Corpus Juris* 2000').

significant differences in the EPPO's scope of competence. At the same time, it would entail a clear position with respect to what is to be considered as the acquis in the PIF sector, as well as an answer to the question whether to limit the scope of EPPO's competence to the existing PIF acquis or to move forward, relying on new provisions in the Treaty.[9]

Criticism of the reference to the PIF directive is easy to imagine, considering that herewith the scope of competence of a supranational investigatory and prosecutorial authority, while requiring some basic common provisions, is completely left to a legal text which in its very nature is merely harmonizing national provisions. Consequently, the exact limits of the EPPO's competence will conclusively depend on the implementing legislation adopted by Member States. As a consequence, the applicable substantive law will presumably vary very much depending on the legal system of the Member State where investigations and prosecutions will be conducted by the EPPO. That state of affairs will not only affect the core of the project as originally conceived in the *Corpus juris*. It will also risk to undermine the overall legitimacy of the project because such a legal patchwork is bound to create significant friction with respect to the principle of legality, established as a fundamental right in the EU's Charter, its central requirements of "accessibility and foreseeability" being seriously affected in the situation described above.

Moreover, looking at four years of negotiations on the proposed directive, one can also conclude that the link established between the directive and the scope of competence of the EPPO had a quite detrimental effect on the progress of negotiations. That link presumably contributed to stifle the perspective of having a legally binding text not only enshrining the acquis but also benefiting from the potential of the provisions introduced by the Lisbon Treaty. Indeed, provided that the reference is considered dynamic in nature, any step forward in the directive would imply an extension of the scope of competence of the EPPO, which Member States clearly wanted to avoid.

In any case, negotiations in the Council fully revealed the sensitive nature of the issues involved in the PIF sector, in addition to the stubborn opposition of most of the Member States with respect to any proposed provision which could affect the competence (and the discretion) of national authorities.[10] In the end, affecting Member State's competences and discretion is the goal of a project aiming to overcome the current inefficiencies of the fight against crimes affecting the financial

[9] Sicurella 2013a, pp. 880–888.

[10] In particular, negotiations showed that there is much sensitivity regarding the relation between criminal investigations on the one hand and powers of inquiry belonging to fiscal authorities on the other hand. This relation can indeed be affected by the setting up of the EPPO.

interests of the Union. These inefficiencies are mostly caused by the lack of harmonization in the field, and by the unacceptably large scope of discretion left to Member States' authorities. The opposition evidenced in the negotiations proved to be highly detrimental to formalizing the PIF *acquis* in the directive. Furthermore, this attitude may also pave the way for an institutional struggle between the Commission and the Council.

The ECJ judgment in the *Taricco* case is emblematic of the burning issue at stake.[11] It also shows the intention of the ECJ to play an active role in the matter,[12] and to influence the negotiations concerning the PIF directive which had come to a standstill with respect to some particularly controversial issues. First and foremost, this concerns the inclusion of VAT related frauds in the notion of frauds damaging the EU's financial interests. The outcome of the last year of negotiations clearly reflects the impact exerted by the ECJ's very determined position on the Member States. It also reflects the 'messages' sent by the judgment to the Member States at different levels. Firstly, these were directed to the Member States as being involved in the on-going negotiations on the PIF directive. Secondly, these messages more in general concerned the Member States as addressees of the obligation to guarantee that domestic legal orders fully comply with the obligations stemming from EU law.

Against this background the present chapter first looks into the development of the PIF directive from the Commission proposal to the Council General Approach (Sect. 7.2). Then it analyses the impact of the *Taricco* judgment on the negotiations (Sect. 7.3) and makes an assessment of the compromise as concluded between the Council and the European Parliament (Sect. 7.4). Finally, some remarks are made on the unsatisfactory legal framework, combining provisions in the PIF directive with provisions in the EPPO regulation defining the conditions for exercising its competences (Sect. 7.5) before concluding (Sect. 7.6).

[11] Case 105/14, *Taricco et al.* 2015.

[12] As the Court already did in the past when it considered that crucial issues of EU integration were at stake, for instance in the ECJ decision issued on the 13 September 2005 in the so-called environmental case (Case C-176/03). That decision was confirmed two years later by the decision in the so-called 'ship source pollution' case (Case C-440/05). Here, the Luxembourg Court established in fact the competence of the EU to adopt provisions binding the domestic legislature to introduce criminal sanctions. Such a competence was provided for by the Constitutional Treaty, which was abandoned after the referenda in France and The Netherlands. In doing so, the ECJ introduced one of the most essential novelties of that treaty. The same the ECJ did with its decision in the *Pupino* case (Case C-105/03) extending the scope of the obligation on the judge for a consistent interpretation of domestic law also with respect to provisions in Framework Decision. This decision resulted in eroding the distinction between the first and the third pillar, and anticipated the abolition of the pillar structure which is the most significant feature of the Lisbon Treaty.

7.2 Establishing the Foundations of a Criminal Law Directive in the PIF Sector: From the Commission Proposal to the Council General Approach

Discussions on adopting a directive in the PIF sector introducing criminal provisions date back to the beginning of the 2000s. At that time, the Commission adopted a first proposal for a directive introducing criminal provisions,[13] which aimed at reacting to the very unsatisfactory way in which financial interests of the Union were protected. This proposal was triggered by the lack of implementation by all the Member States of the various third pillar legal texts adopted in the 1990s. These texts comprised the so called PIF Convention of 1995,[14] supplemented by the two additional Protocols on corruption and money laundering, adopted in 1996 and 1997 respectively.[15] The 2001 Commission proposal for a directive was part of a set of proposals which aimed to introduce provisions establishing obligations on the Member States to adopt criminal sanctions in different sensitive sectors: the environment,[16] ship-source pollution,[17] and intellectual property.[18] This strategy intended to intensify the stringency of obligations resulting from directives through criminal sanctions which were to be implemented by Member States. The obligations resulting from these proposals mostly excluded Member States' traditional discretion to choose the sanctions to be provided, and compelled them to establish sanctions of a criminal nature. The negotiations on the 2001 proposal never reached the end, whereas the directive and the framework decision in the environment law sector gave rise to an institutional struggle resulting in the ECJ judgment in the case concerning protection of the environment.[19]

The current proposal for a Directive in the PIF sector[20] was adopted by the Commission in 2012, after the entry into force of the Lisbon Treaty which provided for enlarged criminal law competences. Therefore, expectations were high as to its contents. However, the proposal appeared to be very shy, often reproducing provisions of the 2001 proposal. It closely follows the well-established *acquis* at the time, and thereby runs the risk to be out-of-date fifteen years after the adoption of that proposal. In particular, it refrains from fully exploiting the possibilities opened up by the Lisbon Treaty. Definitions of PIF crimes, referring to fraud, corruption

[13] COM(2001) 272.

[14] *OJ* C 316, 27-11-1995.

[15] *OJ* C 313, 23-10-1996; *OJ* C 221, 1-7-1997.

[16] COM(2001) 139.

[17] COM(2003) 92.

[18] COM(2005) 276.

[19] Case C-176/03, *Commission v Council*, see also Case C-440/05, *Commission v Council* on the competence to impose criminal sanctions in the enforcement of measures against ship-source pollution.

[20] COM(2012) 363.

and money laundering essentially reproduce the definitions in previous legal texts,[21] which require an actual or at least a potential harm being done to the financial interests of the EU. Moreover, the proposal appeared to follow the trend of the criminal law directives that had already been adopted, in that it simply establishes the obligation for the Member States to provide for criminal sanctions for types of behaviour which can be qualified as an attempt or a participation to the offence, without establishing any common criterion to decide when they can be qualified as such.[22] This method, while it is supposed to harmonise national law, paradoxically obliges Member States to establish criminal sanctions without providing a clear account of the contents of the notions identifying the object of the obligation to establish criminal sanctions in the obligations. The obligations to harmonise national law are supposed to be based on an assessment of necessity and proportionality of such measures, but the types of behaviour concerned are not directly considered at EU level: these are defined in the different legal systems of the Member States.

However, some novelties of the proposed PIF directive can be highlighted. These provisions do not only concern types of behaviour to be defined as criminal offences by the Member States, but also the sanctions that are to be provided, together with common standards concerning responsibility of legal entities and prescription of offences.

Regarding the types of behaviour covered by the proposal, a step forward compared to the PIF *acquis* is realized through including two new situations. These concern fraudulent behaviour in public procurement or grant procedures and the misappropriation of funds. Moreover, for these offences an actual or potential harm to financial interests of the Union is not a requirement. This appears to rely on an extensive notion of the expression "crimes affecting the financial interests of the Union" employed in Article 86(1) TFEU, as covering acts which are detrimental to the EU financial interests even indirectly.

The proposed PIF directive also contained provisions regarding the liability of legal entities and penalties which can be imposed on them. It shows the intent to establish a first European model of criminal responsibility of legal entities (through a legally binding legal text), providing for criteria to assess that responsibility on the basis of employee behaviour and acts of people having a leading role. However, as in existing EU legislation these provisions completely disregard the sensitive issue of establishing when the legal entity itself can be considered 'guilty', especially when this guilt is of a criminal nature.[23]

---

[21] For money laundering, see Directive 2005/60/EC, *OJ* L 309, 25-11-2005.

[22] This only matters with respect to the offences of fraud and misappropriation. Basic definitions of the remaining offences are considered to already cover the attempt.

[23] See Articles 5 and 6 of the Council Framework Decision (FD) 2003/568/JHA of 22 July 2003 on combating corruption in the private sector, *OJ* L 192/54. The concerned Articles 6 and 9 of the proposed PIF directive are virtually identical to those of the FD with the exception of omitting para 2 of Article 6 of the FD on the punishability of lack of supervision or control by authorities in charge of the legal person.

The proposed directive also contains innovative provisions on penalties. While Article 7 states in line with longstanding case law that penalties must be "effective, proportionate and dissuasive",[24] Article 8 sets out an imprisonment threshold, and it refers in particular to mandatory minimum penalties. The latter are of the utmost importance in pursuing the aim of harmonizing sanctions, because the minimum sanction better reflects the seriousness of the offence. Nevertheless, the objection can easily be raised that this provision establishes a single minimum threshold for various different offences. Moreover, it should not be underestimated that such a provision can provoke resistance from legal systems which do not provide for minimum penalties. Also, such provisions could have a limited impact on the concrete sanctions that will be imposed, as the sentencing process in the Member States is influenced by many heterogeneous elements.

Finally, there is an interesting provision in Article 12, dealing with common thresholds concerning the prescription of offences. This provision can be considered the first attempt to harmonise the prescription regime in the European Union. It proposes a time frame of at least 5 years from the moment the offence was committed before the prosecution may be time barred. In addition, it provides for an obligation to ensure that the prescription shall be interrupted by any investigative act, at least until ten years have expired after the commission of the fact.

However, the most crucial issue is the Commission's choice for Article 325 TFEU as the directive's legal basis. In choosing for this legal basis, the Commission establishes Article 325 TFEU[25] as the specific legal basis for any measure to be adopted in the PIF sector, even when it is of a criminal nature. Furthermore, this approach bypasses Article 83 TFEU, which is considered as the general legal basis for measures to be adopted in criminal matters.[26]

The Council's General Approach of 6 June 2013[27] significantly watered down the text of the Commission's proposal. It further limited the scope of the offences aimed to be harmonized,[28] it radically changed the approach with respect to the harmonisation of punishment and it abandoned all references to minimum sanctions, adopting instead the classical paradigm of the minimum of the maximum

[24] Cf. among many others Case 68/88, Greek maize, pt. 24.

[25] This Article is the successor of Article 280 TCE, and before that of Article 209 A of the Maastricht Treaty, formalizing in a Treaty provision the main findings of the ECJ judgment on the Greek maize case.

[26] Sicurella 2013b, pp. 896–897; see also Klip 2012, p. 367; Mitsilegas 2016, p. 66.

[27] Council document 10729/13 of 10 June 2013.

[28] In particular, the new offence in public procurements was erased, and additional requirements have been added to some of the proposed definitions, such as the infringement of an official duty in the definition of corruption, or the need for an actual damage to European funds in the definition of misappropriation.

penalty. Furthermore, the General Approach significantly softened the constraints on time limitation and it erased the criminal nature of legal persons' responsibility.

However, the two most significant amendments brought about by the Council in June 2013, related firstly to the change of legal basis of the directive and secondly to the explicit exclusion of VAT related frauds from the scope of the directive.[29]

Article 325 TFEU, the originally proposed legal basis, was substituted by Article 83 TFEU. According to the Council's Legal Service,[30] Article 83 TFEU has been established as the special legal basis for any measure directly affecting criminal law. It prevails on Article 325 TFEU, which continues to apply when measures other than of a criminal nature would be at stake. Compared to Article 325 Article 83 TFEU stipulates more stringent conditions for the adoption of legal measures. Only "minimum rules" may be laid down concerning the definition of criminal offences and sanctions (instead of "any necessary measure" as provided for by Article 325 TFEU) and these measures have to be "essential", rather than "necessary" as prescribed in Article 325 TFEU. In addition, the emergency brake procedure provided for in Article 83(3) typically highlights the specific nature of the EU competence in criminal matters. This mechanism allows for a high level political, intergovernmental/diplomatic intervention by the European Council in the legislative procedure. This might be seen as quite remarkable where the PIF is at stake, that is to say an area which always has been considered as a European interest *par excellence* implying a wider harmonizing and sanctioning power of the European institutions. It is therefore astonishing that the European Parliament (EP) has not raised any objection to the alteration of the legal basis, accepting Article 83(2) TFEU in its legislative resolution of 16 April 2014.[31]

However, in its opinion the EP did not follow the Council with respect to the other important amendment of the Council expressly excluding VAT fraud from the scope of the directive. Although the Council does not directly object to viewing VAT as a part of the EU budget, the Council proposes to exclude VAT from the scope of the directive. It argues that harmonization of VAT would not be in compliance with the principle of proportionality as one of the basic criteria for the EU to exercise its competences. The reason for this is that only a little part of the VAT revenue is to be considered as the EU's own resources. Moreover, following the principle according to which no deficit is admissible for the EU budget,

[29] The absence of an explicit reference to VAT fraud in the Commission's proposal—which simply refers to "any income, any expense and goods ….a) of the Union budget; and b) institutions …. – relates to the fact that VAT has expressly been recognised as a component of the EU own resources by the ECJ since its judgment in Case C-539/09 [2011], pts 71–72 *et seq.*, confirmed in Case C-617/10 [2013], relying on the direct link between VAT revenue collection and availability to the EU budget of the corresponding VAT resource; therefore, VAT is included in the general reference to the entries/incomes of the EU budget.

[30] Opinion of the Legal Service 15309/12, 22 October 2012.

[31] European Parliament legislative resolution of 16 April 2014 on the proposal for a Directive of the European Parliament and of the Council on the fight against fraud to the Union's financial interests by means of criminal law, A7-0251/2014.

contributions from the Member States to the EU budget are established in order to compensate any loss; therefore no actual damage to the EU budget can flow from VAT frauds.

The inclusion of VAT related frauds, as required by the EP, turned out to become the burning issue in the negotiations. The EP regarded it as a prerequisite for agreeing with both the proposed directive and the proposed regulation establishing the EPPO.[32] In its first reading resolution the EP requested other amendments which aimed at clarifying the notion of the Union's financial interests and of the concept 'public official'. These furthermore aimed at clarifying and sometimes extending the scope of the related fraud offences in Article 4 of the proposal.[33] The EP amendments have been the object of various trilogue meetings held from October 2014 to June 2015, which apparently showed the progressive rapprochement of the two co-legislators. This however came to an end because of insurmountable disagreements about the inclusion of VAT-related fraud in the scope of the draft directive. These disagreements debouched into a decision to wait for the judgment of the ECJ on a preliminary reference under Article 267 TFEU, which was referred to the Court by an Italian court (Tribunale di Cuneo) in the context of criminal proceedings brought against Mr Taricco and others for having formed and organized a conspiracy to commit various offences in relation to value added tax. This is the beginning of the *Taricco* saga.

7.3 The Contribution of the CJEU to the Negotiation on the PIF Directive: The *Taricco* Case

7.3.1 The Taricco *Case: Facts and Considerations*

The facts in the *Taricco* case offered a welcome occasion to the ECJ to send a clear message to Member States' representatives in the negotiations. The request of the Italian judge concerned the interpretation to be given to a number of EU law provisions, especially the provisions in Council Directive 2006/112/EC on the common VAT system, in their function as a basis for the obligation for national courts to assess the compliance of national legislation in areas of EU competence, including the obligation to disapply such legislation when it infringes EU law. More precisely, the Italian judge's request was aimed at assessing the compatibility of certain provisions in the Italian Penal Code on the prescription of offences with Italy's obligations under EU law. The Italian Penal Code regulates in Article 160, last paragraph, in conjunction with Article 161, the cases in which the period of prescription is interrupted and subsequently extended by in no case more than a

[32] See the document of the Presidency 12686/1/16 REV1.

[33] E.g. frauds in public procurement or grant procedures and corruption with respect to the condition of the sanctioned behaviour not necessarily in breach of official obligations.

quarter of its initial duration. According to the referring court, such provisions imply a de facto immunity, when applied in criminal proceedings in relation to tax evasion involving complex investigations. The referring court considered that this could be the case because these investigations take a considerable amount of time already at the preliminary investigation stage, and therefore quickly run out of the prescription period. These provisions could therefore infringe EU law obligations for Member States to guarantee an effective protection of EU financial interests, provided that VAT frauds come within the scope of EU law because of the fact that a part of the VAT collected by Member States falls into the EU's own resources.

The ECJ ruled that national provisions such as those at stake are "liable to have an adverse effect on fulfilment of the Member States' obligations under Article 325 (1) and (2) TFEU if that national rule prevents the imposition of effective and dissuasive penalties in a significant number of cases of serious fraud affecting the financial interests of the European Union, or provides for longer limitation periods in respect of cases of fraud affecting the financial interests of the Member State concerned than in respect of those affecting the financial interests of the European Union, which it is for the national court to verify. The national court must give full effect to Article 325(1) and (2) TFEU, if need be by disapplying the provisions of national law the effect of which would be to prevent the Member State concerned from fulfilling its obligations under Article 325(1) and (2) TFEU".[34]

The judgment provoked strong reactions, especially among Italian scholars and practitioners. They focused in particular on the second part of the decision of the Court, concerning obligations stemming from the relevant EU law provisions on the national court dealing with the case.[35] The fierce reaction from most of the Italian lawyers is essentially provoked by the obligation the ECJ imposes on the national court to disapply national provisions on prescription in case of VAT fraud, whenever the judge can reach the conclusion set out by the Court in the above quotation. This obligation is regardless of whether this would have a negative impact on the accused. Critics essentially point out that the decision of the Court appears to clash with the well-established position of the Italian Constitutional Court holding that provisions on prescription possess a substantive nature.[36] These provisions would therefore be subject to the legality principle and consequently also to the prohibition of retrospective application of any solution that would entail a detrimental effect for the accused.[37] Moreover, because of its quite undetermined

[34] Case C-105/14, *Taricco*, judgment of 8 September 2015, pt 58 and pt 1 of the operative part.

[35] An enormous number of commentaries have been issued on the ECJ judgement on the *Taricco* case. For an overall picture of the various positions expressed, please see the collective volume edited by Bernardi 2017. Among the few commentaries by non-Italian scholars, Billis 2016, p. 20 ff; Lassalle 2015; Peers 2015.

[36] Corte costituzionale 275/90; 393/2006; 324/2008; 23/13; 143/14; 45/15.

[37] For a quick but effective presentation of questions arising in the Italian legal order, see Giuffrida 2016, especially pp. 109–111.

character,[38] this obligation would result in conferring on the domestic judge an extremely wide discretionary power, which is incompatible with the nature of the activity of the judiciary in the Italian legal order, and the limits it encounters which are grounded on the principle of legality. The same effect does, however, not occur when one considers both the abovementioned principles in the form they are recognized at European level. This was expressly stated by the ECJ where it excluded the relevance of Article 49 of the Charter for the *Taricco* case.[39] This point therefore gives rise to the sensitive issue of the differences in scope of such principles at the European and at the national level.

As other Italian courts dealing with cases where the *Taricco* jurisprudence would have to be applied,[40] also the Supreme Court (Corte di Cassazione) referred a case to the Constitutional Court.[41] The Italian Constitutional Court was asked to assess whether the Italian law adopting the Treaty of Lisbon, because it would infringe the legality principle as established in Article 25 of the Italian Constitution, could be opposed on constitutional grounds. According to the Supreme Court, the infringement would be caused in particular by Article 325 TFEU in its interpretation by the ECJ, to the extent that it constitutes the legal basis of the obligation on the national court to disapply domestic provisions on prescription, which has detrimental consequences for the accused. As mentioned above, because of the qualification of prescription as a piece of substantive criminal law, such an obligation would clash with the prohibition of retrospective application of the law. By this referral, the Italian Supreme Court invoked the so-called "counter-limits" doctrine: following the theory elaborated by the Italian constitutional doctrine since the nineteen seventies, it is possible to suspend the "limitation of (national) sovereignty" which is laid down in Article 11 of the Constitution, and which is considered to be the constitutional basis to allow the European integration process, whenever the acceptance of European law in the Italian legal order can be questioned on the grounds that it affects the "constitutional identity of Italy".[42] On 26 January 2017, the Italian Constitutional Court referred a preliminary question on this point to the ECJ.[43] According to its reference, the Constitutional Court appears to expect an overruling by the CJEU. In particular, it seems to expect an

[38] This critic mainly refers to the statement of the Court where it establishes the obligation on the national judge to disapply any conflicting national provision whenever "that national rule prevents the imposition of effective and dissuasive penalties *in a significant number of cases of serious fraud* affecting the financial interests of the European Union".

[39] Ibidem, pts 54–57.

[40] See Court of Appel of Milano, II sezione penale, 18 September 2015.

[41] Corte Cassazione, III sezione penale, 30 March 2016. However, the same Court had previously judged differently, expressly excluding that an infringement of the principle of legality as established in Article 25 of the Italian Constitution occurred: Corte di Cassazione III sezione penale, 15 September 2015. See also Corte di Cassazione IV sezione penale, 25 January 2016.

[42] On the Italian counter-limits doctrine, see also Judge Ezio Perillo's Foreword to this volume.

[43] Order 24/2017.

interpretation allowing the principle of legality in the way it is recognised in the Italian legal order to prevail on EU law.[44]

The decision of the ECJ in *Taricco* touches certain crucial issues. The reasoning of the Court is in fact not fully convincing; above all it appears to disregard the sensitiveness of the issue at stake, which involves the protection of fundamental rights at EU and national level. However, in order to properly deal with critics of the Court's decision, one has to bear in mind that the ECJ's judgment was a decision relating not to guarantees, but to the effectiveness of European law. In that perspective, according to well-established reasoning of the ECJ in its case-law on the matter, guarantees of individuals come into consideration as a possible limit to the general primacy of EU law. In line with this jurisprudence, the Court states in *Taricco* that where the relevant provisions of EU law have the effect of rendering automatically inapplicable any conflicting provision of national law, the national court that decides to disapply the national provisions at issue, must also ensure that the fundamental rights of the persons concerned are respected.[45] Therefore, not applying national law is far from an automatic consequence of the national court's assessment on the incompatibility of the national provision with the obligation to effectively protect the financial interests of the EU. Although not unequivocally expressed, the obligation on the national judge to disapply any conflicting national provision rests on the condition that "the fundamental rights of the persons concerned are respected". The Court's reference to fundamental rights is not merely a reminder of general principles. The Court indeed stresses the fact that in the concrete case before the referring judge "penalties may be imposed on those persons which, in all likelihood, would not have been imposed if those provisions of national law had been applied".[46] By doing so, the Court clearly reaffirms a precise obligation for the national court which necessarily joins the obligation to guarantee the effective protection of EU interests. More precisely, the judgment in the *Taricco* case brings significant progress for the legal framework compared to the *Berlusconi* case.[47] *Taricco* clearly establishes the obligation for the national court to disapply national law even when this would entail a change of the overall legal context that could be detrimental for the accused.[48] However, the decision does not entail an automatic retrospective application of the law to the concrete person who is on trial

---

[44] A collection of commentaries on the order issued by the Italian Constitutional Court to the ECJ can be found in the volume edited by Bernardi and Cupelli 2017; in particular, see Sicurella 2017 pp. 405–433.

[45] Ibidem, pts 52–53.

[46] Id. pt 53.

[47] Case C-387/02 [2003].

[48] According to the established CJEU case-law, neither a directive (Case C-80/86, *Kolpinghuis Nijmegen*, [1987]), nor a regulation when it empowers the Member States to adopt penalties to punish infringements of the regulation itself (Case C-60/02, *X*, [2004]) can of itself and independently of a national law adopted by a Member State for its implementation, have the effect of determining or aggravating the liability in criminal law of persons who act in contravention of its provisions. The same could be said in relation to provisions of the Treaties.

before the national court. The ECJ avoids this consequence by also obliging the domestic judge to assess whether fundamental rights, other than the legality principle established in Article 49 of the Charter, are affected. In doing so, the ECJ seems to indicate that such a situation could imply that the national judge would not be under an obligation to disapply national law whenever this would entail a violation of fundamental rights recognised in the EU legal order.[49]

7.3.2 *Impact of the* Taricco *Case on the PIF Directive Negotiations*

One has to look at the first part of the judgment of the Court to find the arguments that can have an impact on the negotiations on the PIF Directive. These arguments indeed have significantly influenced the negotiations. Actually, the gist of the judgment can only be fully appreciated when considering the very peculiar moment at which it was issued. It was clear that the Court intended to have an impact on the ongoing negotiations on the PIF directive, which almost came to a halt because of the issue whether or not VAT fraud should be included in the scope of the directive. This institutional context can also explain why the impact of its decision in the *Taricco* case on national criminal justice systems, and especially on the Italian one, appears to have been quite underestimated by the ECJ. The decision was primarily viewed as a means to an end, serving the Court's goal to deliver a precise message to the Member States as parties in the negotiating process and in their capacity as legislators, who are under the obligation to implement EU law and in general guarantee the full compliance of their respective legal systems with EU law. It was that perspective which predominated in the Court's decision in the *Taricco* case rather than the intention to realize progress in defining the obligations of the domestic judge.

---

[49] Although guarantees are not the focus of the decision of the Court, the latter does have a significant impact on the way guarantees have to be considered and implemented in the dynamics of the relationship between European and domestic legal orders. Indeed, the ECJ's decision in *Taricco* seems to confirm and develop the approach in *Melloni* (C-399/11) showing the most recent view of the Court which is less keen of derogating to the general principles regulating relationships between EU/domestic orders (even) when fundamental rights are at stake; and so because EU legal order now rests on a significantly developed system of protection of fundamental rights (which has raised much more solid and detailed contents than few decades ago when the above mentioned jurisprudence was established), implying that reference to national systems of protection became unnecessary. Finally, the principle of the better law, still among the fundamental ones, cannot be employed when a conflict arises between the two concurrent systems (European and national) of protection of fundamental rights. Article 53 Charter, indeed, when stating that "nothing in this Charter shall be interpreted as restricting or adversely affecting human rights and fundamental freedoms as recognized [...] by Member States' constitutions" expressly refers to "their respective field of application"; the same solution does not apply when the issue at stake falls in the scope of EU competence, as it was the case in *Taricco* and before that in *Melloni*. Generally speaking, here it is a conflict of competence which is at stake (not a conflict of values).

Analysing the ECJ's judgment where it purports to frame the relevant EU law is particularly telling. Following the position by Advocate General Kokott, the Court ends up 'manipulating' the legal context as described by the referring judge which, in itself, is not unusual. The Court focuses on the common system of VAT (in particular on Directive 2006/112/EC) and completely disregards the other provisions which the referring court brings into the picture: Articles 101, 107 and 109 TFEU. In addition to Directive 2006/112/EC, the Court grounds its decision on a set of provisions, including provisions of the Treaty establishing EU general principles, which were not considered by the referring court.

More precisely, the Court starts by confirming its decision in the *Åkerberg Fransson* case.[50] It indicates that the legal basis for Member States' obligations to effectively protect EU financial interests with respect to VAT (in particular by correctly collecting VAT and combating VAT frauds) can be found in the combination of Directive 2006/112/CE and the general obligation in Article 4(3) TEU to take appropriate legislative and administrative measures to actively contribute to achieve EU objectives.[51] As a prerequisite, the Court also reiterates that a part of VAT falls into the EU's own resources, and therefore matters relating to VAT come within the scope of EU law, as the ECJ expressly recognized in 2011.[52] Additionally, in its reasoning, the Court links Article 4(3) TEU to Article 325 TFEU, being the treaty provision specifying the general obligation of loyal cooperation into the PIF sector. Finally, it makes a further step forward. The ECJ recalls that Member States are in principle free to choose the applicable sanctions while criminal sanctions may be essential to combat certain serious forms of fraud. However, it connects Article 325 TFEU with the obligation to provide for criminal sanctions as laid down in Article 2 of the PIF Convention, which is considered as the specific criminal law element of the Member States' obligations to counter illegal activities affecting EU financial interests. In doing so, the Court finds that the Member States' obligations in the framework of VAT fraud, and in the framework of PIF in general, find their legal basis in EU primary law. In particular, it refers to Article 325 TFEU as a provision that imposes "a precise obligation as to the result to be achieved that is not subject to any condition regarding the application of the rule".[53] This is one of the most intensely debated points of the decision, since Article 325 TFEU is indicated as satisfying the two requirements for direct applicability of a provision, even if this is not explicitly stated by the Court. This is to be seen in the Court's reasoning with respect to Article 325(1) and (2) TFEU, which "have the effect, in accordance with the principle of the precedence of EU law, in their relationship with the domestic law of the Member States, of rendering

---

[50] *Åklagaren v ÅkerbergFransson*, Case C 617/10.

[51] Case 617/10 [2013], pt. 25.

[52] Case C-539/09, Commission v Germany, judgment of 15 November 2011.

[53] *Taricco*, pt. 51. The words 'not subject to any condition regarding the application of the rule' refer to pt. 49 urging the national court to give full effect to EU law 'without having to request or to await the prior repeal of those [provisions] by way of legislation or any other constitutional procedure'.

automatically inapplicable, merely by their entering into force, any conflicting provision of national law".[54] The reference by the Court to the PIF Convention is even more straightforward. This implies that the concept of fraud as laid down in this Convention includes VAT fraud, despite the absence of an explicit reference in the text, and despite the opposite position expressed by the Council on this specific point in its 1997 Explanatory Report on the Convention.[55] This furthermore implies that all Member States are under an obligation to combat VAT fraud on the basis of the provisions in the Convention. By using such an argument, the Court sends a clear message, influencing the negotiations on the new PIF Directive. This message was specifically aimed at the definition of fraud related to EU financial interests. On that point, the Commission proposal was amended by the Council in its General approach. The General Approach added to Article 2 of the proposal, defining the concept of EU financial interests, a phrase stating that "VAT is excluded from the scope of the directive". However, following the reasoning of the Court in *Taricco*, the intrusive obligations as clarified in that decision will compel Member States to do so, regardless of the fact that a directive is adopted in this field, since they flow directly from Treaty provisions and the PIF Convention already in force, binding all the Member States.

This argument was of the utmost importance for the ongoing debate on the PIF directive. Including VAT fraud in the scope of the proposed PIF directive turned out to be in the interest of Member States, as this is the only way to regulate and thereby circumscribe EU competences in this field in accordance with the principle of conferral. Consequently, regulating these obligations could protect the scope of competences of national authorities.

Indeed, the unequivocal turning point in the *Taricco* judgement consisted of the Court's assertion that Article 325 TFEU is directly applicable. At the same time, from a strictly legal perspective the foundation for this conclusion is controversial. The objections that were raised against the Court's reasoning essentially put into question that the wording of Article 325 TFEU really establishes "precise and unconditional" obligations on domestic authorities.[56] Moreover, the consequences the Court draws from recognizing such a nature of Article 325 TFEU radically innovate the traditional case law of the Court dealing with direct effect of EU/EC provisions. As a matter of fact, the case law traditionally conceives direct effect as a basis for extending the rights and guarantees of individuals, notably vis-à-vis Member States' authorities. In *Taricco* however, attributing direct effect to Treaty provisions such as Article 325 TFEU turns out to be detrimental to the individual.

[54] *Taricco*, pt. 52.

[55] See also the position of the Advocate General Kokott in this respect, paras 94–98.

[56] Bin 2017, p. 291 ff.

The outcome of that reasoning has therefore been qualified as a "reverse direct effect".[57]

These objections have been refuted by some authors,[58] although all agree on the lack of a clear and adequately articulated reasoning by the Court on these crucial issues. The argument is put forward that the Court generally adopts a much less rigorous approach when assessing the precise and unconditional nature of treaty provisions for the purpose of recognizing their direct effect.[59] Following such an approach, Article 325 TFEU can, despite its quite wide wording, be considered to be more than a mere programmatic provision. As such, it establishes sufficiently "precise and unconditional" obligations since it clearly determines the goal to be achieved—the protection of a fundamental interest of the Union—and the specific addressees of such obligations: EU institutions[60] and Member States. Moreover, with respect to the objection that direct effect of Article 325 TFEU would result in a detrimental effect on the individual, thereby departing from traditional case law and doctrine and radically affecting the original function and *raison d'être* of direct effect, the argument is put forward that no statement by the Court can be found which expressly holds that no EU provision at all, having direct effect, may have detrimental consequences for an individual. To back up that statement, it is submitted that the well-known case law of the Court[61] on direct effect excludes the possibility that criminal responsibility of an individual essentially rests on provisions in a *directive*. Additionally, one can also stress that this line of reasoning in the Court's case law has traditionally been read as the consequence of the fact that the EU does not enjoy a competence in criminal law.[62] However, after the entry into force of the Treaty of Lisbon this lack of competence in criminal matters cannot be anymore a valid argument, as it entails provisions to harmonise criminal law (see Article 83 TFEU). Therefore, this prohibition of direct effect establishing criminal responsibility can be read as an exception to the doctrine of direct effect of directives, especially applying to criminal law matters where Member States were long considered to enjoy an exclusive competence. Moreover, this case law cannot give conclusive answers to the question whether treaty provisions can have detrimental consequences for the individual whenever they are recognized as having direct effect. Detrimental consequences could anyway only be admitted under the condition that fundamental rights, as established in the EU legal order, are respected.

[57] Ciampi 2015, p. 113 ff.

[58] Cannizzaro 2016, p. 46.

[59] Schütze 2015, p. 84 ff.

[60] The institutions are recognized, by consequence, with precise competences in the field.

[61] Cf. for instance the case law referred to in footnote 54.

[62] This reading can explain the fact that the same conclusion was drawn with respect to provisions in a regulation Case C-60/02, X, [2004].

7.4 The Compromise: Back to Good Weather After the Storm? Not Really

The ECJ's *Taricco* judgement was quite successful in reviving the negotiations on the proposal for a PIF Directive. This was attained by its clear statement that VAT-related fraud is already covered by the notion of PIF fraud as defined in the PIF Convention of 1995. That assertion also implies that VAT fraud naturally falls into the scope of the proposed directive which aims to replace the 1995 Convention. In case the proposed directive would not be adopted, the 1995 Convention would continue to apply, including to VAT-related fraud. After seventeen months of interruption, essentially because the EP refused to accept a text excluding VAT-related fraud from the scope of the directive, negotiations could be relaunched. In that stage of the negotiations, the main issue was to decide on the extent to which VAT fraud would fall into the scope of the directive. This required that precise criteria should be established in order to draw the demarcation line between the EU's and the Member States' competences in this area. The Council reached a common position to proceed with the negotiations on the PIF directive in line with decision of the Court, though including only the most serious forms of VAT related frauds. Then, discussions focused on the question whether major frauds should be defined by a threshold or by other criteria, such as the transborder nature, or by a combination of the two. Moreover, discussions at all levels immediately showed that Member States were very concerned about the impact of the '*Taricco* amendment' on the competences of their administrative and fiscal authorities. In this respect, the negotiations resembled the negotiations on the Market Abuse Directive (MAD).[63] In addition, the Council took the position that, if the text of the directive would be amended in order to cover VAT fraud, the directive should not affect the structure, organization and functioning of the tax administration. In general, the directive was not supposed to change anything in the domestic rules of the Member States, which mostly set apart VAT procedures as being special, without a criminal nature, and consequently deprived of criminal law guarantees.

The text agreed by the Council on 8–9 December 2016 was approved by the EP in February 2017, and adopted by the Council as its position at first reading on 5 April 2017.[64] This text unequivocally confirms a restrictive approach to the fundamental EU competence of the fight against fraud. While the version agreed in the 2013 General Approach expressly excluded revenues from VAT from the scope of the directive, the final agreed text repealed this exclusion. Furthermore, it amended Article 3, para 2 (c) and (d) introducing a specific provision on VAT fraud. On the other hand, none of the weaknesses which were present in the Commission proposal appears to have been improved. Moreover, the compromises which were achieved on the most controversial issues stifle all progress in the fight against crimes

[63] See Herlin-Karnell 2018, Chap. 5 of this volume, on EU financial criminal law (including among others MAD) and the EPPO project (including the PIF directive).

[64] Council document 6182/17 of 5 April 2017.

affecting the financial interests of the Union. In particular, the quite limited scope of the directive, combined with the imprecision and vagueness of various provisions, will presumably bring about an extremely weak effect on the Member States' legal systems, and will consequently barely improve the protection of EU financial interests.

In the sixth trilogue in November 2016, the EP put forward multiple propositions for changing the draft Directive. These related to the definition of VAT fraud, the reintroduction of the autonomous offence on procurement fraud, and the lengthening of the prescription period. The Parliament's propositions were all dis-regarded. This was compensated by the introduction of new review clauses in Article 18 of the proposed directive. These clauses originally referred only to the threshold provided for in Article 2(2) of the Directive, but now establish (Article 18 (4)) that the Commission, "[five years after the date of adoption of this directive]" shall make an assessment "with regard to the general objective to strengthen the protection of Union's financial interests". This assessment must inquire whether (1) the threshold in Article 2(2) is appropriate; (2) the provisions on limitation periods in Article 12 are sufficiently effective; and (3) the Directive effectively addresses the cases on procurement fraud. The text that was agreed confirms the solution indicated by the Council on the various controversial issues, and shows that the Parliament's propositions were not followed. According to the Council, this is in line with the subsidiarity principle: amendments on these points of the text would be discussed if less intrusive solutions would, after a certain amount of time, prove to be insufficient.

Finally, the issue of the legal basis of the directive still remains a sensitive one. Although negotiations after the ECJ's decision in the *Taricco* case did not touch that issue,[65] the reasoning of the Court behind the crucial decision to establish Article 325 TFEU as the key provision in the PIF sector seems to imply that the same provision is the basis for both obligations on the Member States and on the EU institutions to act with the aim to enhance the effectiveness of the fight against PIF offences. Since it establishes a shared competence in these matters, the same legal basis should apply with respect to any initiative in this field, regardless of whether it comes from the Member States or EU institutions. This reasoning could take the ECJ to revise the balance between the Council and the Commission in the PIF sector, in case the latter will question the legal basis of Article 83 TFEU in a procedure before the Luxembourg Court.[66]

---

[65] In the text agreed between the Council and the Parliament, Article 83 TFEU was confirmed as the legal basis for the proposed Directive.

[66] As was the case in *Commission v Council* on 13 September 2005 (the so-called environmental case). Indeed, the Commission already expressed its intention to refer to the ECJ whenever the choice of Article 83 TFEU would have been confirmed in the final draft of the proposed PIF Directive. See the document of the General Secretariat of the Council 7929/17 ADD 1, Statements, Brussels 10 April 2017.

Some remarks must be made concerning offences falling into the scope of the directive.[67] With respect to the controversial definition of VAT-related fraud, the text closely follows the definition of "serious offences against the common VAT system" lastly proposed by the Council. This definition "requires an *i*nfringement to the common VAT system" and combines the structural requirement of the "trans-border nature of the fraud" with the quantitative threshold of "a total damage of at least EUR 10 million". The trans-border nature of the fraud is evident in the requirement that "intentional acts or omissions" as indicated in Article 3(d) must be "connected with the territory of two or more Member States of the Union". This provision is important, as it is the result of the fierce institutional and diplomatic struggle mentioned above. However, its wording runs the risk of marginalizing the competence of the EU. This could be the case since these three requirements are included in the definition of VAT-related fraud as cumulative requirements, and not as alternative requirements, as suggested by the Parliament. In particular the choice for a quantitative threshold of 10 million EUR in total damage appears to be too high. It continues to be so even in the light of recital no. 4 which now clarifies that this threshold refers not only to the damage done to the EU but to the entire fraud scheme. Thereby the threshold pertains to the combined estimated damage for the financial interests of the Member States concerned and the Union.

At the official reopening of negotiations with the Parliament, a provision was added to Article 2(3), stating that the "structure and functioning of the tax administration of the Member States are not affected by [the] directive". This provision is aimed to expressly meet Member States' concerns in the negotiations on the inclusion of VAT-related fraud. If this provision will be interpreted strictly, it could weaken Member States' loyal cooperation duties in the fight against crimes affecting the EU's financial interests. Indeed, the general objective of the directive to improve effectiveness logically implies that rather than remaining unaffected Member States' administrations improve their procedures of collecting and managing revenues, next to providing for offences and sanctions.

Article 4 of the proposed PIF Directive provides for some other offences as well. Regarding the definition of the offence of corruption, a request of the Parliament was granted, deleting the element of breach of duty as an essential component of the *actus reus*.[68] However, recital no. 17 retains an ambiguous phrase which declares that the Directive "does not criminalise behaviour which is not also subject to disciplinary penalties or other measures concerning a breach of official duties, in case where such disciplinary penalties or other measures can be applied to the person concerned". The choice to maintain the misappropriation of EU funds as an autonomous offence is clearly to be welcomed. This offence covers (Article 4(3)) "the action of a public official who is directly or indirectly entrusted with the management of funds or assets to commit or disburse funds or appropriate or use

[67] For a useful presentation, see Giuffrida 2017b, para 4 ff.

[68] This point was positively stressed by most of the scholars. See in particular Picotti 2013, pp. 80–81; Sicurella 2013b, p. 43.

assets contrary to the purpose for which they were intended in any way which damages the Union's financial interests." However, the draft Directive contains an important limitation with respect to the original provision in the Commission's proposal. This limitation is caused by the provision that the listed types of behaviour only constitute an offence when they have produced a "damage" to the EU budget.

The absence of an autonomous offence covering illegal activities and omissions in the framework of public procurement procedures is one of the most deceiving elements of the last text agreed. This offence was originally provided for by the Commission's proposal, and its inclusion in the Directive was strongly advocated by the Parliament after the Council had decided to delete it in its General Approach. This offence concerns a type of expense which plays a very significant role in the EU budget. At the national level, offence definitions vary significantly. Therefore a need exists to harmonise this offence. The *Corpus Juris* study strongly advised this, and proposed to establish an autonomous offence covering public procurement fraud. This suggestion was essentially followed by the Commission in its proposal for the PIF Directive. However, many objections were raised during the negotiations about possible clashes with EU competition law and equivalent national law. Because of that, a reference can only be found in Article 3(2)(b), which defines "fraud affecting the Union's financial interests", as expressly including fraud "in respect of procurement related expenditure", "at least" when acts "were committed in order to make an unlawful gain for the perpetrator or another by causing a loss to the Union's financial interests". Clearly, such a choice limits the scope of the directive and excludes all situations where there is no fully provable fraud offence. These situations do not only occur when the requirement of damage to the Union's financial interests is not met, but especially when the submitted bid meets all necessary criteria while relying on non-public information, illegally received from the tendering body, and relating to the awarding of a Union grant or procurement. Moreover, the requirement of the specific objective "to obtain an unlawful gain" excludes those types of bid-rigging (originally covered by the Commission's proposal) which, even if they are not supported by such a specific objective, aim at distorting or bypassing admissibility criteria, or at benefitting from insider information in any other way. This behaviour also affects the best allocation of EU funds, but it is considered to primarily affect fair competition. For that reason, it is left outside the scope of the Directive.

Finally, the definition of "public official" is unclear. Conforming to the Commission's proposal, Article (5)(a) establishes that this term shall mean "any person exercising a public service function involving the management of or decision concerning the Union's financial interests in the Member States or third countries". It is doubtful whether such a definition can be considered as covering *de facto* public officials. In favour of the inclusion one can read recital no. 10 which refers more explicitly to private persons managing EU funds, such as contractors.

Except for the offences mentioned above, all provisions of the draft Directive dealing with the definition of PIF offences are identical to the offence definitions in previous texts.[69] The only improvement that the Directive brings with respect to these provisions is that they will be enshrined in a legal text fully binding the Member States to properly implement it. As a consequence, they will be supported by the possibility for the Commission to bring infringement procedures.

The provisions of the general part have essentially remained unchanged since the General Approach. As already stressed, this excludes that a real harmonisation is realised with respect to crucial topics such as attempt or conspiracy. A special mention deserves Article 12 on limitation periods for criminal offences, which was the issue at stake in the *Taricco* case. The situation experienced in that case with respect to the Italian regulation clearly appeared to hinder the effective protection of the financial interests of the Union. The *Taricco* situation, however, would comply with the current version of Article 12 of the Directive. The judgment should effectively have led to a rewording of this provision with the aim to provide a common prescription regime including the consequences of interruption and suspension of the relevant timeframes.

Looking at the outcome of the analysis conducted above, the Directive brings very few positive achievements. These mostly relate to the clarification and partial extension of the crucial notions of "EU financial interests" and "public officials". These probably necessitate the amendment of national provisions in order to cover all categories of persons addressed by the proposed directive. Apart from that, the provisions of the directive cannot be expected to have a significant effect on the most crucial issues impeding an effective and coherent protection of the financial interests of the Union. Currently, the various legal systems of the Member States form a patchwork of solutions all of which are supposed to respond to illegal activities affecting the EU's budget. The problems of this patchwork-approach are not adequately overcome by the Directive. In particular, this is caused by the very limited scope of PIF offences as defined in the agreed text In addition, there are no common definitions of notions such as 'incitement', 'aiding' and 'abetting', nor of 'attempt'. As all of these concepts are crucial for defining the scope of competence of the EPPO, the Directive will not substantially overcome the patchwork of legal solutions in national law that currently exists. It seems that a very minimal harmonisation is achieved with respect to penalties, and also with respect to prescription of offences. However, many crucial issues remain unsolved in the very heart of the strategy to effectively protect the financial interests of the Union.

[69] Articles 3(a) and (c) concerning the conducts constituting EU fraud and Article 4(2) on corruption are based on Article 1(a) and (b) of the 1995 PIF Convention and Articles 2 and 3 of its First Protocol, respectively, while Article 4(1) on money laundering simply refers to the definition in the 2015 Directive on the same topic. The latter choice, relying on a direct reference to a specific piece of legislation, is to be criticized because it results in an 'inflexibility' of the text of the Directive with respect to upcoming developments with regard to money laundering.

7.5 The 'Side' Effect of the PIF Directive: An EPPO Lost in Translation?

The present state of the PIF Directive will have a significant impact on the work of the EPPO. Presumably, it will hinder the EPPO in effectively performing its duties as an authority charged with more than cooperation and coordination duties. The PIF offences are conceived to be the core of the competence of the proposed EPPO. Indeed, the exact scope of competence of this European investigating and prosecuting authority will emerge from national legislation, being decisive in setting the boundaries of individual responsibility in the concrete case.[70] This is of course also something that radically affects the idea of protecting supranational interests.

Some provisions of the draft Directive appear quite striking against the backdrop of the future EPPO's competence. One of these is the provision that the Member States succeeded to introduce excluding tax procedures and the competences of national tax authorities from the effect of the Directive. This exclusion could paradoxically result in emptying the *raison d'être* of the proposed Directive, which was supposed to improve the effectiveness of the fight against fraud. This fight is currently quite ineffective due to the actual situation in the various Member States.[71] Yet, these national authorities will be the ones that will have to inform the EPPO on concrete cases. Because of their varying nature and of their lack of cooperation, these authorities can evidently not have an overall picture of the facts. This will make it harder for them to assess that the threshold of 10 million Euros requested by the Directive for a VAT-related fraud to fall into the scope of the Directive is reached. The EPPO's competence absolutely depends on the assessment of national authorities on this point and their prompt and complete reporting to the EPPO. The EPPO must rely on this information in order to decide to evoke the case from the hands of national authorities. This is the consequence of the fact that unlike the Commission's proposal, providing for an exclusive competence of the EPPO, the current text of the draft Regulation clearly opted for a system of "shared competence" between the EPPO and the national authorities,[72] where the competence of the EPPO should "as a general rule take priority over national claims of competence".[73] Moreover, the requirement in the draft PIF Directive that a fraud offence has a transborder nature clearly affects the original idea of the EPPO as a 'European' investigative authority. According to this idea, the EPPO's competences with respect to the protection of EU financial interests should rely on the nature of

---

[70] See also Vervaele 2014, 94.

[71] See Brenninkmeijer 2018 (Chap. 13 of this volume) and European Court of Auditors 2015.

[72] Recital no. 7 of the text of the draft Regulation. See Council document 5766/17 of 31 January 2017.

[73] According to recital no. 51. The EPPO consequently has the right either to initiate investigations or to evoke a case, according to the conditions established in Article 22(a) of the draft Regulation, whenever investigations on PIF offences have been launched already by national authorities.

the protected interest. In that line of thinking, the number of Member States in which the acts were committed should be irrelevant for the competence of the EPPO.

The overall picture of the future EPPO's activities is even more problematic when one takes a look at the provisions in the last version of the draft EPPO Regulation[74] in combination with the Directive. Indeed, once it is established that a concrete situation falls into the scope of competence of the EPPO,[75] it is to be decided whether it is the EPPO that has jurisdiction over the case, or this remains with the national investigative authorities.

Article 17(3) of the proposed EPPO regulation, which was only included in the version of the proposal of 31 January 2017,[76] expressly excludes the competence of the EPPO "for criminal offences in respect of national direct taxes and the structure and functioning of the tax administration of the Member States". This provision matches to some extent the provision in Article 2(3) of the proposed Directive. Both reflect the debate surrounding the *Taricco* decision. But there are other limitations to the EPPO's scope of competence, which can be derived from the provisions of the draft Regulation. Multiple provisions of the draft Regulation indeed appear to have the objective to restrict the jurisdiction of the EPPO. These provisions establish many conditions which are to be met. In particular, one has to pay attention to Articles 20(2) and (3)(b), which deal with the competences of the EPPO defined in Article 17. These competences are comprised of the direct one, concerning PIF offences and the participation in a criminal organization, and the 'ancillary' one, dealing with the "inextricably linked offences". According to the first, "where a criminal offence falling within the scope of Article 17 caused or is likely to cause damage to the Union's financial interests of less than EUR 10 000, the European Public Prosecutor's Office may only exercise its competence if: (a) the case has repercussions at Union level which require an investigation to be conducted by the European Public Prosecutor's Office, or (b) officials or other servants of the European Union, or members of the Institutions could be suspected of having committed the offence.[…]". Following recital no. 51a, "a particular case should be considered having a repercussion at Union level *inter alia* where a criminal offence has a transnational nature and scale, where such an offence involves a criminal organisation, or where the specific type of offence could be a serious threat to the Union's financial interests or the Union institutions' credit and Union citizen' confidence". In compliance with general principles of subsidiarity and proportionality of EU action, this provision and its accompanying recital clearly aim to exclude the competence of the EPPO and, consequently, maintain the competence of the national authorities with respect to offences falling within the scope of Article

74 Giuffrida 2017a; Weyembergh and Brière 2016.

75 According to Article 17 of the draft Regulation, and in particular, concerning PIF, Article 17(1) referring to the PIF Directive. This means for the PIF sector that the situation in the case falls into the scope of the PIF Directive.

76 Council document 5766/17 of 31 January 2017.

17 in situations where the EU budget appears to be only very marginally affected.[77] This consequence was likely the aim also of Article 19(4) of the *Corpus juris* proposal. However, the latter reflects a complete different perspective and relies on very different criteria. In the *Corpus juris* the EPPO is conceived as a European investigative authority enjoying an exclusive competence with respect to PIF offences (which the same text also defined), who nevertheless is able to refer to national authorities "offences which are not serious or which affect principally national interests". That provision was intended to derogate from the obligation to prosecute, which was imposed on the EPPO by the same provision. That provision starts by clearly stating that "the decision to prosecute […] may be taken by the EPP whatever the sum of the fraud involved", and requires such a decision to be based on "special grounds communicated immediately to the person who has informed it, or denounced it to its officials or laid a complaint". Despite the fact that this provision employs the vague notions of "not serious" and "which affect principally national interests", this wording perfectly expresses the idea of the EPPO as an authority protecting the fundament interests of the Union at EU level, regardless of the quantitative impact of an offence. This is evident because the protection of the Union's financial interests *can be* left to national authorities only when the concerned offence can first be qualified by the EPPO itself, on the basis of an overall picture of the facts. Only then the EPPO can make a discretionary decision whether the case is "not serious" in the light of all possible criteria, both objective and subjective. And only then the EPPO can decide if the offence mainly affects national interests. Any concrete offence, even when it has caused or is likely to cause a limited damage to the Union's financial interests, or when it principally affects national interests, will not automatically be outside the competence of the EPPO whenever that body considers action at EU level to comply with the general principles of the action of any supranational authority, first of all subsidiarity and proportionality.

By contrast, the draft Regulation automatically excluded from the EPPO's competence all offences where the lesser seriousness is exclusively based on quantitative criteria. In doing so, the draft Regulation reflects the idea that the focus of EU action in this field is the threat to the economy. Such an approach is confirmed by the fact that the EPPO will by exception be competent to act, even when the damage caused or likely to be caused is less than € 10.000, whenever it manages to justify that the case "has repercussions at Union level which require an investigation to be conducted by the European Public Prosecutor's Office". This situation is met, according to recital no. 51a, "*inter alia* where a criminal offence has a transnational nature and scale, where such an offence involves a criminal organisation, or where the specific type of offence could be a serious threat to the Union's financial interests or the Union institutions' credit and Union citizens' confidence". The concept of "repercussions" at Union level that require the

[77] In the event that such a criminal offence caused or is likely to cause damage to the Union's financial interests of less than EUR 10 000.

competence of the European investigative authority to come into play appears to rely not on the nature of the interest concerned, but on criteria typically relevant in a judicial cooperation perspective. These refer to the "transnational nature and scale" of the offence and to the fact that "such an offence involves a criminal organization". However, the same provision also justifies action from the EPPO when the "specific type of offence [...] could be a serious threat to the Union's financial interests or the Union institutions' credit and Union citizens' confidence". Notwithstanding the vagueness of the notion of a "serious threat", which can result to be problematic in the view of establishing the competent authority, such a reference maintains the possibility that the relevance of the offence at EU level can depend on completely different elements than a quantitative threshold. It can even be in contrast with this last criterion, since an offence can be considered as representing a "serious threat" for some EU interests despite the fact that the damage caused or likely to be caused is less than € 10.000. According to this provision, the seriousness of a PIF offence (and the consequent competence of the EPPO) is to be appreciated at EU level also with respect to the impact on different interests than financial ones, especially on "the Union institutions' credit and Union citizens' confidence". Similarly, the provision in Article 20(2)(b) of the draft EPPO Regulation must be welcomed as it establishes an EPPO competence over PIF offences where, despite a relatively low level of damage, EU officials or other EU servants or members of the Institutions are suspected of having committed the offence. Indeed, such a provision reflects that in these cases it is not only the financial interest of the EU that is at stake, which is of course not 'seriously' affected when considered in a strictly economical perspective. Rather, it is the fundamental interest of the European public function that is at stake. This can justify that prosecutions remain in the scope of competence of the EPPO. Such a provision (partially) compensates the provision of Article 4, restricting the competence of the EPPO for PIF offences committed by EU public officials to offences that resulted in damage or potential damage to the EU's financial interests. Finally, even when the loss to the European budget in an economic sense is not especially relevant, the EPPO can exercise its competence over the case.

Article 20(3)(b) of the draft Regulation is also likely to limit significantly the competence of the EPPO. This provision obliges the EPPO to refrain from exercising its competence when "there is a reason to assume that the damage caused or likely to be caused to the Union's financial interests by an offence referred to in Article 17 does not exceed the damage caused or likely to be caused to another victim". In the text agreed in January 2017, a statement was added excluding such a rule with respect to VAT related frauds. This addition is to be welcomed, since the application of the rule above would have the result of systematically excluding the competence of the EPPO in this field, because the impact of VAT-related frauds on the EU budget is always less important than the damage caused to the concerned Member Stats' budgets. However, the limitation remains in place for other PIF offences. Here as well as in other places, a strict interpretation of the principles of subsidiarity and proportionality lies at the basis of this provision. The result could be that the EPPO's competence is automatically excluded even with respect to PIF offences significantly damaging the Union. There is no room left for a discretionary decision by the EPPO. Contrarily, as shown above, the *Corpus juris* proposal accepted a discretionary decision for the European investigative authority to refer a case to the national authorities when it considered that the offence principally affected national interests. That solution was very different and much less stringent than the automatic exclusion of the EPPO's competence whenever it finds that the damage to the Union's financial interests does not exceed the damage caused to another victim.

7.6 Conclusions

Looking at the overall picture of the legal framework which will be provided for the EPPO, conclusions can only be quite pessimistic about the possibility that it could significantly improve the effectiveness of the fight against fraud and other illegal activities affecting the financial interests of the European Union. The solutions that are now enshrined in the text of the two proposals presented above unequivocally show the progressive weakening of the original idea of the EPPO. The draft PIF Directive, which aims at a very minimalistic degree of harmonization, risks greatly affecting the efficiency of the new office. It essentially confirms the current level of protection of EU financial interests, which is weak and insufficient. As a result of Member States' successes in the negotiations, the draft Directive does not introduce a clear and precise set of offences, essentially leaving the existing patchwork of national offence definitions in place. The fragmented protection of the European budget will thus remain unchanged. Moreover, this continuing situation will clearly result in numerous legal problems relating to the use of coercive powers by the EPPO.

Participants in the negotiations consider the text to be a good achievement. To some extent they are correct: it is a significant improvement that the old third pillar instruments are replaced by a Directive, enabling the CJEU to assess Member States' compliance with their implementation obligations. More importantly however, the negotiations appear to have completely stifled any ambition for a text that should have been the most advanced piece of EU legislation in criminal matters, because of the fact that it deals with the protection of the supranational interest *par excellence*.

References

Bernardi A (ed) (2017) I Controlimiti. Primato delle norme europee e difesa dei principi costituzionali. Jovene, Naples

Bernardi A, Cupelli C (eds) (2017) Il caso *Taricco* e il dialogo tra le Corti. L'ordinanza 24/2017 della Corte costituzionale. Jovene, Naples

Billis E (2016) The European Court of Justice: a "Quasi-Constitutional Court" in criminal matters? The *Taricco* Judgement and Its Shortcomings. New Journal of European Criminal Law 7: 20–38

Bin R (2017) *Taricco*, una sentenza sbagliata: come venirne fuori? In: Berbardi A (ed) I Controlimiti. Primato delle norme europee e difesa dei principi costituzionali. Jovene, Naples, pp 291–300

Brenninkmeijer A (2018) The European Public Prosecutor's Office: A Chronicle of a Failure Foreseen. In: Geelhoed W, Erkelens LH, Meij AWH (eds) Shifting Perspectives on the European Public Prosecutor's Office. TMC Asser Press, The Hague

Cannizzaro E (2016) Sistemi concorrenti di tutela dei diritti fondamentali e controlimiti costituzionali, in margine alla sentenza "Taricco". ASTRID, 14 September 2016

Ciampi A (2015) Il caso *Taricco* impone la disapplicazione delle garanzie della prescrizione: un problema di rapporti fra diritto dell'UE e diritto nazionale e di tutela dei diritti fondamentali, non solo di diritto processuale internazionale. Int'l Lis-Rivista di diritto processuale internazionale e arbitrato internazionale, 3–4:113

Delmas-Marty M (ed) (1997) Corpus juris introducing penal provisions for the purpose of the financial interests of the European Union. Economica, Paris

Delmas-Marty M, Vervaele JAE (eds) (2000) The implementation of the Corpus juris in the Member States. Intersentia, Antwerpen/Groningen/Oxford

European Court of Auditors (2015) Tackling intra-Community VAT fraud: More action needed (Special Report No. 24/2015). Available at http://www.eca.europa.eu/Lists/ECADocuments/SR15_24/SR_VAT_FRAUD_EN.pdf. Accessed May 2017

Giuffrida F (2016) The limitation period of crimes: same old Italian story, new intriguing European answers. New Journal of European Criminal Law 7:100–112

Giuffrida F (2017a) The European Public Prosecutor's Office. King without Kingdom? CEPS, No 2017/03, February 2017

Giuffrida F (2017b) The PIF acquis in light of the new directive. In: Sicurella R et al (eds) EU General Principles for a Common Criminal Law Framework in the EU. A Guide for Legal Practitioners. (on-going publication)

Herlin-Karnell E (2018) The Establishment of a European Public Prosecutor's Office: Between 'Better Regulation' and Subsidiarity Concerns. In: Geelhoed W, Erkelens LH, Meij AWH (eds) Shifting Perspectives on the European Public Prosecutor's Office. TMC Asser Press, The Hague

Klip A (2012) The Substantive Criminal Law Jurisdiction of the European Pubic Prosecutor's Office. European Journal of Crime, Criminal Law and Criminal Justice, 4:367–376

Lassalle M (2015) *Taricco* kills two birds with one stone for the sake of the PIF. europeanlawblog, 27 October 2015

Mitsilegas V (2016) EU Criminal Law after Lisbon. Rights, Trust and the Transformation of Justice in Europe. Hart-Bloomsbury, Oxford/London

Peers S (2015) The Italian Job: the CJEU strengthens criminal law protection of EU's finances. eulawanalysis.blogspot.it, 22 September 2015

Picotti L (2005) La lutte contre la fraude communautaire dans la perspective du Traité établissant une Constitution pour l'Europe. In: La protection des intérêts financiers de l'Union et le rôle de l'Olaf vis-à-vis de la responsabilité des personnes morales et des chefs d'entreprises et l'admissibilité mutuelle des preuves. Bruylant, Brussels

Picotti L (2013) Le basi giuridiche per l'introduzione di norme penali comuni relative ai reati oggetto della competenza della Procura europea. In: Grasso G et al (eds) Le sfide dell'attuazione di una Procura europea: definizione di regole comuni e loro impatto sugli ordinamenti interni. Giuffrè, Milan

Schütze R (2015) European Union Law. Cambridge University Press, Cambridge

Sicurella R (2011) Questioni di metodo nella costruzione di una teoria delle competenze dell'Unione europea in materia penale. In: Studi in onore di Mario Romano. Jovene, Naples, pp 256–264

Sicurella R (2013a) Setting up a European Criminal Policy for the Protection of EU Financial Interests: Guidelines for a Coherent Definition of the Material Scope of the European Public Prosecutor's Office. In: Ligeti K (ed) Towards a Prosecutor for the European Union. Hart Publishing, Oxford, pp 2569–2644

Sicurella R (2013b) Il diritto penale applicabile dalla Procura europea: diritto penale sovrannazionale o diritto nazionale 'armonizzato'? Le questioni in gioco. In: Grasso G et al (eds) Le sfide dell'attuazione di una Procura europea: definizione di regole comuni e loro impatto sugli ordinamenti interni. Giuffrè, Milan

Sicurella R (2017) Oltre la vexata questio della natura della prescrizione. L'actio finium regundorum della Consulta nell'ordinanza *Taricco*, tra sovranismo (strisciante) e richiamo (palese) al rispetto dei ruoli. In: Bernardi A, Cupelli C (eds) Il caso *Taricco* e il dialogo tra le Corti. L'ordinanza 24/2017 della Corte costituzionale, Jovene, Naples, pp 405–433

Vervaele J (2014) The material scope of competence of the European Public Prosecutor's Office: Lex uncerta and unprevia? ERA Forum 1:85–99

Weyembergh A, Brière C (2016) Towards a European Public Prosecutor's Office (EPPO). Study for the LIBE Committee of the EP

Chapter 8
Ancillary Crimes and *Ne Bis in Idem*

Eric Sitbon

Abstract This chapter deals with the issue of the material competence of the European Public Prosecutor's Office and the conditions under which it may extend to offences other than those which fall within the scope of Directive (EU) 2017/1371 on the fight against fraud to the Union's financial interests by means of criminal law (the "PIF Directive"). Since Article 86 of the Treaty on the Functioning of the European Union, on which the future Regulation establishing the European Public Prosecutor's Office (the "EPPO Regulation") is based, limits the material competence of that Office to offences against the Union's financial interests but leaves it to the EPPO Regulation to determine more precisely which offences are covered, this chapter analyses the different categories of offences which may be included in the scope of the EPPO Regulation, in order to preserve the *effet utile* of Article 86 of the Treaty and to take into account the principle of *ne bis in idem*. The first category of offences consists of offences falling within the scope of the PIF Directive. The second category relates to offences regarding participation in a crimination organisation if the focus of the criminal activity of such a criminal organisation is to commit an offence affecting the Union's financial interests. The third category consists of offences which are inextricably linked to a criminal conduct falling within the scope of an offence affecting the Union's financial interests. The concept of "inextricably linked" offences has been clarified in a Recital and the limits of such an "ancillary competence" has been circumscribed by further criteria on the exercise of the competence of the European Public Prosecutor's Office.

The author is Legal Adviser at the Council Legal Service. The views expressed are those of the author and in no way reflect the views of the Council or the European Council. The author availed himself of the almost finalised though not yet formally adopted text of the draft EPPO regulation as available at the proof stage of this volume (October 2017).

E. Sitbon (✉)
Council of the European Union, Rue de la Loi 175, 1048 Brussels, Belgium
e-mail: eric.sitbon@consilium.europa.eu

W. Geelhoed et al. (eds.), *Shifting Perspectives on the European Public Prosecutor's Office*, https://doi.org/10.1007/978-94-6265-216-3_8

Keywords European Public Prosecutor's Office · Competence *ratione materiae* · Principle of *ne bis in idem* · Offences against the Union's financial interests · Inextricably linked offences · Instrumental offences · *Effet utile* · Ancillary competence · Preponderance

Contents

8.1 Introduction

This chapter deals with the issue of the material competence of the European Public Prosecutor's Office and the conditions under which it may extend to offences other than those which fall within the scope of Directive (EU) 2017/1371 on the fight against fraud to the Union's financial interests by means of criminal law (the "PIF Directive"). Since Article 86 of the Treaty on the Functioning of the European Union, on which the future Regulation establishing the European Public Prosecutor's Office (the "EPPO Regulation") is based, limits the material competence of that Office to offences against the Union's financial interests but leaves it to the EPPO Regulation to determine more precisely which offences are covered, this chapter analyses the different categories of offences which may be included in the scope of the EPPO Regulation.

Article 12 of the Commission Proposal[1] gave competence to EPPO in respect of the criminal offences affecting the financial interests of the Union, as provided for by the PIF Directive.

Article 13 of the Commission Proposal gave competence to EPPO for the so-called ancillary crimes which are inextricably linked with crimes affecting the financial interests of the Union, under certain conditions. Recital 22 of the Commission Proposal justified this extension of competence by reference to the principle of *ne bis in idem*.

The possibility or need for the Union legislature to give competence to EPPO to prosecute the so-called "ancillary" crimes on the basis of Article 86 of the Treaty on

[1] COM(2013) 534 final.

the Functioning of the European Union ("TFEU") was extensively discussed within the Council.

The European Parliament has adopted a resolution supporting, under certain conditions, the ancillary competence of the European Public Prosecutor's Office.[2]

In the Council draft text of 30 June 2017[3] (the "draft EPPO Regulation"), ancillary competence is provided for mainly in Articles 22 and 25(3) which are reproduced below:

Article 22

Material competence of the European Public Prosecutor's Office

1. *The EPPO shall be competent in respect of the criminal offences affecting the financial interests of the Union that are provided for in Directive (EU) 2017/1371* [the PIF Directive], *as implemented by national law, irrespective of whether the same criminal conduct could be classified as another type of offence under national law.*
2. *The EPPO shall also be competent for offences regarding participation in a criminal organisation as defined in Framework Decision 2008/841/JHA, as implemented in national law, if the focus of the criminal activity of such a criminal organisation is to commit any of the offences referred to in paragraph 1.*
3. *The EPPO shall also be competent for any other criminal offence which is inextricably linked to criminal conduct that falls within the scope of paragraph 1 of this Article. The competence with regard to such criminal offences may only be exercised in conformity with Article 25(3).*
4. *In any case, the EPPO shall not be competent for criminal offences in respect of national direct taxes including offences inextricably linked thereto. The structure and functioning of the tax administration of the Member States shall not be affected by this Regulation.*

Article 25

Exercise of the competence of the EPPO

[…]

3. *The EPPO shall refrain from exercising its competence in respect of any offence falling within the scope of Article 22 and shall, upon consultation with the competent national authorities, refer the case without undue delay to the latter in accordance with Article 34 if:*

   (a) *the maximum sanction provided for by national law for an offence falling within the scope of Article 22(1) is equal to or less severe than the maximum sanction for an inextricably linked offence as referred to in Article 22(3); unless the latter offence has been instrumental to commit the offence falling within the scope of Article 22(1) or;*

[2] PE546.675v02-00, point 14.

[3] Doc. 9941/17.

(b) *there is a reason to assume that the damage caused or likely to be caused, to the Union's financial interests by an offence as referred to in Article 22 does not exceed the damage caused, or likely to be caused to another victim. Point (b) of the first subparagraph of this paragraph shall not apply to offences referred to in Article 3(2)(a), (b) and (c) of Directive (EU) 2017/1371 as implemented by national law.*

4. *The EPPO may, with the consent of the competent national authorities, exercise its competence for offences referred to in Article 22 in cases which would otherwise be excluded due to application of paragraph 3(b) of this Article if it appears that the EPPO is better placed to investigate or prosecute.*
5. *The EPPO shall inform the competent national authorities without undue delay of any decision to exercise or to refrain from exercising its competence.*
6. *In case of disagreement between the EPPO and the national prosecution authorities over the question of whether the criminal conduct falls within the scope of Article 22(2), or (3) or Article 25(2) or (3) the national authorities competent to decide on the attribution of competences concerning prosecution at national level shall decide who is to be competent for the investigation of the case. Member States shall specify the national authority which will decide on the attribution of competence.*

Recitals 54, 55 and 56[4] read as follows:

(54) *The efficient investigation of offences affecting the financial interests of the Union and the principle of ne bis in idem may require, in certain cases, an extension of the investigation to other offences under national law, where these are inextricably linked to an offence affecting the financial interests of the Union. The notion of inextricably linked offences should be considered in light of the relevant case law which, for the application of the ne bis in idem principle, retains as a relevant criterion the identity of the material facts (or facts which are substantially the same), understood in the sense of the existence of a set of concrete circumstances which are inextricably linked together in time and space.*

(55) *The EPPO should have the right to exercise competence, where offences are inextricably linked and the offence affecting the Union's financial interests is preponderant, in terms of the seriousness of the offence concerned, as reflected in the maximum sanctions that could be imposed.*

(56) *However, the EPPO should also have the right to exercise competence in the case of inextricably linked offences where the offence affecting the financial interests of the Union is not preponderant in terms of sanctions levels, but where the inextricably linked other offence is deemed to be ancillary in nature because it is merely instrumental to the offence affecting the financial interests*

[4] Doc. 5766/17.

of the Union, in particular where such other offence has been committed for the main purpose of creating the conditions to commit the offence affecting the financial interests of the Union, such as an offence strictly aimed at ensuring the material or legal means to commit the offence affecting the financial interests of the Union, or to ensure the profit or product thereof.

This chapter does not address the issue of judicial review on conflicts of competence between EPPO and national competent authorities.

8.2 Legal Framework

Article 86 TFEU, the legal basis for the proposed Regulation, provides that:

1. *In order to combat crimes affecting the financial interests of the Union, the Council, by means of regulations adopted in accordance with a special legislative procedure, may establish a European Public Prosecutor's Office from Eurojust. The Council shall act unanimously after obtaining the consent of the European Parliament.*

   [...]
2. *The European Public Prosecutor's Office shall be responsible for investigating, prosecuting and bringing to judgment, where appropriate in liaison with Europol, the perpetrators of, and accomplices in, offences against the Union's financial interests, as determined by the regulation provided for in paragraph 1. It shall exercise the functions of prosecutor in the competent courts of the Member States in relation to such offences.*

   [...]
4. *The European Council may, at the same time or subsequently, adopt a decision amending paragraph 1 in order to extend the powers of the European Public Prosecutor's Office to include serious crime having a cross-border dimension and amending accordingly paragraph 2 as regards the perpetrators of, and accomplices in, serious crimes affecting more than one Member State. The European Council shall act unanimously after obtaining the consent of the European Parliament and after consulting the Commission.*' (our emphasis)

8.3 Legal Analysis

8.3.1 Preliminary Remarks

Article 86(2) TFEU limits the competence in relation to subject matter (competence *ratione materiae*) of the European Public Prosecutor's Office to 'offences against the Union's financial interests' ('PIF offences'). To extend this competence to include other types of offence relating to 'serious crime having a cross-border dimension', Article 86(4) TFEU sets out a procedure for amending paras 1 and 2 of Article 86 TFEU, under which the European Council is to act unanimously, after obtaining the consent of the European Parliament and after consulting the Commission.

In view of the above, any extension of the EPPO's competence *ratione materiae* beyond PIF offences to include other offences must comply with the principle of conferral of powers set out in Article 5 of the Treaty on European Union (TEU) and the institutional balance provided for in Article 13 TEU. Therefore, for example, any extension of this competence to 'ancillary' offences based on 'identical facts' which is justified solely on the basis of vague criteria with no normative effect, such as 'the interest of a good administration of justice' (Article 13 of the proposal) or 'the interest of procedural efficiency' (Recital (22) of the proposal), would constitute an abuse of the procedure provided for under Article 86(4) TFEU and a breach of Articles 5 and 13 TEU.

In such a case, the requirement of foreseeability in determining the competent prosecuting authority would not be met, which would lead to the application of different penalties[5] according to whether the proceedings jointly concern a PIF offence and an inextricably related ancillary offence (where several offences are committed by a single act) or, on the contrary, deal with a PIF offence or an ancillary offence individually, applying the *ne bis in idem*[6] principle as appropriate. Moreover, using vague criteria, which are therefore left to EPPO to interpret, in order to determine whether the Office, or national prosecution services, should have competence *ratione materiae* as regards ancillary offences, is likely to lead to infringement of the principle of the legality of criminal offences and penalties, as set out in Article 49(1) of the EU Charter of Fundamental Rights (the 'Charter').

However, if it were objectively justified, strictly circumscribed and based on precise criteria, an extension of the EPPO's competence *ratione materiae* to include certain types of ancillary offence based on identical facts or inextricably linked to PIF offences could be compatible with the legal basis of Article 86(2) TFEU, under certain conditions.

Firstly, it follows from a literal interpretation of Article 86(2) TFEU that the EPPO's competence *ratione materiae* is not necessarily limited to offences which fall within the scope of the PIF Directive,[7] which is a directive on minimum harmonisation of substantive criminal law to be adopted on the basis of Article 83 (2) TFEU to cover most (but not all) offences against the Union's financial interests. According to the precise wording of Article 86(2) TFEU, the EPPO's competence

[5] See the judgment of the European Court of Human Rights applying Article 7 of the European Convention on Human Rights (on the principle of the legality of criminal offences and penalties), application No 42931/10, *Camilleri v Malta*, paras 40–45.

[6] Article 50 of the Charter of Fundamental Rights of the Union.

[7] *OJ* L 198 of 28.7.2017, p. 29.

ratione materiae applies generally to the investigation, prosecution and bringing to judgment of the perpetrators of, and accomplices in, offences against the Union's financial interests, as determined by the future Regulation establishing the European Public Prosecutor's Office. Therefore, even if offences ancillary or related to PIF offences which may be prosecuted at the same time as 'pure' PIF offences do not fall within the scope of the PIF Directive, that does not mean that they must automatically and necessarily fall outside the scope of Article 86(2) TFEU. On the contrary, these ancillary and related offences may fall within the scope of Article 86 (2) TFEU.

Secondly, extending the EPPO's competence *ratione materiae* may be justified if it can be demonstrated that such an extension is needed to preserve the effectiveness of Article 86 TFEU.

8.3.2 Justification Based on the Need to Preserve the Effectiveness of Article 86(1) TFEU

First of all, it must be determined to what extent an extension of competence *ratione materiae* is needed in order to preserve the *effet utile* of Article 86 TFEU, and the conditions to be met must be clarified. In this case, it would support the literal interpretation developed above.

The 'functional' interpretation of provisions of the Treaties in light of their *effet utile* (effectiveness) is one of the methods of interpretation employed by the Court, particularly where the literal interpretation leads to a result which is not consistent with the objective pursued by the authors of the Treaties, or to support a literal interpretation. The method of functional interpretation has been used, in particular, in connection with Treaty provisions relating to competition law,[8] environmental law,[9] and criminal justice.[10]

More specifically, it must be established whether, and under what conditions, a functional interpretation of Article 86(2) TFEU would, in light of the objective contained in para 1 of that article, i.e. to 'combat crimes affecting the financial interests of the Union', result in the extension of the EPPO's competence to cover frequent cases of related offences ancillary to PIF offences so as not to deprive Article 86 TFEU of its effectiveness.

---

[8] Judgment of the Court of 23 April 2009, Case C-439/08, *VEBIC*, para 64.

[9] Judgment of the Court (Grand Chamber) of 13 September 2005, Case C-176/03, *Commission v Council*, paras 48 and 51.

[10] Judgment of the Court (Grand Chamber) of 16 June 2005, Case C-105/03, *Pupino*, para 42.

One of the justifications the Commission gives for such an extension appears in recital 22 of the proposal ('possible breach of the principle ne bis in idem') and now in Recital 54 of the draft EPPO Regulation.

In a subsequent communication,[11] the Commission argued firstly that most of the offences prosecuted are not, *sensu stricto*, PIF offences, but other offences (e.g. forgery of documents with the aim of obtaining funds from the Union budget) which are inextricably linked to PIF offences. Secondly, the Commission stated that the prosecution of the two types of offences (i.e. PIF offences on the one hand and other, inextricably linked offences on the other) based on identical facts by two different authorities (the European Public Prosecutor's Office and the national prosecution service) would be inefficient and would, in many cases, defeat the purpose of an EPPO prosecution. Indeed, in the case of parallel prosecutions by these two authorities, the *ne bis in idem* principle as set out in Article 50 of the Charter and Article 54 of the Convention implementing the Schengen Agreement ('CISA')[12] and as interpreted by the Court[13] would oblige the European Public Prosecutor's Office or the national prosecution service to close the proceedings once a final criminal conviction or a final acquittal had been delivered, based on the same facts, with regard to either of the two categories of offences.

Thus, without a rule such as that contained in Article 22 of the draft EPPO Regulation, the EPPO would, in many cases, be unable to exercise its competence over PIF offences if inextricably linked offences being prosecuted in parallel were to end in final discharge or acquittal.

We find the justification put forward by the Commission regarding the *ne bis in idem* principle convincing. Indeed, without strictly regulated ancillary competence, and in light of the *ne bis in idem* principle, the EPPO would *de facto* be prevented from prosecuting PIF offences (including those falling within the scope of the PIF Directive) in many cases, simply because they were accompanied by related ancillary offences (e.g. forgery of documents to misappropriate Union funds) which had already been prosecuted separately by national authorities, resulting in penalties or dismissal.

The conditions under which ancillary competence might be justified must be examined in more detail in light of the case law. In a landmark ruling of 2009, the European Court of Human Rights (ECtHR) held that Article 4 of Protocol 7 of the ECHR prohibits the prosecution or trial of a person for a second offence in so far as it arises from identical facts or facts which are substantially the same.[14] This means that the ECtHR has regard only to whether or not the facts are identical and

[11] See in particular Commission Communication (COM(2013)851 final, para 2.6.2).

[12] *OJ* L 239, 22.9.200, p. 19.

[13] Judgment of the Court of 28 September 2006, Case C-467/04, *Gasparini*.

[14] European Court of Human Rights, judgment in *Sergey Zolotukhin v Russia* (Grand Chamber) of 10.2.2009, para 82 (14939/03).

expressly not to the legal classification of the offence.[15] These facts are defined by the ECtHR as 'a set of concrete factual circumstances involving the same defendant and inextricably linked together in time and space'[16] (our emphasis). This means that the ECtHR is concerned, for example, with ascertaining whether charges brought against an accused person are based on the same conduct on the same date.[17] The ECtHR is guided primarily by the case law of the Court of Justice of the European Union, which has ruled that '(…) the only relevant criterion for the application of Article 54 of the CISA is identity of the material acts, understood in the sense of the existence of a set of concrete circumstances which are inextricably linked together'[18] (our emphasis).

Without strictly regulated ancillary competence, and in light of the *ne bis in idem* principle, the EPPO would *de facto* be prevented from prosecuting PIF offences (including those falling within the scope of the PIF Directive) in many cases. This loss of competence would simply result from the fact that PIF offences would be accompanied by related ancillary offences (e.g. forgery of documents to misappropriate Union funds) which had already been prosecuted separately by national authorities, resulting in penalties or dismissal.

In light of the above, it may be concluded that an extension of the EPPO's competence *ratione materiae* limited to offences arising from identical facts and inextricably linked to facts forming the basis of PIF offences enables the effectiveness of Article 86 TFEU to be preserved, bearing in mind the application of the *ne bis in idem* principle set out in Article 50 of the Charter and Article 54 of the CISA. Any prosecution of such offences by the EPPO at the same time as 'pure' PIF offences would be considered equivalent to prosecutions intended to combat PIF offences within the meaning of Article 86 TFEU.

8.3.3 Conditions Which Have Been Laid Down by the Council to Circumscribe the Competence of, and Its Exercise by EPPO for Ancillary Crimes: Analysis of Articles 22 and 25(3) of the Draft EPPO Regulation

8.3.3.1 Analysis of the First Criterion in Article 22(1)

The first criterion which has been added in Article 22(1) by the Council is not an extension of the competence of the EPPO beyond PIF offences. It actually aims at

[15] Above-mentioned judgment (14939/03), para 81.

[16] Above-mentioned judgment (14939/03), para 84, and European Court of Human Rights, judgment in *Grande Stevens and others v Italy* of 4.3.2014, para 221 (18640/10).

[17] Above-mentioned judgment (18640/10), para 227.

[18] Judgment of the Court of 9 September 2006, Case C-436/04 *Van Esbroeck*, para 36.

reflecting the situation that the same criminal conduct which is classified as a PIF offence as provided for in the PIF Directive as implemented by national law could also be classified as another type of offence under national law.

This situation is known in some legal systems as a *concours d'infractions* which means that several distinct offences based on identical or linked facts may be committed successively or simultaneously by the same perpetrator. In that case, those legal systems require that the several distinct offences would be punished by the most severe sanction applicable to one of the offences committed as opposed to the accumulation of sanctions for each of the offences.

As explained in Sect. 8.3.1, the competence of the EPPO under Article 86 TFEU is not necessarily limited to offences which fall within the scope of the PIF Directive and for this reason, it could capture this situation of cumulative offences.

8.3.3.2 Analysis of the Criterion of 'Participation in a Criminal Organisation' in Article 22(2)

Article 22(2) aims at ensuring that the application of the rules in Articles 22 and 25 (3) of the draft EPPO Regulation does not lead to a circumvention of the material competence of the EPPO for PIF offences where the focus of the criminal activity of a criminal organisation as defined in Framework Decision 2008/841/JHA is to commit a PIF offence, even in cases where the maximum sanction for the participation in such a criminal organisation is more severe than for the pure PIF offence —which is often the case.

This provision—in the same way as Article 22(1)—still limits the competence of the EPPO to offences against the Union's financial interests referred to in Article 86 (2) TFEU but in such a way as to preserve the *effet utile* of Article 86 TFEU.

8.3.3.3 Analysis of the Criterion of 'Inextricably Linked Offence' in Article 22(3) in the Light of the CJEU Case Law

Article 22(3) of the draft EPPO Regulation introduces the criterion of 'inextricably linked' which is in line with the case law of the Court of Justice on the *ne bis in idem* principle, for the reasons set out in Sect. 8.3.2. Recital 54 further specifies this case law; for reasons of legal certainty and foreseeability, the Council has removed the undefined criterion of 'preponderance' from the scope of Article 22.

8.3.3.4 Difficulties Linked to the Use of the Undefined 'Preponderance' Criterion and How They Have Been Overcome by the Council

The criterion of 'preponderance' of PIF offences and the ancillary nature of other offences related to PIF offences is the criterion which was proposed by the Commission without defining it. This reasoning, which distinguishes preponderance from the ancillary nature of the purpose or component of an act, is based on the reasoning developed by the Court with regard to the legal basis applicable when a legal act of the Union has several components or purposes.[19] It probably served to prevent the European Public Prosecutor's Office from encroaching upon the powers of national authorities and of the European Council under Article 86(4) TFEU, whilst preserving the effectiveness of Article 86 TFEU.

However, such a reasoning is not fully applicable to the specific case of the establishment of a Union body to exercise the competence *ratione materiae* which is clearly defined in Article 86(2) TFEU and which can in principle only be extended by a specific procedure as laid down in Article 86(4) TFEU. Having said that it can be used as a basis to which precise criteria can be added in order to identify the preponderance and ancillary components of offences. In this way, PIF offences could be identified as the main or predominant purpose or component of the powers of the European Public Prosecutor's Office whilst other offences would be merely ancillary in cases where they were the instrument through which PIF offences were committed.[20] This has been reflected by the Council in Article 25(3)(a) and in Recital 56 which clarifies the concept of instrumental offences.

It would be problematic to have a lack of criteria in the text or a reference in a recital to a large number of criteria left to the EPPO to interpret, or to a purely quantitative criterion of preponderance based on financial damage.

For this reason, the Council deleted any reference in the operative part to the undefined concept of preponderance and referred to the focus of the criminal activity of a criminal organisation in Article 22(2) and to a list of defined criteria for the exercise of the competence of the EPPO in Article 25(3). Even though preponderance is now defined in Article 25(3) by reference to alternative criteria, i.e. the severity of the sanction,[21] instrumentality of the offence[22] or to the damage caused or likely to be caused to the Union's financial interests,[23] the latter criterion is clearly discarded where the effectiveness of the competence of the EPPO needs to be preserved, e.g. as regards VAT fraud where the damage to the national budget will always be higher than the damage to the Union's budget. This also counts for fraud in respect of non-procurement related expenditure (e.g. structural funds involving co-financing between the EU and national budgets), as well as for fraud in respect of procurement-related expenditure.[24]

---

[19] See for example the judgment of the Court of 8 September 2009 in *Commission v Parliament and Council*, Case C-411/06, para 46, and the judgment of the Court of 6 September 2012 in *Parliament v Council*, Case C-490/10, para 45.

[20] See in particular the judgment of the Court (Grand Chamber) of 6 May 2014 in Case C-43/12, paras 30 and 42, and the judgment of the Court (Grand Chamber) of 22 October 2013 in Case C-137/12, paras 53 and 67.

[21] Article 25(3)(a).

[22] Article 25(3)(a).

[23] Article 25(3)(b).

[24] Second subparagraph of Article 25(3) referring to Article 3(2)(a), (b) and (d) of Directive (EU) 2017/1371 as implemented by national law.

Furthermore, Recitals 55 and 56 specify the Council's intention on 'preponderance'.

8.4 Conclusion

A broad definition of what constitutes offences against the Union's financial interests in Article 86(2) TFEU which goes beyond the scope of the PIF Directive is compatible with the legal basis of Article 86 TFEU, which refers in general terms to investigating, prosecuting and bringing to judgment the perpetrators of, and accomplices in, PIF offences, as determined in the regulation establishing the European Public Prosecutor's Office.

An extension of the EPPO's competence *ratione materiae*, if confined to ancillary offences arising from identical facts and inextricably linked to facts forming the basis of preponderant PIF offences, is compatible with the legal basis of Article 86 TFEU. Moreover, bearing in mind the application of the *ne bis in idem* principle, this limited extension of competence *ratione materiae* would preserve the effectiveness of Article 86 TFEU.

The draft EPPO Regulation has taken these parameters into account. In particular, preponderance has been defined in the draft EPPO Regulation based on precise criteria, such as the criterion of severity of the maximum sanction as provided for in Article 25(3)(a) and Recital 55 of the draft EPPO Regulation.

However, in the absence of unanimity in the Council which has been registered on 7 February 2017, the EPPO Regulation could not be adopted. The authorisation to proceed with enhanced cooperation in accordance with the third subparagraph of Article 86(1) TFEU was deemed to be granted on 3 April 2017 and the EPPO Regulation implementing enhanced cooperation with 20 participating Member States will be adopted by the Council after obtaining the consent of the European Parliament.

Chapter 9
Towards an Inconsistent European Regime of Cross-Border Evidence: The EPPO and the European Investigation Order

András Csúri

Abstract This chapter focuses on the different approaches to cross-border evidence in two future manifestations of judicial cooperation in criminal matters in the EU: the European Investigation Order (EIO) and the proposed European Public Prosecutor's Office (EPPO). In the horizontal context of the EIO, the collection and transfer of evidence is based on a redesigned mutual recognition scheme, while the proposed EPPO model selectively combines elements of horizontal and vertical cooperation for the gathering and the Union wide recognition of evidence. The study sets the emphasis on the potential problems of the mixed EPPO regime and its future co-existence with the EIO. With currently no minimum European rules on the mutual admissibility of evidence, no uniform EPPO powers and the reality of the EPPO being established by enhanced cooperation, the author concludes that initial recourse to the EIO in EPPO investigations might be beneficial for various reasons. It might increase the acceptance of the EIO in practice, the trust in future EPPO investigations, the recognition of EPPO-evidence and the coherence of cross-border investigations in the EU in general.

Keywords European Union · Judicial cooperation in criminal matters in the EU · The *Corpus Juris* study · European Public Prosecutor's Office · European Investigation Order (EIO) · Evidence · Cross-border investigations

---

The author is postdoctoral fellow at the Willem Pompe Institute of Criminal Law and Criminology, Utrecht University.

The author is grateful to Dr. Alicia Hinarejos for her comments. The usual disclaimer applies.

A. Csúri (✉)
3512 BK Utrecht, The Netherlands
e-mail: a.csuri@uu.nl

W. Geelhoed et al. (eds.), *Shifting Perspectives on the European Public Prosecutor's Office*, https://doi.org/10.1007/978-94-6265-216-3_9

Contents

9.1 Introduction

Judicial cooperation in criminal matters has always been a sensitive field of EU integration, given its complex and traditionally strong links to fundamental rights and state sovereignty.[1] One of the most contended issues in this field concerns the necessary level and most practicable scheme of integration, notably, whether coordinated actions between the Member States (horizontal model) or the conferral of certain prosecutorial powers to Union level (vertical model) would be more feasible.

The choice and the balance between these schemes have remained central questions up until the present day with the Treaty of Lisbon referencing both models.[2] Article 82 TFEU defines the mutual recognition principle as the cornerstone of judicial cooperation in criminal matters and Article 85 TFEU strengthens the position of the European Union's Judicial Cooperation Unit (Eurojust). At the same time Article 86 TFEU lays the legal basis for the establishment of a vertical cooperation model, in the form of the European Public Prosecutor's Office (EPPO).

The focus of this article is set on two future manifestations of the different models, on the European Investigation Order (EIO)[3] and on the progressing EPPO negotiations.[4] Special emphasis is set on their different regimes regarding the

---

[1] See for instance Luchtman and Vervaele 2014; Armada 2015; Lohse 2014. With regard to the EPPO, see especially the reasoned opinions issued by various national parliaments in the course of the early warning mechanism. For instance House of Lords, European Union Committee, Third Report, http://www.publications.parliament.uk/pa/ld201314/ldselect/ldeucom/65/6503.htm; the Senate of the Parliament of the Czech Republic 9th Term, 345th Resolution, Senate Press no. N 082/09, http://www.ipex.eu.

[2] Treaty of Lisbon Amending the Treaty on European Union and the Treaty Establishing the European Community, 13 December 2007, *OJ* 2007 C 306/01.

[3] Directive 2014/41/EU of 3 April 2014 regarding the European Investigation Order in criminal matters, 1 May 2014, *OJ* 2014 L130/1.

[4] The analysis is based on the initial Commission proposal and the revised version of the text dated 28 October 2016. Proposal for a Council Regulation on the establishment of the European Public Prosecutor's Office COM (2013) 534 final. Council, Proposal for a Regulation on the establishment of the European Public Prosecutor's Office—Outstanding questions on the full text.

collection and recognition of evidence in cross-border cases. The analysis identifies potential problems concerning the mixed EPPO-scheme on evidence and its future co-existence with the EIO regime. The paper concludes that with currently no minimum European rules on the admissibility of evidence or standardized EPPO procedure, recourse to the EIO in EPPO investigations might increase the acceptance of the EIO among the Member States, the trust in future EPPO investigations and the coherence of cross-border investigations in the EU.

9.2 Rationales and Models of Judicial Cooperation in Criminal Matters in the EU

Judicial cooperation in criminal matters, including the collection of evidence, was traditionally based on formal requests and lengthy political decisions with several grounds for refusal. Over the years, the necessity to simplify, accelerate and improve this scheme emerged, driven and shaped by different rationales.

The distinct stages of this evolution included:

- The Schengen-logic of strengthened legal cooperation
- The concept of vertical cooperation in the 1997 *Corpus Juris* study
- The Amsterdam-logic of mutual recognition of judicial decisions
- The co-existence of horizontal and vertical cooperation in the Treaty of Lisbon.

The Schengen regime aimed to facilitate inter-state cooperation as a necessary compensation of lifting border controls. For that reason the 1990 Convention Implementing the Schengen Agreement (CISA) provided for rules on police and judicial cooperation in penal matters.[5] Article 53 CISA enabled for instance that requests for assistance might be made directly between judicial authorities and not through diplomatic channels.

The objective remained the same under the Treaty of Maastricht (1992).[6] Nevertheless, during this era the Commission also launched an ambitious project in

(Footnote 4 continued)

http://www.statewatch.org/news/2016/nov/eu-council-EPPO-Ful-lText-%2013459-16.pdf. Council doc. No. 13459/16, 28 Oct. 2016. See http://www.statewatch.org/news/2016/nov/eu-council-EPPO-Ful-lText-%2013459-16.pdf.

[5] 1990 Convention implementing the Schengen Agreement of 14 June 1985 between the Governments of the States of the Benelux Economic Union, the Federal Republic of Germany and the French Republic on the gradual abolition of checks at their common borders. The related rules are most notably on mutual legal assistance (Article 53 CISA), extradition (Articles 59 et seq. CISA) and on the *ne bis in idem* principle (Article 54 CISA).

[6] The Treaty on European Union, 7 February 1992, *OJ* 1992 C 325/5.

order to invent a more efficient cooperation scheme to tackle EU budgetary fraud. The results were published in the 1997 *Corpus Juris* study, which envisaged the creation of a single legal area for budgetary fraud cases, based on unified offence definitions and standardized procedures in any part of the Union.[7] To ensure the uniform application of the rules, the study notably proposed the establishment of a central prosecution service: the European Public Prosecutor (EPP) or in later proposals the European Public Prosecutor's Office (EPPO). The seeds of strong vertical cooperation for a limited scope of offences were planted, based on Europe-wide rules for the collection of evidence. Given the slow integration in the field, the *Corpus*-ideas of vertical cooperation and a single legal area proved to have been far too revolutionary at the time.[8]

Next, with the new objective to create an Area of Freedom, Security and Justice (AFSJ) within the EU—inter alia by developing common actions in the field of police and judicial cooperation in criminal matters (Article 29 TEU)—the Treaty of Amsterdam (1999)[9] provided criminal law and judicial cooperation in criminal matters with a European perspective. That said, the Member States continued to support improved horizontal techniques over the vertical cooperation scheme envisaged in the *Corpus Juris*.[10] On the one hand, at institutional level, Eurojust was established with a task to facilitate and coordinate the efforts of the national law-enforcement authorities when dealing with specific trans-border crimes.[11] Contrary to the envisaged EPP, the national members of Eurojust operate under national rules, their decisions are based on intergovernmental mechanisms and their powers are limited to make requests to national authorities. On the other hand, as regards the cooperation scheme, the application of the internal market principle of mutual recognition was extended to criminal matters.[12] In general, the measures based on the mutual recognition principle undeniably simplified and accelerated

[7] Delmas-Marty 1997; Spencer 1998, pp. 77–105.

[8] For initial reactions to the study, see Spencer 2012, pp. 367–371. In 2000 a follow up study was presented that contained detailed information on the criminal justice systems of the then 15 Member States. See Delmas-Marty and Vervaele 2000.

[9] Treaty of Amsterdam amending the Treaty on European Union, the Treaties Establishing the European Communities and Certain Related Acts, 2 October 1997, *OJ* 1997 C 340/1.

[10] The grounds for the improved horizontal cooperation were laid down in the subsequent Tampere European Council of 1999. Additionally, in order to eliminate parallel arrangements of cooperation within the EU, the Schengen *acquis* was integrated into the Treaty.

[11] Eurojust was established by Council Decision 2002/187/JHA [2002] *OJ* L63/1. See also Nilsson 2011, pp. 73–78.

[12] European Commission, Communication on mutual recognition of final decisions in criminal matters. COM(2000), 495 final, 26 July 2000. Council work programme of measures to implement the principle of mutual recognition of decisions in criminal matters. 2001 *OJ* C 12/10. The principle was already embedded in the criminal justice systems of certain Member States (like the UK), in the internal market law (Judgment of the Court of 20 February 1979. Case 120/78) and in the field of civil and commercial judgments (Regulation 44/2001 on Jurisdiction and Recognition of Civil Judgments). The analogy and reference to the internal market principle was subject to various critiques. See Peers 2004, p. 34; Zeder 2014, p. 234.

judicial cooperation in criminal matters by providing for fixed deadlines and a central role for the judicial authorities as well as by reducing the grounds for refusing cooperation. It has also fundamentally changed the role of the cooperating states as the issuing state became the 'owner' of the order, and its decisions took effect as such in the executing Member State. Over the years however, the varying transposition of the measures into national laws together with the lack of harmonization raised serious concerns over the comparability of the final decisions of the national authorities.[13]

9.3 Cross-Border Evidence in the Lisbon Context

The current Treaty context (the Treaty of Lisbon, 2009) provides simultaneously for both horizontal and vertical forms of cooperation in criminal matters. On the one hand it defines mutual recognition along with the complimentary approximation of laws (which may concern mutual admissibility of evidence) as the cornerstone of judicial cooperation in criminal matters (Article 82 TFEU). On the other hand it lays the legal basis for the establishment of the EPPO (Article 86 TFEU), the vertical form of cross-border prosecution within the EU.[14]

In-between Article 85 para 1 TFEU also strengthens the operational position of Eurojust—which some might label as conditional verticalisation—by providing the body with the future possibility to initiate criminal investigations. This however is currently only an option linked to national enquiries and with no powers to initiate criminal prosecutions.

In the following, the paper focuses on questions related to cross-border evidence in the EIO directive and in the EPPO drafts.

9.3.1 The Horizontal Scheme: The European Investigation Order

The first mutual recognition instrument, the European Arrest Warrant (EAW),[15] came into force in 2004 and became the template for subsequent instruments in the field of judicial cooperation in criminal matters. It was driven by the impetus of the 9/11 attacks and was based upon the Amsterdam-logic of cooperation. The emphasis was set on the security objective of the AFSJ and so the EAW provided for nearly

[13] In addition, the mutual recognition model was vague concerning fundamental rights and failed to provide for a standard system of exceptions. See Peers 2014, p. 294; Zeder 2015, pp. 25–26.

[14] Consequently, the current Post-Stockholm multi-annual programme also references both models. European Council Conclusions of 26/27 June 2014. European Council 79/14 Brussels, 27 June 2014. See Peers 2008, pp. 507–529.

[15] Framework Decision 2002/584/JHA on the European Arrest Warrant and the surrender procedures between Member States [2002] L190/1. See also Klimek (2015) and Eurojust News 2013.

automatic execution of foreign judicial decisions to arrest and surrender individuals in another Member State. In order to accelerate proceedings it has provided for fixed deadlines and has reduced the traditional grounds for refusals to cooperate. In particular, the EAW did not provide for refusal grounds based on fundamental rights protection. As all EU Member States were parties to (and presumably conform with) the ECHR,[16] the instrument was based upon practically blind trust in the Member States' mutual commitment to fundamental rights.[17] In fact it took until April 2016 when the CJEU ruled in the joined cases *Aranyosi* and *Căldăraru*, that under certain conditions it is possible to refuse the execution of an EAW for the protection of fundamental rights. Thus, to rebut unconditional mutual trust in each other's legal systems as regards the surrender of an individual in criminal proceedings.[18]

The Directive on the European Investigation Order (EIO) indicates further significant changes in the horizontal model of judicial cooperation.[19] The EIO should accelerate judicial cooperation by introducing deadlines and strict formalities related to the collection and transfer of evidence in cross-border cases. It will presumably facilitate the admissibility of foreign evidence, as a competent authority of the Member State that intends to use the evidence will issue the order.

However, the EIO might also slow down cooperation in individual cases. In order to prevent the issuing authority to bypass national safeguards, the directive limits the former (almost) automatic effect of foreign decisions within the EU. A double equivalency test shall ensure that the measure could be applied to the same offence under the domestic laws of both Member States concerned.[20] Additionally, a proportionality test shall answer whether the executing authority may have recourse to a less intrusive measure if it would achieve the same results.[21] Finally and most notably, in order to protect fundamental rights the Directive also enables to eventually refuse the execution of an EIO. Together, the new guarantees will strengthen the position of the defendant as the presumption of the compliance with Union law and, in particular, with fundamental rights becomes rebuttable.[22]

Altogether, the EIO scheme transforms the horizontal regime somewhere between the traditional inter-state cooperation and the automatism of the mutual recognition principle.[23]

---

[16] European Convention for the Protection of Human Rights and Fundamental Freedoms of 4 November 1950. ETS 5 (ECHR).

[17] See also Mitsilegas 2006, pp. 1277–1311.

[18] Joined Cases C-404/15 and C-659/15 PPU. The refusal of an EAW requires prior consultation of the competent authorities and grounds to believe that due to the detention conditions there is a real risk for the individual being treated in an inhuman or degrading way. See also Mitsilegas 2012, pp. 319–372.

[19] See De Capitani and Peers 2014.

[20] Articles 6(1) and 10 EIO Directive.

[21] Articles 6 and 10 EIO Directive.

[22] Recital 19 and Article 11(1)(f) EIO Directive.

[23] See also Böse 2014, pp. 152–164; Vervaele 2013, pp. 21–56; European Union Agency for Fundamental Rights 2011.

9.3.2 The Desired Vertical Scheme: The European Public Prosecutor's Office

9.3.2.1 The 2013 Commission EPPO Proposal

As pointed out above, the *Corpus Juris* study proposed a truly vertical scheme to prosecute EU fraud. At the central level, the European Public Prosecutor would have made decisions to be enforced by delegated prosecutors at national level according to Union-wide rules of procedure.

The Treaty of Lisbon laid the legal basis for the establishment of the EPPO (Article 86 TFEU), but left it to the future Regulation to define basically all of its features, including its powers and institutional design.[24] The subsequent model proposed by the Commission in 2013 was much like the one advocated by the *Corpus Juris*, but without standardized rules of procedure.[25] Instead, the European delegated prosecutors (EdelP) would enforce the central decisions according to the applicable national laws (Article 26.2), while in cross-border cases the EdelP whom the case was assigned to shall act in 'close consultation' with the EdelP of the Member State, where the investigation measure needs to be carried out (Article 18.2).

Altogether, the nature and scope of the EPPO powers (including the applicable investigative measures) would differ from case to case and from Member State to Member State, the judicial authorisation of investigative measures would be limited to the jurisdiction of the respective national authority, while the application of different regimes of procedural guarantees might also be both beneficial and detrimental for the defendant in the transnational context.[26]

That said, according to the proposal national courts would need to recognize EPPO evidence even in the absence of equivalence of the rules or compatibility of the legal systems between the Member States concerned (Article 30(1)).[27] The Union wide admissibility of EPPO evidence would be indeed desirable, but either on the basis of Article 82(2)(a) TFEU that provides for establishing minimum rules in this area or on the basis of standardized EPPO procedure. The simple fact that the evidence is gathered in EPPO investigations will not automatically balance the different systems of procedural guarantees in the Member States. The arrangement in the proposal set the focus mainly on the enforcement of EPPO decisions within a single jurisdiction.

---

[24] For the discussions on the possible design of the EPPO, see, for instance, Csúri 2012, p. 79; Zwiers 2011; Ligeti 2011, p. 51; Ligeti and Simonato 2013, pp. 7–21.

[25] Proposal for a Council Regulation on the establishment of the European Public Prosecutor's Office COM (2013) 534 final. See also the Impact Assessment Accompanying the Proposal for a Council Regulation on the establishment of the European Public Prosecutor's Office, SWD (2013) 275 final. For a detailed assessment of different aspects of the Commission's Proposal, see Erkelens et al. 2014. See also Csúri 2016, pp. 137–144.

[26] See Luchtman and Vervaele 2014, p. 140. See also Thorhauer 2015, p. 78.

[27] Except if the evidence would adversely affect the fairness of the procedure or the rights of defense as enshrined in Articles 47 and 48 of the Charter of Fundamental Rights.

It failed to address important transnational aspects of EPPO investigations and the significant differences in the national criminal prosecutions, one of the main justifications to establish the EPPO (Preamble Rec. 5). Apart from the obvious risks of such an arrangement, the increased reliance on national laws also questions its added value. Given the considerable differences between the national legal systems, common minimum standards would have been a prerequisite for consistent EPPO investigations and for the admissibility of EPPO evidence in front of the competent trial court.

9.3.2.2 Cross-Border Evidence in the Current Version of the Council Text

The subsequent negotiations in the Council maintained the basic concepts of EPPO decisions being enforced according to applicable national laws (Article 25.3) and EPPO evidence being recognized by national courts as such (Article 31).[28]

The current version of the text however elaborates on the cooperation mechanism in cross-border cases.[29] To some extent it resembles the EIO arrangements but with significant differences. Contrary to the standardized scheme of judicial authorisation in the EIO Directive, the EPPO draft provides for different scenarios. In cross-border cases, the respective measure might be granted by any of the competent authorities concerned (Article 26.3 together with Recital 69).[30] In case the handling authority grants the measure, the arrangement resembles the EIO, while if the assisting authority grants the measure it even takes us back to mutual legal assistance. The EDelP handling the case assigns the respective investigative measure to the assisting EDelP, who in turn undertakes the measure (Article 26). By doing so the assisting authority may apply an alternative measure if it is less intrusive but would achieve the same results, or when the measure does not exist or would not be available in a similar domestic case. The EDelPs concerned would need to consult on such issues with the involvement of the supervising European Public Prosecutor (Article 26(5)). Thus, the draft provides for similar considerations as the EIO, but without real grounds for refusal. In fact, Article 26(3) lays down the only situation, where cooperation is clearly impossible. This occurs, once the competent assisting authority does not grant the judicial authorisation of a measure.

[28] On the evolution of the EPPO concept from the *Corpus Juris* study up to the text endorsed by the 2015 Luxembourg Presidency, see Csúri 2016. For the changes introduced since the Commission proposal, see the Presidency Notes from the Council to the Delegations 2013/0255 (APP). On the proposals of the Greek and Italian Presidencies, see Damaskou 2015, pp. 143–149.

[29] For the latest public version of the text dated 28 October 2016, see http://www.statewatch.org/news/2016/nov/eu-council-EPPO-Ful-lText-%2013459-16.pdf. For a detailed analysis, see Weyembergh et al. 2016.

[30] The text does not specify in which Member State the judicial authorisation should be obtained if more than two Member States are involved but clarifies that in any case there should be only one judicial authorisation (Recital 63).

Even in this case, it would be the EDelP handling the case who withdraws his/her assignment.

As regards the admissibility of evidence, Article 31(1) enables the trial court to examine the evidence (limited to the fairness of the procedure, the rights of the defence or other rights enshrined in the Charter, in accordance with Article 6 TEU), but only where the national law requires so. This new reference to national law limits the original Commission proposal (Article 30) and establishes further differences in the position of the defendants in the Member States.

In essence, the current version of the EPPO text deviates from the existing forms of horizontal cooperation but fails to create a truly vertical model. The draft selectively mixes horizontal cooperation for evidence-gathering and vertical cooperation for the recognition of evidence. This constitutes an inconsistent regime, especially as regards the position of the individuals affected by EPPO investigations, most notably through the almost obligatory recognition of foreign evidence gathered according to various rules and standards.

9.3.3 Interactions Between the Different Schemes

Free movement of judicial decisions requires a considerable comparability of national laws, regardless whether a cross-border investigation is initiated through an EIO or by the EPPO. Therefore a fair level of harmonization of national procedural laws would be inevitable for the proper functioning of either cooperation schemes. Although Article 82 TFEU provides for the possibility to establish minimum rules on mutual admissibility of evidence, no such legislation has taken place as yet.

In order to balance the lack of harmonized rules (and the related lack of trust), the EIO Directive introduces new possibilities to limit cooperation, notably if fundamental rights are at stake. Contrary to that, even in the absence of common rules, the EPPO text reduces the grounds to reject cooperation and imposes the recognition of foreign evidence. Thus, both the EIO Directive and the draft EPPO regulation introduce corrective elements, albeit with very different impact. While putting more emphasis on procedural safeguards, the EIO will strengthen the position of the individuals under investigation. This might slow down cross-border investigations in individual cases but might also increase mutual trust. Conversely, the limited options to reject cooperation in the EPPO text might accelerate cross-border EPPO investigations (not EPPO investigations in general as it will be seriously slowed down by the envisaged chamber-structure),[31] but the proposed rules on the admissibility of evidence could both benefit or detriment the defendant's position. An unfortunate tendency, given the fact that in the current Treaty context the respect for fundamental rights, in particular as regards the rights of suspected and accused persons in transnational criminal proceedings, has gained

[31] On the enlargement of the central decision level, see Csúri 2016, pp. 146–147.

greater emphasis.[32] Beside the already adopted EU legislation concerning the minimum rights of defendants[33] this philosophy also becomes evident in the EIO Directive and in the latest CJEU case law.

So, is there any need for a special scheme of evidence when it comes to EPPO investigations? One of the main arguments for a *sui generis* regime is the assumption that the EPPO will be a single legal office, operating in a single legal area.[34] This would legitimate the idea of a special scheme, especially one different from the mutual recognition mechanism. Nevertheless, the proposed text is far away from establishing a single legal area for EPPO investigations, as the Member States remain reluctant to provide the new Union body with uniform mandate and powers that would ensure the equality, consistency and efficiency of its investigations across the Union. Therefore, as long as the EPPO gathers evidence according to varying national laws, the single legal area-reasoning will be no adequate rationale. Even less, in case the EPPO would be established on the basis of an enhanced cooperation regime.

What if the EPPO would apply the EIO in its investigations? With no minimum European rules on the mutual admissibility of evidence, no uniform EPPO procedure and the possibility of the EPPO being established by enhanced cooperation, recourse to the EIO might be beneficial for various reasons. First, in the absence of uniform EPPO powers, it might strengthen the recognition of EPPO investigations and that of EPPO-evidence as the central European decisions would be enforced and evidence collected on the basis of an already transposed European instrument. Second, requiring national authorities to apply the EIO, while not considering the same measure to be efficient enough for cross-border EPPO cases (for a limited scope of offences) might generally weaken the acceptance of both the EIO and that of the EPPO. Third, in case of enhanced cooperation the EPPO will possibly have recourse to the EIO anyway, when cooperating with EU Member States not participating in the project.

Moreover, the EIO would be not the only horizontal instrument in the EPPO Regulation. The text already provides for the use of the EAW, whenever the arrest or surrender of a person located in another Member State is necessary (Article 28). It is true that the EAW provides for less refusal grounds than the EIO, but in light of the Court's ruling in *Aranyosi* and *Căldăraru*, this might change in the near future. Thus, providing for the use of EAW but not for the EIO creates further inconsistency within the EPPO regime itself.

It seems that the text avoids recourse to the EIO, as it would not assist the desired notion of a central European prosecution service making binding European decisions. It would allow the national authorities to opt for an alternative measure or

[32] See for instance The Stockholm Programme—An open and secure Europe serving and protecting citizens. *OJ* C 115 of 4.5.2010.

[33] EU harmonization measures were adopted with regard to certain defence rights. See Directive 2010/64/EU; Directive 2012/13/EU; Directive 2013/48/EU; Directive 2016/343/EU; Directive 2016/800/EU; and Directive 2016/1919.

[34] Commission Proposal Article 25.1.

even refuse cooperation despite a central decision at Union level. In particular, refusals in order to protect fundamental rights could jeopardize EPPO investigations, given the discrepancies between the national criminal laws concerning procedural safeguards.[35] Though the current version of the text introduces some similar scenarios, but without explicitly defining them as refusal grounds for cooperation.

9.4 Conclusion

The original *Corpus Juris* study based the Union-wide recognition of evidence in transnational fraud cases on a standardised procedure. The EIO Directive and the EPPO drafts provide for significantly different regimes. With no Union-wide minimum rules in the area, the EIO Directive provides for an equivalence check of the measures and presumes the recognition of the foreign evidence due to the congruent jurisdiction of the issuing authority and the authorities that make use of the evidence collected with the help of the EIO. On the other hand, evidence in cross-border EPPO investigations would be gathered according to the different applicable national laws. As a main rule the competent courts would need to recognize such evidence and may examine it only on limited grounds and if the applicable national law requires so. Thus, the recognition of evidence would not be based on uniform European rules or the congruent jurisdiction of the issuing authority and the trial court but exclusively on the circumstance that the evidence was gathered in EPPO investigations. In this chapter it is argued that such a Union-wide admissibility of EPPO evidence would require a uniform EPPO procedure or minimum European rules on the mutual admissibility of evidence. As currently there are no such rules in place, it is hard to imagine, how the EIO and the EPPO would contribute to a stable scheme of recognizing foreign evidence when they deal with the subject matter on such different grounds. Therefore, as long as the EPPO lacks a genuine vertical scheme, recourse to the EIO in EPPO investigations might provide for a more coherent scheme. It could increase the acceptance of the EIO in practice, the trust in future EPPO investigations, the recognition of EPPO evidence and the coherence of cross-border investigations in the EU in general.

References

Armada I (2015) The European Investigation Order and the Lack of European Standards for Gathering Evidence – Is a Fundamental Rights-Based Refusal the Solution? New Journal of European Criminal Law, 6: 8–31

Böse M (2014) Die Europäische Ermittlungsanordnung – Beweistransfer nach neuen Regeln? Zeitschrift für Internationale Strafrechtsdogmatik, 4:152–164

[35] Article 11(1)(f) of the EIO Directive. See Armada 2015, p. 8. See also Luchtman and Vervaele 2014, pp. 141–149.

Csúri A (2012) Naming and Shaping. The Changing Structure of Actors Involved in the Protection of EU Finances. eucrim 2:79–83

Csúri A (2016) The Proposed European Public Prosecutor's Office - From a Trojan Horse to a White Elephant? In: Armstrong K et al. (eds) Cambridge Yearbook of European Legal Studies. Cambridge University Press, Vol. 18, pp 122–151

Damaskou A (2015) The European Public Prosecutor's Office. A Ground-Breaking New Institution of the EU Legal Order. New Journal of European Criminal Law 6: 143–149

De Capitani E, Peers S (2014) The European Investigation Order: A new approach to mutual recognition in criminal matters. EU Law Analysis. http://eulawanalysis.blogspot.co.at/2014/05/the-european-investigation-order-new.html Last accessed 22 March 2017

Delmas-Marty M (ed) (1997) *Corpus Juris* Introducing Penal Provisions for the Purpose of the Financial Interests of the European Union. Editions Economica, Paris

Delmas-Marty M, Vervaele JAE (eds) (2000) The Implementation of the *Corpus Juris* in the Member States: Penal Provisions for the Protection of European Finances, 4 Volumes. Intersentia, Antwerp

Erkelens LH, Meij AWH, Pawlik M (eds) (2014) The European Public Prosecutor's Office An Extended Arm or a Two-Headed Dragon? TMC Asser Press, The Hague

Eurojust News (2013) Interviews with Christine Van Den Wyngaert and Viviane Reding. http://www.eurojust.europa.eu/doclibrary/corporate/newsletter/eurojust%20news%20issue%208%20(may%202013)%20on%20the%20creation%20of%20a%20european%20public%20prosecutor%20office/eurojustnews_issue8_2013–05-en.pdf. Last accessed 22 March 2017

European Union Agency for Fundamental Rights (2011) Opinion on the draft directive regarding the European Investigation Order. http://fra.europa.eu/en/opinion/2011/fra-opinion-draft-directive-regarding-european-investigation-order-eio. Last accessed 22 March 2017

House of Lords, European Union Committee (2013) Third Report: Subsidiarity Assessment: The European Public Prosecutor's Office http://www.publications.parliament.uk/pa/ld201314/ldselect/ldeucom/65/6503.htm. Last accessed 22 March 2017

Klimek L (2015) European Arrest Warrant. Springer, Berlin/Heidelberg

Ligeti K (2011) The European Public Prosecutor's Office: Which Model? In: Klip A (ed) Substantive Criminal Law of the European Union. Maklu Publishing, pp 51–65

Ligeti K, Simonato M (2013) The European Public Prosecutor's Office: Towards a Truly European Prosecution Service? New Journal of European Criminal Law, 4:7–21

Lohse KM (2014) The European Public Prosecutor: Issues of Conferral, Subsidiarity and Proportionality. In: Erkelens LH, Meij AWH, Pawlik M (eds) The European Public Prosecutor's Office An Extended Arm or a Two-Headed Dragon? TMC Asser Press, The Hague, pp 165–183

Luchtman M, Vervaele JAE (2014) European Agencies for Criminal Justice and Shared Enforcement (Eurojust and the European Public Prosecutor's Office). Utrecht Law Review 10: 132–150

Mitsilegas V (2006) The constitutional implications of mutual recognition in criminal matters in the EU. Common Market Law Review 43: 1277–1311

Mitsilegas V (2012) The Limits of Mutual Trust in Europe's Area of Freedom, Security and Justice: From Automatic Inter-State Cooperation to the Slow Emergence of the Individual. Yearbook of European Law, 31:319–372

Nilsson HG (2011) Judicial Cooperation in the EU. Eurojust and the European Public Prosecutor. In: Guild E et al (eds) The Area of Freedom, Security and Justice Ten Years on: Successes and Future Challenges Under the Stockholm Programme. Centre for European Policy Studies, pp 73–78

Peers S (2004) Mutual recognition and criminal law in the European Union: Has the Council got it Wrong? Common Market Law Review 41: 5–36

Peers S (2008) EU criminal law and the Treaty of Lisbon. European Law Review, 33: 507–529

Peers S (2014) EU Justice and Home Affairs Law (Non-Civil). In: Craig P, de Búrca G (eds) The Evolution of EU Law. Oxford University Press, Oxford, pp 269–297

Spencer JR (1998) The *Corpus Juris* project and the fight against budgetary fraud, In: Dashwood A, Ward A (eds) Cambridge Yearbook of European legal studies. Hart Publishing, Oxford, Vol. 1, pp. 77–105

Spencer JR (2012) Who's Afraid of the Big, Bad European Public Prosecutor? In: Barnard C et al (eds) Cambridge Yearbook of European Legal Studies. Hart Publishing, Oxford, Vol. 14. pp 367–371

The Senate of the Parliament of the Czech Republic (2013) 9th Term, 345th Resolution on the Proposal for a Council Regulation on the establishment of the European Public Prosecutor's Office, Senate Press no. N 082/09. http://www.ipex.eu/IPEXL-WEB/scrutiny/COM20120629/czsen.do Last accessed 22 March 2017

Thorhauer NI (2015) Conflicts of Jurisdiction in Cross-Border Criminal Cases in the Area of Freedom, Security and Justice. Risks and Opportunities from an Individual Rights-Oriented Perspective. New Journal of European Criminal Law 6:78–101

Vervaele JAE (2013) Gathering and Use of Evidence in the Area of Freedom, Security and Justice, with Special Regard to EU Fraud and OLAF Investigations. In: Nowak C (ed) Evidence in EU Fraud Cases. Wolters Kluwer Polska, pp 21–56

Weyembergh A et al (2014) The Inter-Agency Cooperation and Future Architecture of the EU Criminal Justice and Law Enforcement Area (Policy Department C). http://www.europarl.europa.eu/RegData/etudes/STUD/2014/510000/IPOL_STU(2014)510000_EN.pdf. Last accessed 22 March 2017

Weyembergh A et al (2016) Towards a European Public Prosecutor's Office (Policy Department C). http://www.europarl.europa.eu/RegData/etudes/STUD/2016/571399/IPOL_STU(2016)571399_EN.pdf. Last accessed 22 March 2017

Zeder F (2014) Gegenseitige Anerkennung in Strafsachen, Teil 1: Status Quo. Journal für Strafrecht 3:233–237

Zeder F (2015) Gegenseitige Anerkennung in Strafsachen, Teil 2: Mängel, Lücken, Entwicklungspotential. Journal für Strafrecht 1:25–26

Zwiers M (2011) The European Public Prosecutor's Office: Analysis of a Multilevel Criminal Justice System. Intersentia, Antwerp

Chapter 10
Forum Choice and Judicial Review Under the EPPO's Legislative Framework

Michiel Luchtman

Abstract The EPPO proposal introduces a new authority that will be competent to act on the joint territories of over twenty Member States. The EPPO structure as it is now is a highly decentralized model. Rules of substantive criminal law and criminal procedure have only been partially harmonized, even after the PIF directive and the Roadmap on defence rights will be fully implemented. The choice of the forum therefore affects the powers, safeguards and remedies of all the actors involved (EPPO, defendants, victims, state authorities). To which extent are/should these forum choices be guided by clear legal rules? Which remedies are available, and if so, for whom and at which level? This chapter deals with these issues and aims to provide an oversight and appraisal of the state of play. It analyses the proposed rules on choice of forum, including judicial review, and seeks inspiration from the Swiss system to propose some amendments.

Keywords Choice of forum · Fundamental rights · European Public Prosecutor's Office

Contents

Unless otherwise provided, the provisions referred to in this chapter are those of Council document 13459/16, 28 October 2016.

M. Luchtman (✉)
Utrecht University, Boothstraat 6, 3512 BW Utrecht,
The Netherlands
e-mail: m.luchtman@uu.nl

W. Geelhoed et al. (eds.), *Shifting Perspectives on the European Public Prosecutor's Office*, https://doi.org/10.1007/978-94-6265-216-3_10

10.1 Introduction

The European Union has set itself the goal of creating and maintaining an Area of Freedom, Security and Justice, wherein free movement of persons is to be reconciled with measures to combat crime (Article 3(2) TEU). The proposal for a European Public Prosecutor's Office is by far one of the most innovative means to achieve that goal. It is, however, also quite controversial. According to Article 3 of the proposal, set up as a single body of EU law, the EPPO has the competence to investigate alleged offences on the whole of the territories of the participating Member States. Unlike most other modes of governance of the AFSJ, it is conceived as a single authority of EU law and not a permanent or temporary cooperative structure of two or more autonomous (national or EU) authorities. In this transnational setting, eventually covering over 20 different Member States,[1] choices of forum determine *in which state* the stages of criminal investigation, prosecution and trial and the execution of sanctions will take place.[2] Thus, the choice of the competent court also determines the applicable criminal law. By allowing to move EPPO investigations (or investigatory acts) from one country to another, the proposed structure automatically has implications for the applicable legal regime and, therefore, the rights and duties of all actors involved. Indeed, forum choices determine the scope of offences and sanctions, the competent courts, and the rules of procedure (including investigatory powers, safeguards and defence rights and remedies).[3]

The key issue, therefore, is how it is determined which European Delegated Prosecutor handles the case. It goes without saying that this subject is extremely relevant not only to the EPPO itself, but also for the national authorities, defendants and their lawyers, victims and third parties (e.g. those persons whose telephones are

[1] After the Brexit and reservations in other Member States, this seems to be the most accurate qualification, for the time being.

[2] The focus of this chapter is therefore on the allocation of competences *ratione territorii* (and its review). The determination of the applicable rules also depends on considerations *ratione materiae*, for instance dealing with inextricably linked offences and 'minor' PIF offences. Those issues also trigger many interesting aspects of judicial review (cf. Article 20(5) of the proposal). They are not dealt with in this chapter.

[3] Article 23 of the proposal determines that the European Delegated Prosecutor handling a case may, in accordance with this Regulation and with national law, either undertake the investigation measures and other measures on his/her own or instruct the competent authorities in his/her Member State.

tapped). Because of the strong impact of such choices of forum on the applicable fundamental rights regimes, but also because of the need to provide for mediators in cases of conflicts between the legal orders involved, the issue of judicial review automatically comes into play.

This chapter focusses on the proposed framework for choice of forum and will make an initial assessment of that framework (Sect. 10.2), including judicial review (Sect. 10.3). Its central argument is that legislative guidance and judicial control of forum choices in a common area of transnational criminal justice are a matter of procedural fairness. As I hope to demonstrate in the following, the proposed framework is not sufficiently developed to adequately protect the interests of the many players involved. This is why, before I make my concluding remarks (Sect. 10.5), some attention is paid to one of the most advanced systems of case allocation/forum choice on the European continent, i.e. the Swiss system (Sect. 10.4).

10.2 Choice of Forum in the EPPO Proposal

Ever since the introduction of the proposal in 2013,[4] Member States have gone to great lengths to decentralize the operational and decision making structures of the EPPO. If adopted, EPPO will consist of a college, Permanent Chambers, a European Chief Prosecutor, European Prosecutors and European Delegated Prosecutors. In such a decentralized system, rules on the determination of the responsible unit within the EPPO structure are very important. Article 22(1) holds that where there are reasonable grounds to believe that an offence within the competence of the European Public Prosecutor's Office is being or has been committed, a European Delegated Prosecutor in a Member State which, according to its national law, has jurisdiction over the offence, shall initiate an investigation.

Less clear, however, is what happens where a case is linked to more than one Member State, or connected to other offences in other Member States, for which the EPPO is also competent. In such instances, according to Article 22(4) the case shall, as a rule, be initiated and handled by a European Delegated Prosecutor from the Member State where *the focus of the criminal activity is*. Alternatively, if several connected offences within the competence of the Office have been committed, the case shall be handled by a European Delegated Prosecutor from the Member State *where the bulk of the offences has been committed*. Interesting interpretative questions arise. How is the 'focus' or 'bulk' determined? Do we only count the number of offences? Or do we also take into account such factors as he legal interests involved, the nature and degree of the offences and/or the penalties? Is the focus or bulk of the offences also determined by the status of the alleged offenders (perpetrator, accomplice, etc.)? Do attempt and the separate criminalization of

[4] COM(2013) 534.

preparatory acts play a role? No doubt that it would have been easier to solve these questions, had the ambitions of the proposed PIF directive been set higher. All these questions are related closely to national legal doctrine and will therefore be very much defined according to national conceptions. This could lead to diverging practices along national lines.

The system becomes even more complicated, because the proposal—rightfully, in my opinion—recognizes that deviations from the main rule should be possible and that there is a need for flexibility. A European Delegated Prosecutor of a different Member State than the state where the focus (or the bulk) of the criminal activity (or offences) is and that has jurisdiction for the case may initiate or be instructed by the competent Permanent Chamber to initiate an investigation where a deviation from these starting points ('focus'; 'bulk') is duly justified. But then, it has to take into account the following criteria, in order of priority: (a) the place where the suspect or accused person has his/her habitual residence; (b) the nationality of the suspect or accused person; (c) the place where the main financial damage has occurred. Here, too, it is not quite clear what precisely is meant. Does this wording imply a mandatory ranking order, i.e. does it mean that the European Delegated Prosecutor of the state of the place of residence of the suspect always has priority above the other two? Or does 'taking into account' also leave room for deviations? Are other criteria no longer allowed? The answer to these questions would have to be determined by the legal interests involved, and by their relative weight. In my opinion, the place of residence as such does not always reflect an unambiguous interest. It may protect many different interests, yet also hopelessly fail to protect many others. Why, then, should it be the first in line? For the sake of clarity? But what purpose does it serve, if the results are not considered to be in the interest of justice? In fact, what are the legitimate interests involved? The proposal is silent on this.

It thus becomes clear that the proposed system will need time and practice to develop a workable policy. It also needs a clear structure to deal with the many potential conflicts. This is done through another provision in Article 22(5), stipulating that until a decision to bring a case to trial is taken, the competent Permanent Chamber may, in cases concerning the jurisdiction of more than one Member State and after consultation with the European Prosecutors and/or European Delegated Prosecutors concerned, decide to: (a) reallocate a case to a European Delegated Prosecutor in another Member State; (b) merge or split cases and for each case choose the European Delegated Prosecutor handling it. According to the proposal such decisions must be in the general interest of justice, which is not defined any further, and be taken in accordance with the aforementioned criteria for choosing the European Delegated Prosecutor handling the case.

The provisions here referred to are relevant for the determination of the applicable legal regime in the initial stages of the investigation. They determine where the investigations will be initiated and conducted, without excluding that certain specific acts of investigation may be needed in other Member States or third states.[5]

[5] Provisions for that purpose are found in Articles 26–28 of the proposal.

The proposal goes on in Articles 29 and 30 with rules on the determination of the applicable legal regime for the stages of prosecution and trial. Article 29 provides that when the European Delegated Prosecutor handling the case considers the investigation to be completed, he shall submit a report to the supervising European Prosecutor, containing a summary of the case and a draft decision whether to prosecute before a particular national court. Where applicable, the report of the European Delegated Prosecutor must also provide sufficient reasoning for bringing the case to judgment either at a court of the Member State where he is located, or, in accordance with the aforementioned rules of Article 22(4) at a court of a different Member State which has jurisdiction over the case.

The final decision on the matter is in the hands of the Permanent Chamber. Where more than one Member State has jurisdiction over the case, the Permanent Chamber shall in principle decide to bring the case to prosecution in the Member State of the European Delegated Prosecutor (already) handling the case. However, it may decide to bring the case to prosecution in a different Member State, if there are sufficiently justified grounds to do so, taking into account the aforementioned criteria. It may also, before deciding to bring a case to judgment, decide to join several cases, where investigations have been conducted by different European Delegated Prosecutors against the same person(s) with a view to prosecution of these cases at the court of one Member State which, in accordance with its law, has jurisdiction for each of these cases (Article 30(2/3) of the proposal).

Quite astonishingly, the position of national courts in this framework is rather unclear.[6] In particular, the proposal leaves doubt as to the scope of the judicial powers in the trial stage to assess the forum choices by the Permanent Chamber. This question is relevant because in most national jurisdictions courts will only assess jurisdiction under national law, not the reasonableness of a forum choice. To that extent, therefore, the EPPO structure is certainly a novelty in transnational law enforcement. But what, then, are the practical consequences of it for the courts? Moreover, there is the issue of whether national courts can assess the actions of an EU body. These pertinent issues have been discussed in the framework of judicial review.

10.3 Judicial Review of the Choice of Forum in the EPPO Proposal

10.3.1 The Provisions of the EPPO Proposal

Article 36 of the proposed EPPO regulation has been substantially amended a few times during the course of the negotiations. One element that has been consistent throughout the negotiating process is that the EPPO's legal basis in Article 86(3)

[6] Cf. Weyembergh and Brière 2016, p. 38.

TFEU seems to have been used to turn the EU system of court organization more or less upside down. Meij has already demonstrated that this system is based on a division of labour between the EU and national courts.[7] As it is a body of the EU, judicial review of the legality of EPPO actions would normally fall to the Court of Justice.[8] Yet the EPPO proposal explicitly puts this responsibility at the national level, on the basis of two main arguments. First of all, the EPPO is a body of criminal justice. Its task is to prepare the case for, in principle, a trial before the national courts: 'The [EPPO] is (…) a Union body whose action will mainly be relevant in the national legal orders. It is therefore appropriate to consider the European Public Prosecutor's Office as a national authority for the purpose of the judicial review of its acts of investigation and prosecution.'[9] Second, it is said that the current approach is necessary in order to avoid the Court of Justice becoming even more overburdened than it already is and to prevent national criminal courts having to wait for a long time for an answer to their preliminary references.

As a consequence, the current version of Article 36(1) now reads: 'Procedural acts of the European Public Prosecutor's Office which are intended to produce legal effects vis-à-vis third parties shall be subject to review by the competent national courts in accordance with the requirements and procedures laid down by national law.' A new recital 78 clarifies the goals of the article further: 'This should ensure that the procedural acts of the European Public Prosecutor's Office adopted before the indictment and intended to produce legal effects vis-à-vis third parties (a category which includes the suspect, the victim, and other interested persons whose rights may be adversely affected by such acts) are subject to judicial review by national courts. Procedural acts relating to the choice of the Member State whose courts will be competent to hear the prosecution, which is to be determined on the basis of the criteria laid down in this Regulation, are intended to produce legal effects vis-à-vis third parties and should therefore be subject to judicial review before national courts at the latest at the trial stage.' Forum choices therefore come within the scope of judicial review.

As we have seen already, the system is not intended to be exclusive, nor does it comprise a harmonization of national remedies. In fact, even if remedies have to be available for the acts referred to in Article 36(1), much depends on the specific arrangements of national law. Some guidance is however offered by the Preamble, stating that 'the national procedural rules governing actions for the protection of individual rights granted by Union law must be no less favourable than those governing similar domestic actions (principle of equivalence) and must not render practically impossible or excessively difficult the exercise of rights conferred by Union law (principle of effectiveness).'[10] These are the well-known Rewe requirements.[11]

---

[7] Meij 2014. See also Inghelram 2014, pp. 132–133.

[8] See Inghelram 2011, p. 225 *et seq.*

[9] Cf. COM(2013) 534, p. 7.

[10] Preamble, recital 79.

[11] Case 33/76 *Rewe*, ECLI:EU:C:1976:188.

Moreover, although the EU system of judicial organization has been turned almost upside down, the system of preliminary references (section 2) and direct action before the EU courts (section 3) are taken aboard in the proposal explicitly, but in a rather limited way.[12] Following section 2, *inter alia*, the Court of Justice of the European Union shall have jurisdiction, in accordance with Article 267 TFEU, to give preliminary rulings concerning the validity of procedural acts of the European Public Prosecutor's Office, in so far as such a question of validity is raised before a court or tribunal of a Member State directly on the basis of Union law. The same goes for the interpretation or the validity of provisions of Union law, including the EPPO regulation, which are relevant for the judicial review by the competent national courts of the acts of the EPPO referred to in Article 36(1). The recitals, however, indicate that, although national courts apply a mixture of EU law and national law, they may not refer to the court 'questions on the validity of the procedural acts of the European Public Prosecutor's Office with regard to national procedural law or to national measures transposing Directives, *even if this Regulation refers to them* [my italics].' Finally, direct actions against forum choices are not open to individuals on the basis of section 3. They may, on the contrary, be open to Member States, European Parliament, Council and Commission under the conditions of the relevant provisions of the Articles 263 and 265 TFEU.

10.3.2 Procedural Acts Intended to Produce Legal Effects Vis-À-Vis Third Parties

Key to the proposed Article 36 are the words 'procedural acts intended to produce legal effects vis-à-vis third parties'. Because of the similarity in wording with Article 263 TFEU (actions for annulment), it is informative to consider what we can learn from the CJEU's case law in this regard. Would forum choices come under the scope of Article 263 TFEU? What arguments would play a role here? What can we learn from this with respect to the interpretation of Article 36? What is of particular interest to this chapter are those types of cases where legal proceedings are transferred from one jurisdiction to another, or cases relating to proceedings that have started under one set of rules and are continued under another. In the absence of specific case law on forum choices,[13] these types of cases come closest to the situation at hand.

Already since *IBM/Commission*,[14] the Court of Justice has been quite consistent in its interpretation of Article 263 TFEU and its predecessors. According to its first

[12] Cf. Meij 2014, pp. 112–113.

[13] The issue of choice of forum was explicitly raised, however too late, in Case T-339/04, *France Télecom SA/Commission* and Case T-340/04, *France Télecom SA/Commission*, both dated 8 March 2007, discussed by Rizzuto 2008, pp. 286–297.

[14] Case 60/81, *IBM v. Commission*, [981] ECR 2639, ECLI:EU:C:1981:264.

paragraph, the Court shall review the legality of acts of bodies, offices or agencies of the Union intended to produce legal effects vis-à-vis third parties. The Court has developed a twofold, cumulative criterion for this admissibility condition.[15] Actions for annulment are open against 'any measure the legal effects of which are binding on, and capable of affecting the interests of, the applicant by bringing about a distinct change in his legal position.' A binding legal nature and a distinct change in the legal position of the party concerned are therefore key.

From the case law with respect to OLAF it is apparent that decisions by OLAF to forward information or the case report to national authorities are not considered to be binding in nature and therefore do not produce such effects on the legal position of the party concerned. National authorities are not obliged to commence criminal proceedings or to give other types of follow-up on OLAF reports,[16] even if they are increasingly held to report back on the actions taken on the basis of the OLAF report.[17]

In the specific OLAF setting, decisions to refer a case for further action to national authorities therefore do not open the way to an action for annulment. Under the EPPO regime, however, a referral to the national courts does have binding effects (cf. Article 30(1) proposal). Nonetheless, the availability of an action for annulment under Article 263 TFEU in such cases may still be considered doubtful. Indeed, in the light of the case law of the Court of Justice, there is reason for doubt whether such a referral brings about a distinct change in one's legal position. In *Philip Morris et al.*, an alleged cigarette smuggling scheme with the involvement of a number of tobacco companies, led the Commission to start civil actions, seeking compensation for the financial losses (customs, VAT).[18] Those proceedings were however not instituted before the Community courts, but before a federal US court. Before the General Court of the EU, the applicants sought to annul the Commission decision to bring the case before the US court. After all, can the Commission unilaterally take an affair outside the EU system of court control? No doubt that these decisions come very close to a forum choice as defined in this chapter.

The Court of First Instance nonetheless declared the action inadmissible. It held that '[t]he commencement of legal proceedings is not without legal effects, but those effects concern principally the procedure before the court seised of the case. The commencement of proceedings constitutes an indispensable step for the purpose of obtaining a binding judgment but does not per se determine definitively the obligations of the parties to the case. That determination can result only from the judgment of the court. The decision to commence legal proceedings does not, therefore, in itself alter the legal position in question (…). When it decides to

[15] Schonard 2012 argues that the former criterion is in fact a specification of the latter.

[16] Case T-193/04, *Tillack v. Commission*, [2006] ECR II-3995, ECLI:EU:T:2006:292, paras 69–70.

[17] See, for instance, Article 11 of Regulation 883/2013 concerning investigations conducted by the European Anti-Fraud Office (OLAF), *OJ* EU [2013] L 248/1.

[18] Joined Cases T-377/00, T-379/00, T-380/00, T-260/01 and T-272/01, *Philip Morris International et al. v. Commission* [2003] E.C.R. II-1, ECLI:EU:T:2003:6.

commence proceedings, the Commission does not intend (itself) to change the legal position in question, but merely opens a procedure whose purpose is to achieve a change in that position through a judgment. In principle, therefore, such a decision by the institution cannot be considered to be a decision which is open to challenge.'[19] From this case, one may derive that it is doubtful that a decision to seize a national court in a setting like that of the EPPO would be a reviewable act under Article 263 TFEU.[20] In fact, from this perspective, the decentralized EPPO system may not even be in contradiction with the present EU system of court organization —as far as Article 263 TFEU is concerned—as long as national courts have the unconditional power (duty) to refer to the ECJ where the validity of EPPO acts is concerned.[21]

But there is more. The Court's case law also leaves room for a different approach. Illustrative is *Rendo v. Commission*.[22] The main difference of that case with *Philip Morris et al.* is, in my view that in *Rendo* proceedings had already commenced. The case concerned competition law and also involved certain import and export restrictions, in which the Commission decided to *suspend* competition law proceedings under (then) Article 85 EEC with respect to certain import restrictions and to proceed under Article 169 EEC (infringement proceedings) against the Member State in question. However, this also meant that the procedural rights of the applicants under the Article 85 proceedings were (temporarily) no longer available to the applicants under the infringement proceedings. In the latter type of proceedings, such private applicants have no standing. In light of this, the General Court held: 'Since the Commission's deferral has the effect of interrupting the procedure initiated under [competition law] for a considerable period, consideration of some of the issues raised by the applicants in their complaint (…) has been taken out of that procedure, in which the applicants have specific procedural rights, and left to proceedings under Article 169 of the Treaty in which the applicants have no such rights. Whilst the procedure under Regulation No 17 is held over, the complainants will be deprived of the effective exercise of their procedural rights.'[23] The General Court consequently declared the application admissible.

Rendo presents evidence for that fact that where the parties lose their status as parties to the proceedings, even if temporarily, a remedy at EU level ought to be open. The question is whether this also applies to cases where, like in the EPPO setting, there is no such loss, but 'merely' a change in the parties' position under substantive and procedural law. In my opinion, it does, because the differences

[19] Joined Cases T-377/00, T-379/00, T-380/00, T-260/01 and T-272/01, *Philip Morris International et al. v. Commission* [2003] E.C.R. II-1, ECLI:EU:T:2003:6, para 79.

[20] Cf. Wasmeier 2014, p. 155.

[21] As seen, that is not the case under the present proposal. It makes a distinction along the lines of the origin of the legal source (national or EU).

[22] Case T-16/91, *Rendo a.o. v. Commission*, [1992] ECR Jur. II-2417, ECLI:EU:T:1992:109.

[23] Case T-16/91, *Rendo a.o. v. Commission*, [1992] ECR Jur. II-2417, ECLI:EU:T:1992:109, paras 53–54.

between the Member States' legal systems are still considerable in the EPPO-setting. Such a change is brought about particularly by forum choices that deviate from the envisaged statutory system of allocation.

The foregoing cases present two different types of arguments for why choices of forum must come within the scope of Article 263 TFEU. The first line of reasoning is that it is the seizing of the national criminal court that is binding in nature and will bring about a distinct change in legal position *per se*, regardless of the trial state that was eventually chosen. This line was rejected in *Philip Morris*, but the setting of a criminal trial and its impact on the defendant are of course completely different than the facts of that case. This is also why I am not unsympathetic to this line of reasoning. But there is also a clear disadvantage. Why would only the transfer from the stages of investigation and prosecution to the trial stage bring about such a distinct change? The position of the individual, it seems to me, is already affected much earlier. Many of the defendant's rights, for instance, become applicable in the stages of the investigation; that stage will certainly affect the individual, too.[24] Are those situations then also covered? If not, the cogency of this argument is in my opinion flawed; but if it would include also the earlier stages of the investigation, it would certainly require a mechanism to prevent judicial review from becoming over-inclusive.[25]

The *Rendo*-line of reasoning does not connect to the stages of the proceedings (the seizing of the national court), but to the choice of the applicable substantive and procedural legal regime. If interpreted in a wide fashion, every determination of the applicable legal regime would bring about a distinct change in legal position, precisely because of the differences within the decentralized EPPO-structure. Yet in a more restrictive way, it would entail that only deviations from the statutory rules in the EPPO proposal bring about such a change.[26] In my opinion, the restrictive line needs to be accepted at any rate and, personally, I am of the opinion that much is to be said for also embracing the wider interpretation, at the least from the stage of prosecution. It would be contrary to fundamental principles of criminal justice, in particular the principle of equality of arms, to accept that one party in the criminal proceedings should be awarded uncontrolled and therefore unfettered discretion to

[24] One only needs to think of the applicability of the procedural safeguards of the Charter that are connected to the presence of a criminal charge (particularly Articles 47 and 48 CFR), for instance the right of access to a lawyer or the privilege against self-incrimination. Those rights start to apply once, in the words of the European Court of Human Rights, a person is 'substantially affected'.

[25] In my opinion, judicial review in the early stages of investigation could be useful in specific cases, for instance to avoid a clear *bis in idem* situation (Article 50 CFR).

[26] Cf. for instance the clarifications to a previous version of Article 36, Council document 11350/1/16 REV 1 of 28 July 2016, providing that (only) '[d]ecisions of the European Public Prosecutor's Office to *reallocate* the case to a European Delegated Prosecutor in another Member State and decisions of the European Public Prosecutor's Office to bring the case to prosecution in *a different Member State* may be subject to judicial review before the national courts, by way of an action or a plea in objection [my italics, ML].'

choose by which set of rules, out of—say—25, it wishes to conduct the proceedings.[27] Therefore, it is a significant improvement that it is now explicitly clarified in the aforementioned Recital 78 that forum choices do come under the scope of Article 36, implying that remedies must be available at the national level.

I assume that this clarification is also of importance for the future interpretation of Article 36. The notion of 'procedural acts intended to produce legal effects vis-à-vis third parties' appears to be an autonomous concept of EU law, despite the references to national law in the following text. After all, though there are some references to national law, none of those references concerns 'the notion of procedural acts intended to produce legal effects vis-à-vis third parties.' It then follows from the need for a uniform application of EU law, and from the principle of equality, that that notion is an autonomous concepts of EU law and to be interpreted uniformly throughout the territory of the European Union.[28] Therefore, the EPPO would apply directly applicable EU law, thus conferring on the CJEU not only the power to interpret the relevant provisions, but also to assess the validity of a forum choice, when interrogated on such issues by a national court.

However, the clarification does not solve all issues. A pertinent question is, for example, whether, in line with *Rendo*, the 'choice of the Member State' only constitutes a reviewable act where the determination of the handling Delegated Prosecutor and hence the relevant legal order deviates from the 'default position' determined by the focus of the criminal activity or the bulk of the offences,[29] or whether it also includes the determination of the 'default forum'. Furthermore, are the remedies available only in the stages of prosecution and trial, or should forum choices in the stages of investigation also be subjected to review? The latter situations are not covered by Recital 78. Furthermore, does review mean that it is limited to review upon request of the parties involved in the proceedings or does it also include an *ex officio* review? What happens when a national court rejects a forum choice? Are only the courts where proceedings are brought competent, or is any court competent if it is capable of exercising jurisdiction according to the law of the Member State in question? How can contradictory decisions by different national courts be prevented (for instance when cases are split as meant in Article 22(5) of the proposal)? These questions still need an answer which the current proposal does not provide. It refers back to national law and national procedural law. The outcome can be no other than that national courts will develop their own approaches to these problems, even if preliminary references are possible.

---

[27] See Luchtman and Vervaele 2014.

[28] Support for this approach may be found in CJEU 24 May 2016, Case C 108/16 PPU, *Pawel Dworzecki*, ECLI:EU:C:2016:346, paras 28–30.

[29] See *supra* Sect. 10.3.1.

10.3.3 Appraisal of the Proposal and Provisional Findings

Though it is a great improvement that (some) forum choices now explicitly come under the scope of Article 36, many issues remain open. I believe that the current set-up of the judicial control of the EPPO structure still constitutes a substantial risk, as long as there are no additional guidelines that guide the interaction between the EU and national courts involved. As said, the existing system of EU Court organization is turned upside down. This is done on the basis of Article 86(3) TFEU, which provides that the EPPO regulations shall determine the general rules applicable to the European Public Prosecutor's Office, the conditions governing the performance of its functions, the rules of procedure applicable to its activities, as well as those governing the admissibility of evidence, and the rules applicable to the judicial review of procedural measures taken by it in the performance of its functions. We have seen the reasons for this.[30] However, doubt remains as to whether these reasons constitute a satisfactory explanation to justify such a marked departure from the system provided for by the Treaties. The EPPO structure will produce, by its very definition, decisions that cannot always be attributed to a single legal order. Forum choices are clearly within this category, particularly because the proposed system does not exclude contradictory national decisions. Examples of such cases may arise where cases against a single (or multiple) defendant(s) are split, and trials take place in different Member States. It is also unclear to which extent remedies are open, e.g. for victims, in legal orders other than the actual trial state. Moreover, the consequences of a decision by a national court that decides that it is not the proper forum in light of the EPPO criteria, are left untouched. Therefore, forum choices being decisions of an EU body, it is unclear why —contrary to *Foto Frost* and the arguments put forward in it—judicial review of those types of decisions is put in the hands of the national courts or, alternatively, why the EPPO system does not include a system of mutual recognition of such decisions and an enhanced system of preliminary references. The proposed system appears to be almost a guarantee for forum shopping and contradictory judicial decisions.

But also regardless of whether legal review is to be offered directly by the EU courts, or by the national courts under European guidance, it is clear that the proposal needs much more clarification on many issues. It will for instance be necessary to reflect further on the consequences of national judicial decisions in the transnational EPPO setting, e.g. through mutual recognition.[31] And we need clear and workable criteria and those criteria need to be clearly linked to legitimate interests. The proposed system works with the rebuttable presumptions of Article 22(1) of the proposal ('focus of the criminal activity', resp. 'bulk of the offences'). Both of these presumptions, and the criteria for deviating from it, are vague or do not identify which interests they protect. This is why it is interesting to refer to the

---

[30] *Supra* Sect. 10.3.1.

[31] Such provisions are for instance included in the project of the University of Luxembourg on the Model Rules for the Procedure of the EPPO, particularly Rule 7 (dealing with judicial authorizations rather than review), http://www.eppo-project.eu/ Last accessed 25 August 2016.

Swiss system of intercantonal forum choices (*Gerichtsstandbestimmung*) a source of inspiration.

10.4 A Different Perspective: The Swiss Experience[32]

Like in the European Union, the Swiss territory is viewed as a single area, where law enforcement is the responsibility of authorities which, in principle, are bound by the territory of their component canton. Intercantonal cases therefore require a lot of mutual coordination. The Swiss scheme of *Gerichtsstandbestimmung* assumes a statutory assignment of cases across the cantons, which—within the federal framework—can themselves organise their cantonal legal systems. The scheme is binding on the police, the public prosecutor and the judiciary.[33] Although the situation in the EU is similar to the one in Switzerland, it is also much more complex. While substantive and, more recently, procedural federal criminal law have been harmonised in Switzerland, such harmonisation has only been achieved to a limited extent in the European Union. At first sight, this fundamental difference in the substantive and procedural law framework hampers a comparison between the two legal orders. However, as until recently procedural criminal law was not harmonized in Switzerland, inter-cantonal differences in criminal procedure used to be a factor of relevance in case allocation. Moreover, the relatively autonomous position of the Swiss cantons in relation to the administration of criminal justice forced the federal legislator to provide for a framework that would avoid positive and negative conflicts of jurisdiction.[34]

With respect to the 'inter-cantonal forum choice', Swiss law therefore includes statutory choice of forum rules which pertain to a variety of situations.[35] They cover the relatively simple situation in which there is one suspect and one offence,[36] the situation in which there is one offence and multiple suspects,[37] the situation in which one suspect has committed multiple offences[38] and, finally, the situation in which multiple suspects have committed multiple offences.[39] The legal system is

[32] This section is to a large extent an update of Luchtman 2011, pp. 99–100.

[33] Articles 340–345 of the Swiss Penal Code (*Strafgesetzbuch*/CH-StGB). Once the Federal Code of Criminal Procedure of 5 October 2007 (*Schweizerische Strafprozessordnung*/CH-StPO, *BBl.* 2007, 6977) enters into force, these articles shall be replaced by Articles 29–41 CH-StPO.

[34] It is remarkable that the relevant rules, until recently, were laid down in the federal Penal Code (*Strafgesetzbuch*/CH-StGB). As such, the issue is more a matter for procedural law. This is explained by the fact that a system of case allocation was considered to be essential for the implementation of substantive federal criminal law; see Schweri and Bänziger 2004, p. 2.

[35] See also Schweri and Bänziger 2004.

[36] Articles 340–342 CH-StGB, replaced by Articles 31–32 CH-StPO.

[37] Article 343 StGB, replaced by Article 33 CH-StPO.

[38] Article 344 StGB, replaced by Article 34 CH-StPO.

[39] In those situations, both Articles 33–34 StPO may be used, see further Waiblinger 1943, p. 81.

designed for related criminal cases preferably to be tried before a single court, even if multiple courts from different cantons would have jurisdiction.[40]

As it would be virtually impossible to cover all possible scenarios regarding the choice of forum by legislation, the legal system explicitly allows for deviations.[41] This is not considered to be in violation of the constitution, i.e. the concept of the *verfassungmässige Richter*, nor is it considered to violate Article 6 ECHR. On the contrary, in situations like these, the right to the *verfassungmässige Richter* protects suspects against arbitrary application of the law.[42] In the very abundant case law and practical experience, which are now codified in the federal *Strafprozessordnung*, it is clear that such deviations from the statutory scheme are subject to strict limitations and are reviewable by the courts, specifically the federal *Bundesstrafgericht*. One obvious limitation is that the authorities (courts and prosecutors) cannot themselves establish their territorial jurisdiction; they must already have jurisdiction under the law.[43] Moreover, deviations from the statutory scheme are only possible if there are compelling reasons (*triftige Gründe*) which 'automatically come into play' (*gebieterisch aufdrängen*).[44] This power to deviate from the statutory rules may therefore only be exercised if a strict application of the statutory rules would be contrary to the purpose of that law.[45] The *Bundesstrafgericht* held that it is not enough to only take considerations of prosecutorial efficiency into account,[46] and that deviations from the statutory rules must always take account of:

1. the interests of the place where most of the damaging effects of criminal conduct were felt;
2. those of the courts, which must be put in the position to obtain, as far as possible, a complete overview of both the person of the accused and his actions;
3. those of the suspect (and his counsel) to effectively defend himself; and we may possibly add the victim to this list;
4. and those of a speedy and efficient administration of justice.[47]

---

[40] In Swiss legal doctrine and case law, this is called the *Vereinigungsprinzip*; cf. BGE 95 IV 32 (35); Article 29 CH-StPO; Schweri and Bänziger 2004, p. 6.

[41] See for instance Articles 262 and 263 of the *Bundesgesetz über die Strafrechtspflege*/BStP, meanwhile replaced by Article 38 CH-StPO.

[42] Standard case law, cf. BGE 105 Ia 172 (175) and BGE 119 IV 102.

[43] Standard case law, cf. BGE 120 IV 280 and BGE 119 IV 250 (252–253).

[44] Standard case law, cf. Bundestrafgericht 30 March 2009, BG.2008.22 and BGE 119 IV 250. See also Article 38 CH-StPO.

[45] Standard case law, cf. Bundesstrafgericht 8 January 2009, no. BG.2008.26 and BGE 123 IV 23 (25–26).

[46] See also Schweri and Bänziger 2004, p. 148; Guidon and Bänziger 2007.

[47] Cf. Bundesstrafgericht, 13 January 2015, no. BG.2014.34; Bundestrafgericht 9 October 2013, BG.2013.20; Bundesstrafgericht, 21 October 2004, no. BK_G 127/04. Literally: 'Wird vom gesetzlichen Gerichtsstand abgewichen, sollten jedoch folgende Bedingungen erfüllt sein: Die Tat sollte dort verfolgt werden, wo das Rechtsgut verletzt wurde; der Richter sollte sich ein möglichst vollständiges Bild von Tat und Tater machen können; der Beschuldigte sollte sich am Ort der Verfolgung leicht verteidigen können; das Verfahren sollte wirtschaftlich sein.'.

The system of statutory assumptions—which are, admittedly, much more refined than in the EU setting—and the room for deviations under which the prosecution has to demonstrate, also before the courts, that their forum choice is well-balanced in light of the clearly defined interests at stake, also offers inspiration to the EU. In this system, the role of the judiciary is not to 'second guess' the decisions of the prosecutors, but to check for their reasonableness. Obviously, the interests that are defined often point in completely different directions. But they do force the prosecution authorities to issue a reasoned opinion on which the forum state is, in their minds, the best placed for prosecution and trial.

10.5 Conclusions

This chapter provides an analysis and appraisal of the proposed provisions on choice of forum, including judicial review, in the proposal to set up an EPPO. The draft provisions on these issues have been changed many times during the negotiations. My starting point was that legislation on and judicial control of forum choices are a matter of procedural fairness. The EPPO structure is unique to the extent that we are dealing with a single authority with the competence to operate under potentially 25 different sets of criminal law and criminal procedure. In that setting, statutory rules and judicial control on forum choices are an issue of the utmost importance. It is good that forum choices—after initial lack of clarity on the matter—are now taken within the scope of Article 36. As the concept of 'procedural acts intended to produce legal effects vis-à-vis third parties' is laid down in directly applicable Union law, the Court of Justice will have full interpretative powers on this concept and I assume it will also have the power to assess the validity of these decisions through preliminary references. Certainly, this will have important organizational consequences for that court in order to guarantee trials at the national level within a reasonable time.

Nonetheless, I conclude that the proposed system leaves much to be desired for, not only because the criteria are vague and seem to cover divergent interests, but also because comprehensive judicial review is still not guaranteed under the proposal. The proposal introduces a significant deviation from the existing EU court system without apparently paying attention to the reasons justifying that system, including the wish to avoid contradictory rulings by national courts and forum shopping. It is inevitable in the EPPO setting, that judicial oversight has both a vertical and a horizontal dimension. Comprehensive judicial oversight implies that the tasks and responsibilities of national courts are clearly demarcated *vis-à-vis* their foreign colleagues, as well as between the national and EU courts. It also needs to deal with the consequences of the decisions by one court for another. A failure to do so can only result in forum shopping, unnecessary duplication of work or even contradictory decisions on the same case.

Above, I presented the Swiss system as a source of inspiration. In my opinion, there are three lessons to be learned from it, even though the AFSJ does not even come close to the level of harmonization achieved by the Swiss federal legislator. First of all, it turns out that even one of the most advanced European systems of forum choices recognizes that a full statutory system is a utopia. The EPPO legislator rightly reached the same conclusion. Second, I consider it wise to refine the system of statutory assumptions and to develop different default positions for different types of cases (one offender, one offence; one offender, multiple offences; multiple offenders, one offence; multiple offenders, multiple offences).[48] Finally, and most importantly, forum choices that deviate from the statutory assumptions should be possible only when it can be demonstrated by the EPPO that such deviations serve a number of clearly defined legitimate interests better than the statutory system does. The onus is on the prosecution. The task of the courts—national and/or European—is to assess the reasonableness of that decision, *ex officio* or upon request of the defendant.

References

Guidon P, Bänziger F (2007) Die aktuelle Rechtsprechung des Bundesstrafgerichts zum interkantonalen Gerichtsstand in Strafsachen. Jusletter May 2007

Inghelram JFH (2011) Legal and institutional aspects of the European Anti-Fraud Office (OLAF). Europa Law Publishers, Groningen

Inghelram JFH (2014) Search and seizure measures and their review. In: Erkelens LH, Meij AWH, Pawlik M (eds) The European Public Prosecutor's Office: An Extended Arm or a Two-Headed Dragon? TMC Asser Press, The Hague

Luchtman MJJP (2011) Choice of Forum in an Area of Freedom, Security and Justice. Utrecht Law Review, pp 74–101

Luchtman M, Vervaele J (2014) European Agencies for Criminal Justice and Shared Enforcement (Eurojust and the European Public Prosecutor's Office). Utrecht Law Review, pp 132–150

Meij AWH (2014) Some explorations into the EPPO's administrative structure and judicial review. In: Erkelens LH, Meij AWH, Pawlik M (eds) The European Public Prosecutor's Office: An Extended Arm or a Two-Headed Dragon? TMC Asser Press, The Hague

Rizzuto F (2008) Parallel Competence and the Power of the EC Commission under Regulation 1/2003 According to the Court of First Instance. European Competition Law Review, pp 286–297

Schonard P (2012) Judicial Review of EU Acts Affecting Criminal Proceedings. European Criminal Law Review, pp 62–77

Schweri E, Bänziger F (2004) Interkantonale Gerichtsstandsbestimmung in Strafsachen. Stämpfli Verlag, Bern

Waiblinger M (1943) Die Bestimmung des Gerichtsstandes bei Mehrheit von strafbaren Handlungen oder von Beteiligten. ZStr 57

Wasmeier M (2014) The Choice of Forum by the European Public Prosecutor. In: Erkelens LH, Meij AWH, Pawlik M (eds) The European Public Prosecutor's Office: An Extended Arm or a Two-Headed Dragon? TMC Asser Press, The Hague

Weyembergh A, Brière C (2016) Towards a European Public Prosecutor's Office – Study for the LIBE Committee. European Parliament, Brussels

[48] *Supra* Sect. 10.4. To a certain extent the EPPO proposal already does this (albeit in a very modest way), introducing the criterion of the 'bulk of the offences'.

Chapter 11
Relations Between the EPPO and Eurojust—Still a Privileged Partnership?

Anne Weyembergh and Chloé Brière

Abstract Once it is established, the EPPO will not operate as an isolated actor, but it will integrate itself in the already existing network of EU agencies and bodies. In this context, its relations with Eurojust are of fundamental importance. Both actors are active in the field of judicial cooperation in criminal matters, and the Treaty itself (Article 86 TFEU) provides for a special link between them. Provisions organising their relationship can be found in the EPPO's and Eurojust's proposals for regulations, which are still under negotiation. The present chapter analyses the modalities of their cooperation, as they are currently envisaged, with the aim to assess whether the two actors are privileged partners. This analysis is divided in three steps: it examines firstly their institutional relationship; secondly their management and administrative links and finally their operational cooperation. The analysis reveals that it is at the moment difficult to consider Eurojust as the EPPO's privileged partner. A better clarification of their bilateral relations should be included in the draft proposals, and Eurojust's expertise should be better taken into consideration. A further clarification of the distribution of competences between the EPPO, Eurojust and OLAF is also advisable, especially to avoid unnecessary tensions between the different actors.

Keywords European Public Prosecutor's Office · Eurojust · OLAF · Interagency cooperation · Administrative and management links · Exchange of information · Operational cooperation

A. Weyembergh (✉)
Institute of European Studies and European Criminal Law Academic Network (ECLAN), Université Libre de Bruxelles, avenue F.D. Roosevelt 50, 1050 Brussels, Belgium
e-mail: aweyembe@ulb.ac.be

C. Brière
Institute of European Studies, Université Libre de Bruxelles, avenue F.D. Roosevelt 50, 1050 Brussels, Belgium
e-mail: cbriere@ulb.ac.be

W. Geelhoed et al. (eds.), *Shifting Perspectives on the European Public Prosecutor's Office*, https://doi.org/10.1007/978-94-6265-216-3_11

Contents

11.1 Introduction

Several agencies and bodies coexist within the Area of Freedom, Security and Justice (AFSJ), and some are active in the protection of the Union's financial interests. The establishment of the European Public Prosecutor's Office (EPPO) will clearly impact the current landscape, including the other EU agencies and bodies competent in this field. The importance of inserting the EPPO in the AFSJ in a coherent and efficient way has been and must be stressed. As M. Coninsx rightly pointed out, the EPPO "should not be conceived as an isolated actor, but rather seen in the context of part of a multilevel interaction".[1] If the purpose of its establishment is to ensure an efficient fight against offences affecting the Union's financial interests, then complementarity, consistency and smooth and close cooperation between all EU agencies/bodies will be crucial. However the integration of the EPPO's work within the existing system of institutions, in particular with Eurojust, is one of the main difficulties of its establishment.[2]

The relations between the EPPO and Eurojust are indeed of fundamental importance.[3] Not only the two actors are both active in the field of judicial cooperation in criminal matters, but their special link has also been provided for in the Treaty itself, via the final wording of Article 86(1) TFEU referring to the establishment of an EPPO "from Eurojust". As it is well known, the exact meaning of such expression is far from clear and its concretisation has been extensively debated.[4] Nevertheless, it implies that the two entities shall—at the very minimum—form

[1] Coninsx 2014, p. 28.

[2] Commission staff working document, Impact assessment accompanying the proposal for a Council Regulation on the establishment of the European Public Prosecutor's Office, SWD (2013) 274 final, 17 March 2013, p. 5.

[3] The importance of their relations has been highlighted in two research papers written for the LIBE Committee of the European Parliament: see Weyembergh et al. 2014 and Weyembergh and Brière 2016.

[4] See among others, Conclusions of the Strategic seminar organised by Eurojust and the Belgian Presidency (Bruges, 20–22 Sept. 2010), "Eurojust and the Lisbon Treaty, towards more effective action?", Council Doc. No. 17625/10 REV 1, 9 Dec. 2010; Eurojust/ERA conference "10 years of Eurojust. Operational achievements and future challenges", The Hague, 12 and 13 Nov. 2012,

a privileged partnership. The present chapter intends to analyse the modalities of the cooperation relationship between the EPPO and Eurojust, as they are currently envisaged in the EPPO draft Regulation, with the aim to assess whether they are indeed privileged partners.

The moment is particularly timely to address the issue of their cooperation. Concerning the EPPO, a Commission Proposal for a Council Regulation on the establishment of the European Public Prosecutor's Office[5] was finally published on the 17 July 2013, after years of discussions and consultations. The Commission also published the same day the proposal for a Regulation on the European Union Agency for Criminal Justice Cooperation (Eurojust).[6] Both proposals are at the moment of writing still under negotiations. However, whereas the negotiations on Eurojust Regulation have somehow been paused for more than a year,[7] those on the EPPO have been intensified more and more. The objective was indeed to adopt a general approach on the full text by the end of 2016.[8] Considering that the negotiations of the provision in the draft Eurojust Regulation are paused while awaiting progress on the draft EPPO Regulation, the discussion will focus on the content of Article 57 of the draft EPPO Regulation. References to the current version of the EPPO proposal refer to the latest public version of the draft Regulation, dated of 28 October 2016.[9]

The issue of their bilateral cooperation has been explicitly addressed by the two proposals put forward by the Commission. In each of these drafts, a specific provision, whose wording is not yet final, is devoted to their bilateral relations: Article 57 of the draft Regulation for the establishment of the EPPO,[10] on the one hand, and Article 41 of the draft Eurojust Regulation,[11] on the other hand. In addition, the principle of sincere cooperation, enshrined in Article 4 TEU, will apply to their relations. By virtue of this principle, the relevant Union bodies, including Eurojust, "should actively support the investigations and prosecutions of the EPPO, as well as cooperate with it to the fullest extent possible, from the moment a suspected offence

(Footnote 4 continued)

Council document 8862/13, 26 April 2013, pp. 15 and 16; Hamran and Szabova 2013, particularly pp. 46 and ff.

5 COM(2013) 534 final.

6 EPPO Commission Proposal 2013.

7 No further development since the adoption of a partial General Approach in February 2015 (Council, Proposal for a Regulation of the European Parliament and the Council on the European Union Agency for Criminal Justice Cooperation (Eurojust)—General Approach, Council doc. no. 6643/15, 27 Feb. 2015). See especially para 10, p. 3.

8 EPPO Council Proposal 2016. At the time of writing the latest version of the proposal dated of 28 October 2016.

9 Ibidem.

10 *Supra* note 6.

11 Commission, Proposal for a Regulation of the European Parliament and the Council on the European Union Agency for Criminal Justice Cooperation (Eurojust), COM (2013) 535 final, 17 July 2013.

is reported to the EPPO until it determines whether to prosecute or otherwise dispose of the case" (current text, Preamble, Recital 59).

The wording of this provision in the Commission's proposal was particularly representative of the special and privileged link between the two agencies. In contrast with its relationship with Europol and OLAF, the initial EPPO proposal dealt rather extensively with the cooperation with Eurojust, as evidenced by the number of references to each other in the respective proposals. Eurojust was also the only EU agency benefiting from a provision dealing exclusively with its cooperation with the EPPO. The EPPO's relations with other EU agencies/bodies, such as Europol or OLAF, were envisaged in a catch-all and far less detailed provision (Article 58—Relations with Union institutions, agencies and other bodies). This differentiated treatment was justified in the explanatory memorandum accompanying the proposal, by the fact that "special rules apply to the relationship of the EPPO with Eurojust given the special links that tie them together in the area of operational activities, administration and management".[12]

However, the content of the regulation has evolved substantially in the course of the negotiations. The provisions organising the EPPO's relations with its partners do not depart from this trend. The relations between the EPPO and Eurojust are no longer the only ones being the object of a specific provision, and it can be questioned whether according to the currently available text of the Regulation Eurojust can still be considered to the EPPO's privileged partner. New provisions dealing with the relations between the EPPO and OLAF and between the EPPO and Europol have indeed been inserted, and they envisage with a certain degree of detail the modalities of their bilateral cooperation. Furthermore, the provision dealing with the relations between the EPPO and Eurojust has been substantially amended.

In a first part, their relationship will be analysed from a broad perspective, i.e. addressing their institutional relationship (Sect. 11.2). Their administrative and management links will then be examined (Sect. 11.3). Finally, their operational cooperation, including the exchange of information between the two bodies, will be addressed (Sect. 11.4).

11.2 General Overview of the EPPO-Eurojust Relations

From an institutional point of view, three main scenarios have been envisaged when designing the structural relations between EPPO and Eurojust.[13] The first option saw the EPPO as a separate and autonomous entity, with its own budget, distinct

[12] Commission, Explanatory memorandum, in Proposal for a Regulation on the establishment of the EPPO, COM (2013) 534 final, 17 July 2013, 63 pages, p. 8.

[13] In this regard, see for instance Conclusions of the Strategic seminar organised by Eurojust and the Belgian Presidency (Bruges, 20–22 September 2010), 'Eurojust and the Lisbon Treaty, towards more effective action?", Council Doc. No. 17625/10 REV 1, 9 Dec. 2010, especially workshop 6, pp. 22 ff. See also Ligeti and Weyembergh 2015; see also White 2012, p. 73.

from Eurojust.[14] Under the second option, the EPPO would have been a part of Eurojust, e.g. a specialised unit within Eurojust,[15] and they would have thus shared one budget. In the third option, the EPPO and Eurojust would have been two separate entities, with common services (for instance IT services). From the very beginning, i.e. the publication of the Commission's proposal, the choice has been made in favour of creating the EPPO as an independent body distinct from Eurojust, and thus disregarding the second option. The current version of the EPPO regulation reveals that the choice has been further reinforced in favour of the first option. In other words, EPPO and Eurojust remain separate and independent entities, with distinct budgets, but that will cooperate with each other.[16]

The first paragraph of Article 57 of the draft EPPO regulation organises the general framework of their cooperation. It has been modified during the negotiations and now reads: "The European Public Prosecutor's Office shall establish and maintain a close relationship with Eurojust based on mutual cooperation *within their respective mandates* and the development of operational, administrative and management links between them as defined below" (emphasis added). The provision does no longer refer to a special relationship, but only to a close one. This new formulation constitutes a first sign that the relations between the EPPO and Eurojust are no longer to be envisaged as being qualitatively different from those with other EU agencies/bodies. The text provides indeed that the EPPO should also establish and maintain a close relationship with OLAF (Article 57a(1)) and Europol (Article 58(1)). The insertion of a reference to their respective mandates, which is also present in the provision on EPPO OLAF relations, must be particularly welcomed. This clarification is indeed essential in order to prevent and avoid overlaps and potential competition and tensions between the two bodies.[17]

This provision has been further complemented by a clause foreseeing that the European Chief Prosecutor and the President of Eurojust shall meet on a regular basis to discuss issues of common concern (Article 57(1)). This mirrors an informal practice already existing between for instance the Director of Europol and the President of Eurojust; these meetings are perceived as a way to facilitate cooperation between EU agencies.[18] One should note that Eurojust is the only agency for which such regular meetings are envisaged, and it can be explained notably by the fact that the two entities are supposed to develop administrative and management links between each other.

[14] Many argued that this is the most straightforward solution in terms of accountability and internal organisation. It would have the further advantage that since the two entities (EPPO and Eurojust) would be kept completely separate it would be clear that there is one unit for judicial cooperation in general whereas the other one is for investigating and prosecuting EU fraud.

[15] In this case the EPPO would be located on Eurojust's premises in order to be able to use Eurojust's facilities, but it would function independently from Eurojust.

[16] This independence between the two has been clearly confirmed by Commissioner Jourova at the JHA Council meeting of 14 October 2016.

[17] See Weyembergh et al. 2014, p. 59.

[18] Ibid., p. 17.

11.3 Administrative and Management Links Between the EPPO and Eurojust

The administrative and management links are covered in the last paragraph of Article 57 of the draft EPPO Regulation. The text of the paragraph seems to have been the object of intense negotiations. This provision remained unchanged during most of the time and listed the services to be provided by Eurojust to the EPPO (which include technical support, security, information technology, financial management, and 'any other services of common interest') and left the details to an agreement to be concluded between the two bodies.

However, it has been changed at a later stage of the negotiations. This becomes clear in the version of that provision of July 2016[19] and its wording at that time. Indeed, whereas the Commission's proposal stipulated that "Eurojust ***shall*** provide the following services", the version of July 2016 provided that "Eurojust ***may/shall*** provide **[any of]** the following services". Furthermore, the text referred to a suggestion made by France, and supported by Germany and Luxembourg, that Eurojust "shall provide services of common interest to the EPPO", and that the provision shall continue in providing "the details of this arrangement shall be regulated by an agreement" without listing them explicitly.

The most recent version of the text, i.e. of 28 October 2016 at the time of writing, seems almost final, and indicates which compromise has been reached within the Council. Article 57(5) now reads: "The EPPO may rely on the support and resources of the administration of Eurojust. To this end, Eurojust may provide services of common interest to the EPPO. The details shall be regulated by an arrangement". The provision is thus far less detailed than the one contained in the Commission's proposal, and it is drafted in vague terms. The use of the word "may" as well as the choice to leave the details to the conclusion of a posterior administrative arrangement, can be interpreted as signs of the sensitivity of the issues at stake, which are linked to two very politically delicate points, which will impact the support that Eurojust will furnish to the EPPO.

The first point relates to the localisation of the seat of the EPPO, which is one of the most sensitive political questions. The Commission's proposal (Preamble, recital 49) simply referred to the decision adopted by the Heads of State and Government level the 13th December 2003, in which they determined that the seat of the EPPO would be Luxembourg.[20] Such reference was present in the text until

[19] Council, Proposal for a Regulation on the establishment of the EPPO—Consolidated text: update of the provisional version, 28 July 2016, Council Doc. No. 11350/1/16 REV 1.

[20] On this issue see also the Presidency Conclusions, European Council of Laeken, 14 and 15 December 2001, para 57, referring to the Decision 67/446/EEC of 8 April 1965 of the representatives of the Governments of the Member States on the provisional location of certain institutions and departments of the European Communities (notably Article 3).

December 2016 (Preamble, recital 112, now deleted).[21] Should the agreement of 2003 apply, establishing the EPPO in Luxembourg would have important consequences, particularly endangering the idea of the EPPO being supported by Eurojust in its daily functioning.[22] A location close to Eurojust would be better suited to guarantee such an objective, since it would be a more efficient and less expensive solution. However, and in spite of the huge impact the decision on the EPPO's seat will have in this regard, the final decision will most probably only be taken at the very end of the negotiations on the EPPO Regulation. This relative uncertainty[23] might explain the success of the proposal made by France, and supported by Germany and Luxembourg not to list the forms of support Eurojust would bring to the EPPO, thereby ensuring some flexibility to the choice of the EPPO's seat. In this regard, the European Parliament stated in its 2016 Resolution that it "believes that it would best for the EPPO and Eurojust to operate in the same location if the cooperation and information exchange between them is to operate efficiently".[24]

The second issue relates to the numerous references in several documents, including in the Commission's proposal, to the fact that the envisaged EPPO will come at "zero cost". Whereas this declaration sought to reassure Member States in a time of financial crisis, no one really believed that the creation of such an EU body would require no additional EU expenses. The changes in the EPPO's structure introduced by the Council will also impact the cost of establishing the EPPO,[25] but the idea remains nonetheless to limit the expenses as much as possible and to rationalise available resources.[26] According to the Commission, these benefits include the dissuasive effect of establishing an EPPO, which is expected to significantly reduce impunity of EU fraudsters, and in terms of recovery of defrauded

[21] The version of the text we refer to is Council Doc. No. 15 200/16 of 2 December 2016, in which the former recital 112 has been deleted. The removed recital read as follows: "the Representatives of the Member States, meeting at Head of State or Government level in Brussels on 13 December 2003 have determined the seat of the European Public Prosecutor's Office."

[22] Coninsx 2014, p. 38.

[23] However, even if the location of the EPPO's seat seems to be the one agreed upon in 2003, "nothing could be considered to have been agreed before an overall agreement on the text was reached" (Press release, JHA Council meeting of 9 and 10 June 2016, p. 5).

[24] European Parliament, Resolution of 5 Oct. 2016 on the EPPO and Eurojust (P8_TA(2016) 0376), para 10.

[25] Whereas at the decentralised level the European Delegated Prosecutors have been maintained, new layers have been added to the "central" level (Article 7(3)). The central office now consists of the European Chief Prosecutor, his/her deputies, the College, the Permanent Chambers, and the European Prosecutors (one per Member State).

[26] See for an updated costs/benefits analysis the presentation by Commissioner V. Jourova in front of the JHA Council on 14 October 2016. Video available at: http://video.consilium.europa.eu/en/webcast/6917239d-893d-40ad-b2a2-339306dcb322.

EU money that would come back to the EU budget.[27] In that regard, and more fundamentally, one should pay particular attention to the new structure at the EPPO's central level, which will cost more than the initially envisaged model, and will imply important fixed costs. Despite the Commission's belief, one may doubt whether such an increase of costs will be compensated by the decreased number of cases with which it will deal given EPPO's shared competence with national authorities. Moreover, the search for savings will necessarily impact interagency relations in the field of the protection of the Union's financial interests, and notably the relations between the EPPO and Eurojust. Indeed, the more restraints are placed on the EU budget, the more important reliance on Eurojust's resources becomes. Eurojust rightly fears that its other tasks will suffer if no extra money is devoted to its supporting missions to the EPPO. M. Coninsx underlined in May 2016 before the LIBE committee that there is a need to join forces, and that Eurojust is keen on cooperating with the EPPO. However, as she stated, in the event that new tasks are assigned to Eurojust, then corresponding resources must also be allocated in order to avoid prejudice to the rest of Eurojust's work.[28] In this regard, it must be noted that non-participating Member States have already opposed the idea of a detrimental effect to the other EU agencies and bodies as a consequence of the establishment of the EPPO.[29] Should Eurojust's resources (human or financial) be transferred to the EPPO, this would be highly detrimental for the EU area of criminal justice as a whole. Eurojust's expertise does not only cover PIF crimes, but includes other forms of serious crime (including other forms of financial crime),[30] for which its services will continue to be required in cross-border cases. Moreover, the involvement of Eurojust in PIF cases will continue to be relevant in cases concerning non-participating Member States. The costs linked to these activities will still have to be covered.[31]

In definitive, the current version of the text seems to grant to both entities a large margin of flexibility, potentially explained by the sensitivity of the abovementioned underlying issues. The lack of details in the regulation itself implies that careful attention will have to be paid to the content of the arrangement that they shall conclude in the future, especially to ensure that Eurojust's resources are not drawn off by the EPPO.

[27] See intervention of Commissioner Jourova at the JHA Council meeting of mid-October 2016.

[28] Coninsx 2016.

[29] House of Lords, The impact of the EPPO's on the United Kingdom, 4th Report of session 2014–2015, p. 26, para 76.

[30] As an example, see Eurojust, Annual Report, 2015, p. 28: Eurojust registered in 2014 around 1850 cases. Whereas the agency registered 69 PIF cases, it also registered 647 fraud cases (including excise fraud and VAT fraud) and 90 corruption cases.

[31] For more details, see Weyembergh and Brière 2016, p. 52.

11.4 The EPPO-Eurojust Relations in Operational Matters

In operational matters, the mandate and tasks of the EPPO and Eurojust will differ substantially. Whereas the EPPO shall be able to exercise directly operational decisions, through its European Delegated Prosecutors, Eurojust shall remain an agency only supporting the operational cooperation between national judicial/prosecutorial authorities. Nevertheless, their operational cooperation would be of crucial importance and deserves close attention. It would indeed be necessary to ensure that overlaps between the two entities' mandates and tasks are avoided.

11.4.1 Preliminary Remarks

As a first preliminary remark, one should stress the important changes introduced in this respect to the text during the negotiations. Some provisions of the initial Eurojust proposal could give the impression that the EPPO would be a sort of "29th Eurojust member"—albeit one with limited powers. This impression resulted especially from Article 41(2) of the Eurojust proposal, according to which requests for support by the EPPO should be treated by Eurojust as if they had been received from a national authority.[32] This impression seems however less valid today, since the general approach on the EPPO Regulation does not follow such orientation. Such evolution will presumably lead to a system of operational cooperation between two clearly distinct EU bodies.

As a second preliminary remark, it is important to highlight that once the EPPO will be established, there will continue to be cases linked to offences affecting the Union's financial interests, in which Eurojust will play a role. This is especially true since it has been decided that the competence of the EPPO in PIF cases is no longer of an exclusive nature.[33] In this regard, some uncertainty resulting from the wording of Eurojust's

---

[32] It was further confirmed by other provisions, such as Articles 12(3) and 16(7) providing EPPO the possibility to participate in Eurojust's College and Executive Board meetings [wherever issues relevant to its functioning were discussed–albeit without the right to vote. According to Article 16 (8), the EPPO may also address written opinions to the Executive Board, to which it shall respond in writing without undue delay].

[33] Article 14 of the initial Commission EPPO proposal provided that the EPPO shall exercise its exclusive competence to investigate and prosecute any criminal offence referred to in Articles 12 and 13 (Directive PIF and ancillary competences).

Article 3 Eurojust GA (unchanged from the proposal) «However, its competence shall not include the crimes for which the European Public Prosecutor's Office is competent». EPPO GA—Article 17 «The European Public Prosecutor's Office shall be competent in respect of the criminal offences affecting the financial interests of the Union which are [provided for in Directive 2017/xx/EU, as implemented by national law] 57, irrespective of whether the same criminal conduct could be classified, under national law, as another type of offence.»

competences as phrased in the draft Eurojust Regulation should be removed ("its competence shall not include the crimes for which the EPPO is competent").[34]

The cooperation between the two bodies in the field of the protection of the Union's financial interests will be especially important in the situations described hereafter.[35] Firstly Eurojust may continue to play its classic facilitator role with regard to cases concerning participating Member States in the event of minor frauds,[36] or wherever the EPPO does not exercise its competence. Secondly, Eurojust will maintain its current competence in PIF files with regard to cases that exclusively concern non-participating Member States. At first sight, in such cases, the EPPO will not be involved, and there will thus be no need for the two bodies to cooperate. However, if one deepens a bit the reflection, such cooperation might be useful anyway, especially in order to detect potential links between cases in non-participating and participating States. Thirdly, Eurojust will play a role in PIF cases concerning participating and non-participating Member States.[37] Finally, Eurojust may play a role in the relations between the EPPO and third countries.[38] Indeed, the draft EPPO Regulation, i.e. both the Commission's proposal and the latest version of the text, foresees that the EPPO may request the support of Eurojust in the transmission of its decisions or requests for mutual legal assistance in cases involving third countries (Article 57(2) (b)). That provision must be read in combination with Article 41(3) of the Eurojust proposal providing that Eurojust shall make use of its agreements with third countries and its liaison magistrates to support the cooperation of the EPPO with third countries.[39] But, it should be noted that, like Eurojust, the EPPO will also be able to establish working arrangements

[34] The General Approach of the Eurojust regulation of February 2015 still contains this sentence, however it is placed between brackets and considered outside the general approach (Article 3(1), footnote 18).

[35] Besides the four hypotheses mentioned in the corpus of the text, Eurojust could also play a role in hybrid cases where PIF offences are connected to other offences (the so-called "ancillary offences"). Indeed, Articles 13(2) and 57(2) c) of the Commission's proposal for an EPPO regulation foresaw a role for Eurojust in the determination of the competent authority to deal with the ancillary offence (EPPO or the Member State concerned). In the event that the EPPO would not be competent over such offences, then cooperation between the EPPO and Eurojust could become essential, as Eurojust's assistance would be essential to liaise between the EPPO and the competent national authorities. If by contrast the EPPO would take over the investigation and prosecution of ancillary offences, then there could be a role for Eurojust as an advisor/expert in judicial cooperation issues relating to those ancillary offences. It is however important to note that the relevant provision (Article 57(2) c)) has been deleted during the negotiations in the Council. There is thus some uncertainty as to the role of either body—and their cooperation—in relation to ancillary offences.

[36] Article 20(2) of the draft EPPO regulation.

[37] See *infra* Sect. 11.4.2.

[38] On the risk of diminishing Eurojust's relations with third parties in light of the proposal for a Eurojust Regulation, see Deboyser 2014, p. 93.

[39] These elements are provided for in provisions outside the scope of the General Approach on the Eurojust regulation. They can be considered as being still valid, yet potentially subject to amendments once the negotiations on the Eurojust regulation restart.

with third countries and international organisations (including the secondment of liaison officers to the EPPO), and may designate contact points in third countries.[40] As a consequence, the assistance provided by Eurojust in this form of cooperation will most likely be of a temporary nature, until the EPPO has concluded its own agreements with third countries. This appreciation is reinforced when reading Article 59 of the EPPO draft regulation, which envisages extensive possibilities for the EPPO to cooperate with authorities located in third countries, including on the basis of cooperation agreements concluded by participating EU Member States.[41]

11.4.2 Modalities of Their Cooperation in Operational Matters

Concerning the precise modalities of their cooperation in operational matters, two issues are particularly important: the exchange of information between them, and the situations envisaged in the regulation itself.

The draft EPPO regulation provides that the institutions, bodies, offices and agencies of the Union, including Eurojust, and the authorities of the Member States competent in accordance with applicable national law shall report without undue delay any criminal conduct in respect of which it could exercise its competence (Article 19(1)).[42] The EPPO may also under certain conditions request further relevant information available to these entities (Article 19(5)).[43] Compliance with this reporting obligation would require that EU institutions and bodies, as well as national authorities, report cases as soon as possible, i.e. as soon a suspicion of an offence within the EPPO's competence is identified and even if the assessment of some criteria, such as the level of damage, or the applicable penalty, is not immediately possible (text of 28 Oct. 2016, Preamble, Recitals 46–48). The effective implementation of that provision would ensure that the flow of information smoothly reaches the EPPO. Indeed, the importance of the transmission of information to the EPPO should not be under-estimated, as it is key to its functioning and at all levels of intervention, including the very beginning of a case.

The first relevant issue concerns the exchange of information between the EPPO and Eurojust. Provisions of the draft EPPO Regulation, such as Article 19, concern the exchange of information in general terms between the EPPO and other bodies, including Eurojust. For instance, it results from Article 19 para 1 that Eurojust shall report without undue delay to the EPPO any criminal conduct in respect of which it

[40] Article 59 EPPO COM proposal.

[41] For more details, see Weyembergh and Brière 2016, pp. 37–38.

[42] EPPO Council Proposal 2016b.

[43] These requests may concern infringements which caused damage to the Union's financial interests, other than those within the competence of the EPPO, where it is necessary to establish links with a criminal conduct on which the EPPO has exercised its competence.

could exercise its competence. However, the exchange of information between the two entities may be further developed on the basis of Article 57(3). This provision indeed envisages an indirect access of the EPPO to the Eurojust's case management system on the basis of a hit/no hit system. Such provision is interesting[44] and seems at least at first sight more easily readable and understandable than the initial provision proposed by the Commission.[45] It must be noted that the EPPO shall have the same indirect access to the databases of OLAF (Article 57a(5)), and it remains to be seen whether Eurojust would obtain similar access to the EPPO's Case Management System.

The second issue concerns Article 57(2), which generally frames the EPPO-Eurojust bilateral operational cooperation. A comparison between the version of this provision in the Commission's proposal and in the current version of the text reveals significant changes.

Whereas the Commission proposal mentioned the possibility for the EPPO to associate Eurojust to its activities concerning cross-border or complex cases, the general approach of the Council only mentions such possibility concerning cross-border cases and not anymore concerning complex cases. This raises the question of consistency with Eurojust's regulation, more precisely Article 3 para 4 which foresees the competence of Eurojust in cases affecting one Member State only if they have repercussions at Union level.

Furthermore, the number of situations, in which operational cooperation between the two bodies are listed, has been significantly reduced in the course of the negotiations. The Commission proposal provided no less than six situations in which the EPPO could associate Eurojust in its activities concerning cross-border or complex cases: sharing information in its investigations; requesting Eurojust to participate in the coordination of specific acts of investigation; facilitating the agreement between the EPPO and Member States regarding ancillary competence; requesting Eurojust to use its powers regarding certain acts of investigations falling outside the competence of the EPPO; sharing information with Eurojust on prosecution decisions and requesting Eurojust the transmission of its decision or requests for mutual legal assistance to non-participating Member States or third countries (Article 57(2)). The current version of the text (of 28 October 2016) envisages only two of these situations: sharing information in its investigations (including personal data) on EPPO's investigations (a) and inviting Eurojust to provide support in the transmission of its decision or requests for mutual legal assistance to non-participating MSs or third countries (b). In the second situation envisaged, Eurojust would cooperate with the EPPO in cases involving non-participating Member States and third countries. Eurojust may be able to offer

[44] It is comparable to the system established between Eurojust and Europol.

[45] Article 24 of the Eurojust proposal foresees that the CMS and its temporary work files shall be made available for use by the EPPO. At the same time, Article 22 of the EPPO proposal provides for the establishment of a 'Case Management System, index and temporary files' for the EPPO. It is, however, unclear how the two systems would interact. The proposals envisage a system of automatic cross-checking of data.

some of its services to support the EPPO's cooperation with these countries, such as the assistance for setting up a Joint Investigation Team, the organisation of coordination meetings, etc. However, the text only refers to one possibility: the support that Eurojust or its competent national members may provide in the transmission of the EPPO's decisions or requests for mutual legal assistance. One should note that the wording of the provision has slightly changed. Whereas in the Commission proposal the EPPO "*may request*" such assistance, in the scrutinised version of the text, the EPPO "*may invite*" Eurojust to provide its support. The exact impact of this change remains far from clear, but it seems confer a broader margin of manoeuvre to Eurojust.

Although the current wording of the provision presents these two options of cooperation, as a non-exhaustive list,[46] its shortening raises concerns. The provision does not reflect Eurojust's scope of competence in operational matters, ignoring for instance the possibility to set up coordination centres or to offer analysis of cases in order to identify issues requiring special attention, such as conflicts of jurisdiction. It must however be noted that coordination of investigative measures in respect of cases handled by Eurojust has been added to the Preamble (recital 97). Moreover, with regard to the second form of cooperation envisaged, that is, assistance in the transmission of mutual legal assistance requests to non-participating States, this task also falls within the mandate of the European Judicial Network, which could offer such assistance to the EPPO. As it is well known, Eurojust and the European Judicial Network (EJN) have suffered from some overlaps.[47] Efforts have been made to overcome these. EJN's competence and expertise seem to have been overlooked here. The insertion in the Regulation of a reference to EJN's assistance could thus be considered, illustrating how the EPPO integrates itself in the AFSJ becoming part of a multilevel interaction and cooperation system.

The provisions relating to the EPPO-Eurojust cooperation in operational matters thus suffer from several flaws. Not only it fails to address shortcomings identified in the initial proposal of the text, but the current version of the text also raises new concerns. The main criticism concerns the organisation of their cooperation in very vague terms, and with a wording that does not take into consideration Eurojust's valuable expertise and experience, especially in operational matters.

[46] The wording "including by" indicates this. The provision is furthermore complemented by a recital in the preamble (recital 97, which reads as follows: "*The European Public Prosecutor's Office and Eurojust should become partners and should cooperate in operational matters in accordance with their respective mandates. Such cooperation may involve any investigations conducted by the European Public Prosecutor's Office where an exchange of information or coordination of investigative measures in respect of cases* ***within the competence of*** *Eurojust is considered to be necessary or appropriate. Whenever the European Public Prosecutor's Office is requesting such cooperation of Eurojust, the European Public Prosecutor's Office should liaise with the Eurojust national member of the Member State of the handling European Delegated Prosecutor. The operational cooperation may also involve third countries which have a cooperation agreement with Eurojust.*").

[47] Weyembergh et al. 2014, op. cit., pp. 28–30.

11.5 Conclusions

While the negotiations in the Council on the EPPO regulation might be reaching their final stage, the provisions on the relations between the EPPO and Eurojust could still be the object of further improvements. The Council seems indeed to fail to address one of the concerns raised by the European Parliament in its 2015 and 2016 Resolutions: a better clarification of the EPPO's bilateral relations, especially with Eurojust, taking into due consideration their respective expertise, "in order to differentiate between their respective roles in the protection of the EU's financial interests".[48] One could hope that the European Parliament, from which the Council must obtain the consent for the adoption of the Regulation, will notably insist upon such clarification of competences before giving its consent to the text.

The reason why the provision on the EPPO's relations with Eurojust is significantly less developed and less detailed than the provision relating to the cooperation between the EPPO and OLAF (Article 57a)[49] remains obscure and is difficult to justify. The idea that Eurojust would become a privileged partner for the EPPO does not appear to be reflected in the provision detailing their bilateral cooperation. The provision on EPPO's relationship with OLAF is significantly more developed when it comes to EPPO-OLAF cooperation in the course of an investigation (Article 57a para 3). Such a difference is difficult to understand considering that Eurojust has always been presented as the privileged partner of the EPPO; the current version of Article 57 does not really reflect this privileged partnership anymore. It looks empty when it comes to describing the substance of their bilateral operational cooperation. It may even be questioned whether Eurojust is still the privileged partner of the EPPO, or whether in a way OLAF has taken this position. Furthermore, the provision on EPPO-OLAF relationship seems to take better into consideration the specific expertise of OLAF. Such imbalance is surprising, especially considering that Eurojust was primarily envisaged as the EPPO's privileged partner. As a consequence, coming back to the question raised in the Introduction of this chapter, i.e. whether a special link exists between the EPPO and Eurojust as provided in the Treaty, the answer has to be negative at the current stage of the negotiations.

Further clarification of the distribution of competences, especially between the EPPO, OLAF and Eurojust, would thus be needed to reduce the risks of tensions between EU agencies/bodies. Such clarification is furthermore essential to ensure that the costs generated by the establishment of the EPPO do not exceed the benefits expected from EPPO's actions. The idea of covering EPPO's costs by drawing from

---

[48] European Parliament, Resolution of 2015, para 29 and European Parliament, Resolution of 2016, para 9.

[49] For more details about the relations between the EPPO and OLAF, see Weyembergh and Brière 2016, pp. 32–34.

Eurojust's (and/or OLAF's) resources should be handled very carefully, as it may generate unnecessary tensions. Furthermore, should Eurojust's resources (human or financial) be transferred to the EPPO, this would be highly detrimental for the EU area of criminal justice as a whole. Eurojust's expertise does not only cover PIF crimes, but includes other forms of serious crime (including other forms of financial crime),[50] for which its services will continue to be required in cross-border cases, and/or in PIF cases involving non-participating Member States. The costs linked to these activities will still have to be covered. More generally, the multiplication of agencies/bodies in the field of judicial cooperation, without ensuring good relations among them, might lead to a dangerous fragmentation and consequent weakening of EU actors within the AFSJ. This will further deepen the already worrying imbalance between judicial and police actors at EU level, since one powerful agency already benefits from larger resources in the police field, i.e. Europol.[51] Establishing a complex and costly new EU prosecutorial body, which would "undo" pre-existing actors and/or have bad relations with them, would not only be detrimental to the AFSJ and the fight against crime (including PIF crime) but would also give relevant and concrete arguments to Eurosceptics.

Finally, besides the uncertainties relating to the EPPO Regulation, the question remains how the evolution of the EPPO draft regulation will be taken into consideration in the Eurojust Regulation. One can but underline the importance of having complementary and consistent provisions in both regulations. Furthermore, should the establishment of the EPPO be postponed to a more distant (and uncertain) futurc, EU institutions could envisage an interesting alternative option to improve the efficiency of fighting PIF offences, namely strengthening Eurojust by using the possibilities provided for in Article 85 TFEU. As is well known, the 2013 Commission proposal for a Eurojust Regulation did not make use of the full potential of Article 85 TFEU. However, Eurojust could be granted some limited binding powers vis-à-vis national authorities, e.g. the powers to initiate criminal investigations (Article 85(1)a) TFEU),[52] at least regarding PIF offences. This provision presents the advantage of providing for the adoption of a Regulation via the ordinary legislative procedure. This is a positive element, as it means that the European Parliament is on an equal footing with the Council and it can potentially orientate the negotiations towards granting these powers to Eurojust.[53]

---

[50] As an example, see Eurojust, Annual Report, 2015, p. 28: Eurojust registered in 2014 around 1850 cases. Whereas the agency registered 69 PIF cases, it also registered 647 fraud cases (including excise fraud and VAT fraud) and 90 corruption cases.

[51] About such imbalance, see Weyembergh et al. 2014, *op. cit.* p. 60.

[52] About Article 85 TFEU and its potentialities, see for instance Weyembergh 2013, pp. 177–186; Weyembergh 2011, pp. 75–99.

[53] About Article 85 TFEU and its potentialities, see for instance Weyembergh 2013, pp. 177–18 and Weyembergh 2011, pp. 75–99.

References

Coninsx M (2014) The European Commission's legislative proposal: an overview of its main characteristics. In: Erkelens LH, Meij AWH, Pawlik M (eds) The European Public Prosecutor's Office: An Extended Arm or a Two-Headed Dragon? TMC Asser Press, The Hague

Coninsx M (2016) Intervention before the European Parliament, Public Hearing on "The EPPO and the Eurojust", Session 2: "Enhancing Eurojust and the relations between EPPO, Eurojust and Olaf". Available at http://www.europarl.europa.eu/ep-live/en/committees/video?event=20160524-1500-COMMITTEE-LIBE, Last accessed 24 January 2017

Deboyser C (2014) European Public Prosecutor's Office and Eurojust: 'Love match or arranged marriage'? In: Erkelens LH, Meij AWH, Pawlik M (eds) The European Public Prosecutor's Office: An Extended Arm or a Two-Headed Dragon? TMC Asser Press, The Hague

EPPO Commission Proposal (2013) Commission for a Regulation of the European Parliament and the Council on the European Union Agency for Criminal Justice Cooperation (Eurojust), COM (2013) 535 final, 17 July 2013

EPPO Council Proposal (2016a) Council, Proposal for a Regulation on the establishment of the EPPO – Consolidated text: update of the provisional version, 28 July 2016. Council Doc. No. 11350/1/16 REV 1. Available at http://data.consilium.europa.eu/doc/document/ST-11350-2016-REV-1/en/pdf. Last accessed March 2017

EPPO Council Proposal (2016b) Council, Proposal for a Regulation on the establishment of the European Public Prosecutor's Office – Outstanding questions on the full text. Council doc. No. 13459/16, 28 Oct 2016. Available at http://data.consilium.europa.eu/doc/document/ST-13459-2016-INIT/en/pdf. Last accessed March 2017

Hamran L, Szabova E (2013) European Public Prosecutors Office – Cui Bono? NJECL, Vol. 4, issue 1–2

House of Lords (2014) The impact of the EPPO's on the United Kingdom. Available http://www.publications.parliament.uk/pa/ld201415/ldselect/ldeucom/53/5302.htm, Last accessed 20 January 2017

Ligeti K, Weyembergh A (2015) The European Public Prosecutor's Office: Certain constitutional issues. In: Erkelens LH, Meij AWH, Pawlik M (eds) The European Public Prosecutor's Office: An Extended Arm or a Two-Headed Dragon? TMC Asser Press, The Hague

Weyembergh A (2011) The Development of Eurojust: Potential and limitations of Art. 85 TFEU. New Journal of European Criminal Law 2:75–99

Weyembergh A (2013) Coordination and initiation of investigations and prosecutions through Eurojust. ERA Forum 14:177–186

Weyembergh A, Armada I, Brière C (2014) The interagency cooperation and the future architecture of the EU criminal justice and law enforcement area, study for the European Parliament, DOI:10.2861/452825

Weyembergh A, Brière C (2016) Towards a European Public Prosecutor's Office, study for the European Parliament, DOI:10.2861/874675

White S (2012) A Decentralised European Public Prosecutor's Office - Contradiction in Terms or Highly Workable Solution? EUCRIM 2:67–74

Part III
Summa Summarum: Assessing EPPO's *Raison d'Être* in the Light of the Debates

Chapter 12
EPPO's *Raison d'Être*: The Challenge of the Insertion of an EU Body in Procedures Mainly Governed by National Law

Hubert Legal

Abstract EPPO's framework has had to adjust itself, through legislative deliberations, to reflect the diversity of the unharmonised legal environments in which this instrument of EU policy is called upon to act. This makes it more complex but—the author suggests—not necessarily weaker for that. Being a factor of progressive integration rather than of imposition is an asset for its future.

Keywords Legislative procedure · Efficiency · Sovereignty · Prosecutor · Criminal justice · Legality control

Quite briefly, I will try to answer a few questions on the assessment of EPPO's *raison d'être*.

I wish to thank you, Professor John Vervaele, for these questions, and Arjen Meij, my former colleague in the General Court in Luxembourg, for inviting me to sit with you in the Asser Instituut, which I regard as a distinct privilege.

The Council Legal Service has actively participated in the elaboration of the Council's views on the draft Regulation—you have heard this morning my colleague and compatriot Eric Sitbon who has been our man at working party meetings and the primary author of our several opinions on matters of law during the process—which I have of course personally endorsed. I also pay tribute to the intelligent and sophisticated contribution of the Commission's services throughout the exercise. Now that the proposal is entering the final phase of its deliberation, with a prospect of being finalised before the end of the year (2017), I can only command to you the efficiency of the Union's decision-making processes—particularly in the legislative sphere.

The author is the Legal Counsel of the European Council and of the Council, Director General of the Legal Service. He is a former member of the General Court of the European Court of Justice.

H. Legal (✉)
Council of the European Union, rue de la Loi 175, 1048 Brussels, Belgium
e-mail: hubert.legal@consilium.europa.eu

W. Geelhoed et al. (eds.), *Shifting Perspectives on the European Public Prosecutor's Office*, https://doi.org/10.1007/978-94-6265-216-3_12

The legal basis of Article 86 has barely six years of existence, the proposal has only been on the Council table for two years. There are faster procedures, admittedly—concerning banking crises or refugees, but the prosecutor's office can hardly be regarded as the response to a crisis, rather as a subject for which one says, sometimes with a degree of bad faith that quality should prevail over speed.

The Treaty terms, that devote ample consideration to what may happen in the absence of the required unanimity in Council for the establishment of an EPPO, do not indicate confidence that this will be an easy job. Enhanced cooperation was probably felt to be the likely outcome. It still is—but with the focus being put on bringing on board the largest possible number of Member States—an indication that keeping the Union together is a widely shared concern. And particularly when it comes to giving a common interpretation to our core values—the rule of law, bringing crime to justice in a decent and effective manner, moving towards a common perception of fundamental rights—what the European Court of Justice has held to be the integration force of the unified interpretation of human rights in its famous opinion on the EU's accession to the ECHR.

No doubt the core purpose of the EPPO is to be the judicial arm of the protection of the financial interests of the Union. In schematic terms, it is the procedural arm of the policy of which the substantive side is to be found in the "PIF" (protection of EU financial interests) directive. It serves a financial or budgetary purpose and not the purpose of being a model of criminal prosecution—for which there is no need. But it is not the end of the story, as para 4 of Article 86 spells out. There may be a second episode. And the yellow card issued by some national parliaments regarding subsidiarity at the outset of the process indicated an awareness of the potentially far-reaching consequences of the initiative in terms of indirect limitations to the Member States' procedural autonomy—in other words sovereignty.

We are talking about what could—without gross unfairness—be qualified as a monstrosity, an abnormality—an EU body called upon to exercise the functions of prosecutor in national criminal courts. If there were any suspicion that such a body could act as a power-grabbing tool in the hands of the Union institutions that would have been the end of it. The justice scoreboard approach, made famous by the former Commissioner Viviane Reding, caused so much irritation that it almost killed the project in its early days, presenting an EU minister of justice as the only way to bring any interest for the peoples' needs in our ignorant democracies terrorised by medieval courts. It took a new Commission, with a Dutch first Vice-President, and several successive patient and hard-working presidencies of the Council—with the Luxembourg and Dutch presidencies particularly active in the crucial phase—to put the boat back afloat. The idea has survived—a sign (that we should bear in mind) that confidence may be restored if the Union's purpose is clearly to strengthen national governments and not to make them irrelevant.

Some may think the office has lost its strength and character by becoming too much of an emanation of the judicial structures of the Member States. I disagree. In its current form, convoluted as its drafting may be in places, it is neither a Trojan horse, nor a syndicate. It is not a mere cooperation structure; it is not directly a harmonising device. It has the power to act in the common interest of the Union;

it has the capacity to insert itself without causing collateral damages in the court systems of which it will become an agent. A specific and autonomous agent, but not a missionary preaching the name of God to wild tribes in the bush, rather a fish in water—a big fish, admittedly, but one that will not be a foreign force, that will be at home—and very efficient because very well aware of how things work in the law of the land—which is actually how Europe should be altogether.

Acceptance of this imported structure will therefore depend on its capacity to converge with national prosecutors and reinforce them. It also requires assurance that, in the exercise of all its functions, a proper judicial review of its conduct be in place—through national channels as concerns actions contributing directly to criminal justice, with the possibility of referrals for preliminary rulings since a national court may not determine the irregularity of the acts of a Union body; and through direct legality control by the European Court of Justice for acts that cannot be controlled via the criminal trial. It would be paradoxical that an instrument that is intended to strengthen the rule of law makes exception for its own workings to the principle that all EU bodies are submitted to judicial review of their acts having legal effects. To bring a case to a national court rather than to another, by applying criteria that contain little automaticity, is—in particular—a decision that cannot be made with unchecked discretion. A prosecutor is not a judge and is not at liberty to develop its own case-law, let alone a jurisprudence.

So, on these last words, let me thank you for allowing me to deliver my brief remarks to the lovely civilised presence of distinguished academics and other informed personalities on a subject well worth a sustained diplomatic effort.

Chapter 13
The European Public Prosecutor's Office: A Chronicle of a Failure Foreseen

Alex Brenninkmeijer

Abstract One of the crucial principles of the European Union is the principle of loyal cooperation. This principle seems to be weakly applied in the EU's daily work. The discussions on the construction of EPPO are testifying thereof, for example regarding the question how competences regarding VAT fraud should be dealt with. The underlying problem seems to be the nationalistic approach of the Member States, neglecting the many mechanisms EU law already provides and thereby hampering European cooperation required to combat more effectively VAT fraud. As a response to this ineffective fight against VAT fraud, the European Court of Auditors (ECA) recommends on the basis of a Special Report to integrate VAT fraud in the PIF directive. A complex initiative like the establishment of EPPO should be evaluated on the basis of a multidisciplinary investigation. Questions regarding its organizational effectiveness and its cooperation with other organizations demand for such an approach. The issue 'Is that value for money for EU citizens' should be an important element of a multi-disciplinary audit by ECA on the effectiveness and cost-effectiveness of a mechanism such as EPPO. The most probable outcome thereof would be: a chronicle of a failure foreseen.

Keywords Principle of loyal cooperation · State sovereignty · Shared competences · Area of Freedom, Security and Justice · EU criminal law · VAT fraud

I would like to highlight some perspectives from the European Court of Auditors (ECA) and start with two general observations. Firstly, I observe that the most crucial element of the European cooperation, which is the principle of loyal cooperation, laid down in Article 4 of the Treaty, is very weakly applied in the daily

---

The author is a Member of the European Court of Auditors.

A. Brenninkmeijer (✉)
European Court of Auditors, 12, rue Alcide De Gasperi, 1615 Luxembourg, Luxembourg
e-mail: alex.brenninkmeijer@eca.europa.eu

W. Geelhoed et al. (eds.), *Shifting Perspectives on the European Public Prosecutor's Office*, https://doi.org/10.1007/978-94-6265-216-3_13

work in Europe.[1] On many occasions in my work in the Court of Auditors, I am very disappointed. I mention this in the current context of our discussions on the setting up of a European Public Prosecutor's Office (EPPO), because it gives us an insight into what the struggle on the construction of EPPO is about. Well, it is primarily about loyal cooperation or non-loyal, non-cooperation. That is, I think, a first fundamental insight. Furthermore, loyal cooperation becomes an even bigger challenge when it is placed in this specific context of European criminal law which relates to several issues. Historically, ever since the Age of the Enlightenment, when the nation state arose, it is considered that the nation state is the only competent authority to prescribe, adjudicate and enforce criminal law within the boundaries of its territory. With the rise of the European Union, sovereignty became increasingly shared between the national and the European level. At the same time the notion of cooperation became more and more important. This cooperation especially increased in 1997 when the Treaty of Amsterdam established an 'Area of Freedom, Security and Justice' (AFSJ).[2] The rationale behind this concept is that cooperation between the European Union and its Member States is required in order to face the new challenges to security and peace. This struggle between powers shared between Member States and the EU (and its Institutions) on the one hand, and the demand of cooperation in a common area on the other hand results in a tense relationship. Furthermore, the fear of Member States to transfer operational powers to a European Office makes the move towards a European criminal justice system with its own EPPO difficult, as it arguably touches upon the most sensitive field of all Union law.

My second observation is that if we evaluate all initiatives leading to EPPO, I think it is important to choose for a more multidisciplinary approach. At this conference we are discussing EPPO in a more legal context and I think that from the point of view of effectiveness of an organization and the cooperation between organizations, a multidisciplinary approach is extremely important. In my evaluation hereafter I will apply this idea of a more multidisciplinary approach.

---

[1] Article 4(3) TEU 1992: "Pursuant to the principle of sincere cooperation, the Union and the Member States shall, in full mutual respect, assist each other in carrying out tasks which flow from the Treaties.

The Member States shall take any appropriate measure, general or particular, to ensure fulfilment of the obligations arising out of the Treaties or resulting from the acts of the institutions of the Union.

The Member States shall facilitate the achievement of the Union's tasks and refrain from any measure which could jeopardise the attainment of the Union's objectives."

[2] Treaty of Amsterdam 1997, Article K.1: "Without prejudice to the powers of the European Community, the Union's objective shall be to provide citizens with a high level of safety within an area of freedom, security and justice by developing common action among the Member States in the fields of police and judicial cooperation in criminal matters and by preventing and combating racism and xenophobia."

I have listened carefully to what one could call the 'pleading note' of Mr. Legal.[3] On the one hand, in the case of EPPO, I have been a judge for a very long time and I highly appreciate the beautiful construct of this pleading note. But on the other hand, to be honest, the most important issue is that this pleading note is the result of what we can call 'the EU context', within which negotiations are conducted in the Council, which is doing its utmost to make of EPPO what is feasible in the European context. And that is my greatest concern. Because, as also has been stated by the representative of the Commission at this conference, the EU context leans towards a realistic or, maybe, even a bit cynical approach. However, we must admit it is the best we can achieve.

What can be observed in the European context is the dominance of a strong nationalistic approach. It is extremely important to note that all Member States, encouraged by the idea of sovereignty, are pushing forward their own position, and are increasingly taking steps and making decisions in which they shape their nationalistic approach. The watering down of the whole construct of EPPO is caused by this nationalistic approach. So what can be seen is that many officials and politicians, together with a coalition of the willing around EPPO, are building a sand castle, like young boys. Just as you can see happening only one kilometer away from here on the beach of Scheveningen. A sand castle can have some strength, but when the tide is incoming, the sand castle will fall apart and will even be washed away completely. Everybody knows that, at a certain moment, the tide will rise. And that is my fear in relation to the construct of the EPPO. In this case, what is the incoming tide? The incoming tide equals to the perspective of the European citizens. We are constructing, with a lot of energy, an EPPO. However, this office is constructed with many constraints ensuing from the overly nationalistic approach of the Member States. In presenting it, at the end of the day, can we be serious to citizens and say: "Well, this is a very strong construct."? Or should we be honest and say: "It is the best we can get. Please give it a try and we will see whether we can improve it in the future."? It resembles a situation of buying a car with many problems, in the knowledge that you have to repair it the very moment you have acquired it. I think this is a serious problem and it is the heart of the matter when it comes to Euroscepticism. On the one hand, there is the nationalistic approach of national governments and on the other hand, we must admit that this is the best we can construct. But such an approach and what comes out of it, is nowadays not convincing anymore for modern citizens.

Therefore, the question comes up: "Is this value for money for EU citizens?" This question relates to the other perspective that is also connected to the multidisciplinary approach. The Court of Auditors is not only, as is often said, responsible for financial and compliance audits, but also for the auditing of the performance of EU institutions and bodies. Through performance audits the ECA examines the quality of their financial management measured on the basis of the principles of economy, effectiveness and efficiency. And the ECA has conducted many of these performance audits, for instance on how the EU's institutions and bodies are dealing with VAT matters. So what makes

[3] See Chap. 12.

VAT such a preferable topic to be audited? The completion of the internal market of the European Community involved among others the removal of all border controls for intra-Community trade.[4] From 1 January 1993, the controls justified by the varying VAT rates from one country to another were no longer carried out at borders but within each State by the national tax authorities.[5] This created the risk that the exported goods remained untaxed in the supplying state as well as in the state of consumption. This risk now appears to have come true: Member States annually face over 40-60 billion euro of losses. In its capacity as the external audit body of the EU budget, the Court of Auditors has the task to respond to this important finding.[6]

And what seems to be the problem with VAT? Well, the EU has many beautiful mechanisms in place to fight intra-Community VAT fraud, but the Member States do not apply them. There is a nationalistic approach if it comes to VAT fraud. But everybody knows that VAT fraud is not only a national issue but also a European issue. So European cooperation is demanded; however, there are many reasons why this cooperation is not coming off the ground. This is for example illustrated by the inefficient cooperation between Member States in exchanging information on tax authorities. Again, I am disappointed when it comes to the way in which the principle of loyal cooperation is applied within the European Union. As a response to this disappointment, the Court of Auditors recommends among others to initiate a coordinated effort by Member States to establish a common system of collecting data and statistics on intra-community VAT fraud and to focus on the enhancement of the timeliness of Member States' replies to information requests.[7]

At the end of the day, it can be concluded that the fight against VAT fraud is not effective in Europe. One of the changes which could make it more effective is the integration of VAT fraud in the PIF directive. This was one of our recommendations made on the basis of our performance audit tackling intra-community VAT fraud.[8]

My last point is that when we are posing the question: "Is that value for money for EU citizens?", the Court of Auditors would, from its perspective, put forward the question: "What kind of questions do we have to pose when auditing the effectiveness and the cost-effectiveness of a mechanism like EPPO?" And then I must admit, if I analyze the contribution of Professor André Klip—that he already drafted—what is called in terms of the Court of Auditors—an 'audit planning memorandum'. His contribution was not very welcoming for everybody here. As

[4] Commission of the European Communities 1985. A direct consequence of this programme was to remove all barriers to the free movement of goods, services, people and capital.

[5] CVCE (2016).

[6] European Court of Auditors 2015, p. 9.

[7] European Court of Auditors 2015, recommendation No. 8.

[8] European Court of Auditors 2015, recommendation No. 14: In order to effectively protect the financial interests of the European Union, "the European Parliament and the Council should: (a) include VAT within the scope of the proposed directive on the fight against fraud to the Union's financial interests by means of criminal law (PIF directive) and the regulation on the establishment of the European Public Prosecutor's Office (…)".

such, Klip starts his contribution with addressing several arguments which illustrate the controversial nature of EPPO.

Firstly, he mentions the difficult development of the increased shared sovereignty between the national and the EU level. Secondly, he mentions the common area in which the EU bodies need to work. As such, the debate on EPPO concerns the division of power between the national and EU level, but moreover includes also the protection of common interests in a common area. Thirdly, Klip mentions the scope of offences the EPPO would be dealing with. The actual problem reaches beyond this scope including many other offences which occur within the common area. This evokes fear by Member States as it opens the door, without knowing where we will get with this. Fourthly, Klip brings forward the fear of Member States that national operational powers are transferred to a higher level. Lastly, he mentions the fact that the model of the EPPO is not the same as the institution of the public prosecutor in every Member State.

Next to addressing these arguments addressing the controversial nature of EPPO, Klip argues that the problem with EPPO is that after 30 years of discussion, people still do not have a clear picture of the phenomenon. As a potential field of interest for EPPO, he mentions VAT Fraud. The problems relating to this topic concern the data and information flaw between the authorities dealing with VAT, while VAT fraud is a transnational topic.

I think the answers to all the points Klip raised are already given. Therefore, the Court of Auditors could start already now, today, with an audit of EPPO. The conclusion should be a chronicle of a failure foreseen.

References

Commission of the European Communities (1985) Completing the Internal market. White Paper from the Commission of the European Council. Doc. COM(85) 310 final. Available at http://www.europa.eu/documents/comm/white_papers/pdf/com1985_0310_f_en.pdf. Last accessed January 2017

CVCE (2016) The removal of barriers to intra-Community trade. Available at http://www.cvce.eu/content/publication/2003/3/27/d9c4a1fa-be1a-44fb-a1d6-05b022b2eeb3/publishable_en.pdf. Last accessed January 2017

European Court of Auditors (2015) Tackling intra-Community VAT fraud: More action needed (Special Report No. 24/2015). Available at http://www.eca.europa.eu/Lists/ECADocuments/SR15_24/SR_VAT_FRAUD_EN.pdf. Last accessed January 2017

Treaty on European Union and Treaty Establishing the European Community (1992) *OJ* C 224/6, 31.8.92

Treaty of Amsterdam (1997) amending the Treaty on European Union, the Treaties establishing the European Communities and certain Related Acts, *OJ* C 340/ 1, 10. 11. 97

MIX
Papier aus verantwortungsvollen Quellen
Paper from responsible sources
FSC® C105338

If you have any concerns about our products,
you can contact us on
ProductSafety@springernature.com

In case Publisher is established outside the EU,
the EU authorized representative is:
Springer Nature Customer Service Center GmbH
Europaplatz 3, 69115 Heidelberg, Germany

Printed by Libri Plureos GmbH
in Hamburg, Germany